...ot already requ
y be renewed in person, in
new, please quote the
new online a P'

Just Follow the Floodlights!

About the Author

Brian Kennedy is a part-time writer for *The Munster Express* and full-time football fanatic. He is author of several previous books including *Confessions of an Exeter City Nut* and *Blow It Up Ref!* He lives in Waterford.

JUST FOLLOW THE FLOODLIGHTS!

The Complete Guide to League of Ireland Football

Brian Kennedy

The Liffey Press

Published by
The Liffey Press
Ashbrook House, 10 Main Street
Raheny, Dublin 5, Ireland
www.theliffeypress.com

A catalogue record of this book is
available from the British Library.

ISBN 978-1-908308-03-0

Printed in Spain by GraphyCems.

Contents

Acknowledgements

I am writing this at 4.37 am on a July Sunday morning from my bath, laptop in one hand, Jack Daniels in the other. I've just completed 2,856 miles of travelling around to 21 League of Ireland grounds in the name of research so I need a wash and a drink badly!

On my travels I've had 27 burgers, 14 chips and 9 battered sausages. Amount of times I got lost – 6. Amount of times SatNav left my window – 4. Total amount of wrong turns – 352. I stayed in 9 hotels, counted 6 road kill, collected 2 penalty points and was chased by 1 bull whose relentless pursuit of me unfolded in full view of the watching Monaghan and Dundalk fans at a League Cup game in Gortakeegan.

I felt the only way to write this book was to travel to each ground and chat to the fans, staff, historians and people associated with the clubs to get a feel of what their club meant to them. I am indebted to so many people for their help, all of whom I would like to thank now.

For their contribution to the histories of each club, statistics and photographs I'd like to thank Tadhg Carey, Ray Egan, Chris Enright, Stephen Burke, Michael Duffy, Plunkett Carter, Gerry Desmond, Mick McBride, Brian Dunleavy, Eddie Mahon, Brian Whelan, Tom Reilly, Jim Murphy, Bartley Ramsey, Tommy Shields, Brian O'Brien, Aidan Corr, Bernard and Gary Spain, Martin Stapleton, Tony Gee, Tiernan Dolan, Terry Flaherty, William Henry, Declan and Mary McDonnell, Ronan Kilmurry, Pete Kelly, Robert Goggins, Eoghan Rice, Chris Sands, Frank Young, Pat O'Callaghan, Joe Molloy, Anthony Kilfeather, Keith O'Dwyer, Declan Hughes, Stephen Joyce, Philip Bourke, Sean Ryan, Simon Aust and the lovely Lucia at Finn Harps.

To the wonderful League of Ireland books that I sourced information (and the odd quote) from and the authors who helped every step of the way: *The Hoops* by Robert Goggins and Paul Doolan; *We are Rovers – An Oral History of Shamrock Rovers* by Eoghan Rice; *DUFC – A Claret and Blue History* by Brian Whelan; *Drogheda United – The Story So Far* by Tom O'Reilly; *The History of Dundalk FC – The First 100 Years* by Jim Murphy; *When We Were Kings* by Tadhg Carey; *A Century of Cork Soccer Memories* by Plunkett Carter; *The Bass Book of Irish Soccer* by Sean Ryan and Noel Dunne; *The Irish Football Handbooks* (various editions) by Gerry Desmond and Dave Galvin; *The Finn Harps Story* by Bartley Ramsey; *A History of Sligo Rovers* by Joe Molloy; *The End of an Era – A History of Limerick Senior Soccer at the Markets Field 1937-84* by Aidan Corr and Bernard Spain; *The History of Mervue United AFC 1960-2010* by William Henry; and *Gods vs Mortals* by Paul Keane.

Thanks to Keith Kelly at the *Connaught Tribune*, Leo Gray at the *Sligo Champion*, Kevin O'Neill at the *Westmeath Independent*, Ann Kearney at the *Irish Examiner*, Ger Lawton at the *Waterford News & Star*, Jamie O'Keeffe at the *Munster Express*, the *Limerick Leader*, Ronan Kilmurry at the *Northern Standard* and of course Arthur Duffy at the *Derry Journal*.

I owe the photographers who contribute to Extratime.ie a big thank you, particularly Andy McDonnell who unselfishly went round to each one of them getting permission for use of the photographs. So thank you Fergus McNally, Sean Dempsey, Gary McGivney, Simon Crowe and Eddie Lennon.

Thanks to the following photographers for pictures and programme covers: David Caldwell, Eimear Taaffe, Ian Anderson at Sportslifephoto.com, Padraig Devaney, Michael Melly, Clive Hynes, Alan Mooney, Eric Barry and Mick Ring at Blinkofaneye.ie, Tony Tobin, Larry McQuillan, David Nail, Paul O'Brien, Vincent Kirwan, Aidan O Toole, Ed Scannell, George Kelly, Michael Tierney, Ian McDonald, Gerard McHugh, Ronan Geary, A. Baldiemann, Barry Gregg, Jimmy Kenny, Jim O'Sullivan.

I'd like to thank the following people who agreed to be interviewed via phone, email or in person and the permission to use some of the wonderful quotes they gave me: John Minnock, Turlough O'Connor, Dermot Keely, John Gill, Rod De Khors, Tony O' Connell, Paul Doolin, Roddy Collins, Stephen Kenny, Pat Fenlon, Brush Shiels, John Coughlan, Donie Wallace, Dave Barry, Johnny Glynn, Pat Dolan, Damien Richardson, Felix Healy, Jim McLaughlin, Peter Hutton, Gavin Dykes, Liam Cullen, Tommy Byrne, Guy Bates, Cathal Muckian, Tommy McConville, Patsy McGowan, Brendan Bradley, Terry Harkin, Jim Sheridan, Con McLaughlin, Eamon Deacy, Tom Lally, Tommy Shields, Tony Mannion, Paul McGee, Eoin Hand, Kevin Fitzpatrick, Des Kennedy, Brian O'Brien, Charlie Walker, Billy Bagster, Alan Kirby, Declan McDonnell, David Goldbey, Seamus Finnegan, Mick Cooke, Emlyn Long, Pete Kelly, Liam Tuohy, Mick Leech, Finbarr Flood, Eric Barber, Freddie Strahan, Chris Rutherford, Ger Carr, Nicky Broujos, Tony McDonnell, Ken O'Doherty, Theo Dunne, Declan Hughes, Alfie Hale, Johnny Matthews, Shamie Coad, Vinny Maguire, Al Finucane, Mick Wallace, Conor Sinnott.

Thanks to Gareth Penrose at Extratime.ie for use of the Paul Osam interview, Ray McManus at Sportsfile and Jim O'Donnell for the hospitality on visiting Derry. To Paul Keane for the photographs, advice and making me feel inferior by writing *Gods vs Mortals*, Pete O'Doherty for the wonderful front cover photograph, effortlessly enhanced by my cousin John Butler, and to Shane Murphy for following up on odds and ends. Finally, to David Givens at The Liffey Press for his faith in me.

Foreword

Whatever level of football you have played, I bet your desire was very much the same as mine. You wanted to be good.

All through my own career, from schoolboy days to the professional ranks, the one sustaining, and at the same time outstanding, factor of motivation was the desire to play at the very highest level possible.

The first steps of this grand ambition are usually taken in one's home town. It is every kid's dream to emulate his local heroes. It is the first sporting ambition we have all held, and it is something that stays with us forever, irrespective of how our individual careers turn out. Over the past hundred years or so League of Ireland clubs have ensured many such dreams were realised.

Because football is in essence a kid's game, the game of the streets and parks all across the globe, it is a game that responds best to a clear heart and an open mind. The beautiful game takes both performer and spectator into a world of excitement and imagination, and elevates the spirit to a level that transcends the mundane and provides an escape from the reality of the world around it.

While this book highlights many decades of dedicated endeavour by clubs and players, it must be accepted that inspiration and imagination are not curtailed by the passing of time. The consequence of this is that those most desirable qualities are still fostered to a quite extraordinary degree, and one only has to gaze around venues like Turner's Cross, Tallaght Stadium or The Showgrounds on any match evening to understand that these special places are still fundamental to who we are. Each one of the League of Ireland clubs contained in Brian Kennedy's superb history of Irish professional football has provided inspiration for generations of young Irish people.

The great virtue of a football club is not just its ability to help us feel pride in moments of triumph. The great virtue of a football club lies in its ability to encourage us in the midst of failure, to motivate us to function even in the depths of despair because there is always another day, another game.

This splendidly researched book is a timeless portrayal of the lives of men and the clubs they created. It highlights legacies that will last as long as the imaginations they ignited and it emphasises the indispensable qualities of hope and the vital significance of optimism.

Finally, I am delighted that clubs long gone have not been forgotten in this book. My father, George, played for Bray Unknowns and Brideville, and one of the original member clubs is Frankfort, amazingly still in existence in intermediate football and playing out of St. Annes Park in Clontarf where I sometimes do a bit of coaching for them.

Damien Richardson
August 18, 2011

Author's Note:

Just as this book was going to press Shamrock Rovers made history by becoming the first League of Ireland team to qualify for the group stages of the Europa League. Whilst we didn't have time to incorporate Rovers' accomplishment into their illustrious history (see page 195), we also couldn't let it go unmarked. So congratualtions to Shamrock Rovers and best of luck doing battle with Rubin Kazan, PAOK and of course Tottenham Hotspur. Long may the adventure continue!

Brian Kennedy
August 29, 2011

Athlone Town

Formed: 1887
Ground: **Athlone Town Stadium**
Capacity: 2,500
Nickname: The Town

"If I'd had a bit more maturity (like I have now!), I'd have looked up, waited for him to commit himself and placed it the other way." – John Minnock on his penalty miss against AC Milan

The oldest club in the league, with a history spanning 124 years of joy, pain and the odd bit of depression, Athlone Town are the grand-daddies of League of Ireland football. A midland club born of humble origins, Athlone found domestic dominance and memorable moments in European football. Even AC Milan were blessed to get out of St. Mel's Park without losing!

Like many, they've basked in glory and traded blows with the bad times, but almost 125 years after the exotically named Orlando Coote placed an advertisement in the *Westmeath Independent* announcing the formation of a new football club, Athlone Town is still a part of the League of Ireland fixture list in 2011.

Having recruited local players through the ad, Coote helped shape the club. Its early days were spent competing locally, playing their games at the grounds of a local school called Ranelagh and winning the Leinster Junior Cup in 1894 and '95. A year after a ship set sail from Cobh en route to destiny with an Atlantic iceberg, Athlone gained entry into the Leinster Senior League, winning the Division 2 title in their first attempt, but the breakthrough on a national scale arrived on January 14, 1922 when the club competed in the inaugural Free State Cup. A brace from John Sweeney, one from Frank Ghent and a winner from Alan Smith gave Town a 4-3 victory over YMCA (minus the Village People) in a match played at Claremount Road in Sandymount, but Bohemians ended any potential fairytale in the next round.

The following season Athlone Town featured for the first time in the League of Ireland, playing at home on September 16, 1922 against League champions St. James Gate. John Sweeney had the honour of scoring the first league goal in that 3-1 defeat, and the side included Tommy Muldoon, a man who went on to carve out a career with Aston Villa and Tottenham Hotspur for the rest of the decade.

The step up to national football didn't faze the club either and they finished a healthy sixth of 12 teams, winning 11 of their 22 games. Amazingly,

The Athlone Town team which played Bohemians in the Free State Cup semi-final in 1924 en route to the club's only cup victory to date. Back row (L-R): Denis Hannon, John Joe Dykes, Terry Judge, Paddy O'Reilly, Joe Monahan and Jimmy Hope. Front row (L-R): Barney Connaughton, Tommy Muldoon, Jim Sweeney, Tommy Collins and Frank Ghent (photo from When We Were Kings: The Story of Athlone Town's 1924 FAI Cup Triumph, *by Tadhg Carey. www.whenwewerekings.ie)*

in only their third attempt, the club won the Free State Cup in 1924. Fellow league side Midlands Athletic were put to the sword in the first round, whilst a 2-0 away win against Shelbourne brought Athlone in the semi-finals and a meeting with Bohemians. The first game played at Shelbourne Park attracted a crowd of 11,000 and ended scoreless, however in the replay Athlone progressed to the final courtesy of Frank Ghent and Norman Lyster goals in a 2-0 victory.

The final pitted Town against Cork side Fordsons. The lads from the Lee still remain one of only a handful of non-league clubs to make it to an FAI Cup final (St. Francis being the last in 1990), though they actually entered the League the very next season – the first Cork club to do so. On the day a single goal by Denis Hannon, shooting through a crowded goalmouth in the 20th minute at Dalymount, was enough to capture Athlone's first and so far only FAI Cup, and also ensure they were the first team in cup history to not concede a goal in the competition (a record that stood until Dundalk's cup campaign of 1958.)

Things turned as sour as sixteen-year-old milk soon after though, and before the end of the decade Athlone had left the league. That final 1927/28 season proved disastrous, winning just two of their 18 games and taking a mere five points. The Ranelagh grounds were deemed not to be up to scratch and the club simply wasn't invited back into the league the next season. Several clubs folded around that period only to make an appearance some years later under a new name (for that, see the eternal chameleons Cork), but Athlone Town didn't return to League of Ireland football for another four decades.

Until then the club had to be content with Junior League football, though they had success at the highest level at that grade, winning two FAI Junior Cups in 1935 and again three years later in 1938. There was also success in the Leinster Junior Cup in 1932 and again 30 years later in the swinging sixties. But playing at the highest level in the Republic was always the main aim and in May 1969 a vote by the League of Ireland Management Committee decided in favour of electing Athlone Town (by the narrowest of margins, seven to six) to the League of Ireland and a 41-year gap was bridged when Billy Young's side played a Presidents Cup match on Sunday, August 3, 1969 in a 2-1 win over Drumcondra.

Athlone held their own that season as well, keeping four teams beneath them and amassing eight wins and 21 points from their first season back in the big time. They also won the Leinster Senior Cup with a 4-0 demolition of Shelbourne in the 1970 final which included a Jackie Mooney hat-trick.

The arrival of former Irish international Amby Fogarty in November 1974 marked an upturn in the club's fortunes, and in that 1974/75 season the club launched their first serious league challenge in their history (mind you, to that date they'd only competed in a dozen full seasons.) In their best showing since just after the Irish Civil War, Athlone managed to finish runners-up for the first time in their history, win 13 games and amass their biggest amount of points in the top flight. All season Fogarty's men, with talents such as Paul Martin, Noel Larkin, Mick O'Brien, Eugene Davis and John Minnock, battled with Bohemians, Finn Harps and Cork Hibernians. They saw off Dave Bazzuci's Leesiders and Patsy McGowan's charges from Donegal, but not Bohemians, ironically now managed by Billy Young, the man who had taken Finn Harps into their first League of Ireland game. Although it was a brave effort, the Dubliners actually won the title rather comfortably by a full nine points. However, there was the prize of UEFA Cup football that autumn.

With clubs such as Liverpool, Marseille, Lazio, Aston Villa and Barcelona on offer in the first round draw, it was probably a bit of a disappointment to draw a Norwegian side on the outskirts of Oslo called Valerenga. At this stage Norwegian football was, well, awful. The national side had been beaten by Holland 9-0 in their qualification group for the 1974 World Cup, and even Luxembourg notched a victory over the Scandinavians. Valerenga themselves had just worked their way back up from the third division so this tie might have been a rarity in the seventies – a League of Ireland club as favourites to progress in Europe!

Roughly 4,000 turned up at St. Mel's Park to see Athlone win 3-1 with goals from Paul Martin and a brace from Eugene Davis. The job was finished a fortnight later with a solid performance in the Bislett Stadium in Oslo, where Martin scored again in a 1-1 draw for an aggregate 4-2 win in front of a crowd of less than 900. Norwegian football has come a long way since – Valerenga now play in a 25,000 capacity stadium with a supporters' club topping 10,000 members!

And then Giovanni rode into town. Now Ireland's national team manager, Mr. Trapattoni was part of manager Nereo Rocca's backroom staff of Italian giants AC Milan – the astonishing reward for Athlone Town in the next round. The Italians played at the 80,000 capacity San Siro, had won Serie A nine times, the Coppa Italia three times and had just played two back to back Cup Winners Cup finals (winning against Leeds in '73, losing to FC Magdeburg of Germany in '74). Athlone played in St. Mel's Park. It held 7,000 and had a few seats. The words "capacity" and "full" didn't often enter the club's vocabulary. They had one national cup to their name, a squad of part-timers and drew 0-0 with Dalkey United in the FAI Cup that season!

Milan had Gianni Rivera, a former European Footballer of the Year in 1969, a man who had played in four World Cups and bore witness to the

If a picture painted a thousand words. The now famous photograph of the AC Milan players arriving at St. Mel's Park and automatically getting those new Italian handmade shoes dirty! (photo credit: Athlone Voice)

greatest footballing side of all time – the 1970 Brazilian team that he played against in that glorious 1970 World Cup final in Mexico.

Whilst he was playing in that final, John Minnock was plying his trade at Charlton. Little did he know a short five years later he'd have the chance to gun down Rivera's club and shock the world of football with, quite possibly, the single biggest spot-kick in League of Ireland history – one which he is aware of!

Despite the obvious choice of switching the game to a bigger stadium like Lansdowne, the club officials decided to stage the game in St. Mel's Park and worked like Trojans to bring the capacity up to around the 9,000 mark. They couldn't tarmac a mile long runway for the Rossoneri to fly a jet into should they have requested it (when the Italians asked, "Where Athlone Airport is?" a club official stated it was two hours away in Dublin), and the Serie A giants were soon put straight on the limitations of St. Mel's!

The game took place on October 22, 1975 with an Athlone Town team that lined out O'Brien, Stephenson, Wood, Duffy, Smith, Davies, Humphries, Daly, Larkin, Minnock and Martin. Looking back, it's still astonishing, and will remain forevermore, that not only did Athlone Town, a side playing Leinster League a mere seven years previously, hold AC Milan to a scoreless draw but had the chance to beat them from a dead ball situation 12 yards from goal. Not that John Minnock will want to be reminded of that for the millionth time.

Nevia Scala's clumsy challenge on Terry Daly in the 30th minute led to that penalty kick – a spot kick to put the Midlanders 1-0 up against Milan. The word pressure was created for such a scenario. Three years ago I took a penalty kick in a second round losers group of the Waterford Factory League. I nearly vomited on the walk up. What in the name of Christ was it like for John Minnock?

> *"I normally struck my penalties to my left (the goalkeeper's right) and I had thought about changing it when I placed the ball for the penalty but to be completely honest I didn't make a great connection anyway, so much so Albertosi had almost been down waiting for it! If I had a bit more maturity (like I have now!), I would have looked up, waited for him to commit himself and placed it the other way."*
> – John Minnock

Despite missing (no shame against Italian national goalkeeper Enrico Albertosi), Athlone hung on to a 0-0 draw and gave a good account of themselves in the replay – the tie was actually still scoreless, and amazingly in the balance until the 63rd minute in Italy. However goals from Vincenzi and a brace from tough nut Romeo Benetti gave the Rossoneri a 3-0 victory in front of over 40,000 fans.

Amby Fogarty left in 1976 (becoming manager of Galway Rovers a year later), however the true golden age of Athlone Town arrived when Turlough O'Connor took charge of the midland club. The former Bohemians striker (still third in the all-time League of Ireland goal scoring charts with 178 strikes) was appointed manager of his hometown club in 1979. He brought in experienced players like Johnny Fullam and Mick Smyth, and added his own brother Padraig from Bohemians, whilst his other brother, 19-year-old Michael, was already at the club.

> *"It was my first manager's job and I really didn't know what to expect. It was also a big challenge as I was going back to my home town having played almost all my career away from Athlone. We were one of the weaker teams at the time and hadn't won a major honour for a long time, but there was a great community spirit about the place. I talked Johnny Fullam out of retirement for a year and added Mick Smyth. These were players who'd won trophies before so their experience was essential. It was also nice having my brother Michael already at the club."* – Turlough O'Connor

> *"Michael was probably the best player I'd ever played with. Absolute top drawer. I must have scored 20 odd goals in my one season at Athlone and I'd safely say he'd rolled almost every one of them to me to just tap in!"* – Roddy Collins

From a mid-table seventh position in 1978/79, Town finished top three in O'Connor's first season in charge behind Dundalk and eventual champions Limerick, and went on to take their first national title since their return to top flight football by winning the League Cup on November 28, 1979, beating St.

Athlone Town with the most distinctive jersey of the seventies!
Back row (L-R): *Pauric Nicholson, John Minnock, Noel Larkin, Mick O'Brien,*
John Duffy, A. McSwiney, Andy Stevenson. Front row (L-R): *Paul Martin,*
Dougie Wood, Joe Healy, Terry Daly and Eugene Davis (photo credit: Athlone Voice)

Patrick's Athletic 4-2 in the final with goals from Joey Salmon and a Pat Whelan hat-trick. It was just the starter to a delightful main course.

The 1980/81 season saw the Midlanders conquer all, losing just two games and winning their first League of Ireland title. There was no last day, heart-stopping, clenched teeth, kicking-the-cat frustration before a final whistle to endure as Athlone finished top by a comfortable six point margin (two points for a win in those days for all you young fellas out there). Eugene Davis's 23 goals were crucial that season, finishing top goal scorer in the league. Padraig O'Connor won the PFAI Player of the year, Turlough the SWAI Personality of the Year but, most importantly, it brought the club back into Europe.

This time around the St. Mel's outfit drew Danish side KB. Another Scandinavian outfit, KB had won 15 league titles to that point (they are now FC Copenhagen) and had a 17-year-old named Michael Laudrup on their books. Despite drawing 1-1 away from home (Michael O'Connor scoring) to set up a tasty second leg, the Danish outfit were 2-0 up after the hour in St. Mel's Park. Amazingly, Eugene Davis replied with two goals in the last 17 minutes to set up a grandstand finish, and had Turlough O'Connor's men found a winner the roof would have blown off St. Mel's and still be orbiting Saturn at this point. Alas, they didn't and The Town went out on away goals. They relinquished their crown a year later to Dundalk but won back the League Cup by denying Shamrock Rovers with a goal from Dom Fitzpatrick in the final.

The following season was the most successful in the club's history to date. Again under O'Connor, Athlone showed an even more ruthless streak. A League Cup campaign that started with a 1-0 win over Longford Town ended on the penultimate day of 1982 with goals from Harry McCue and Noel Larkin in a come from behind 2-1 win against Dundalk to retain their League Cup. The league was just as efficient. With just one solitary loss in 26 games, Athlone took the 1982/83 League of Ireland championship with ruthless efficiency, finishing a massive 16 points ahead of nearest rivals Drogheda. Noel Larkin topped the goal scoring charts with 18 goals to become the third Athlone player in three years to win the Golden Boot, after Eugene Davis in 80/81 and Michael O'Connor a year later with 22 strikes.

Again, the lads were off on their travels, this time drawing Standard Liege in the European Cup. The Belgians had won successive titles with players like Eric Gerets and were managed by Raymond Goethals, who went on to lead Marseille to Champions League glory in the 1993 final.

Now it was policy for every League of Ireland club to take a least one beating in Europe (or two, or three, or four) in the seventies or eighties, but Athlone had avoided this procedure with Milan and KB. Unfortunately, those waffle-making, chocolate-eating, frothy beer-drinking Belgians ruined this record by scoring 11 goals against the run of play over both legs against Athlone in their 1983/84 European cup tie. In the home leg, both Roddy Collins and Martin Salmon scored but a penalty by Belgian international Gerard Plessers on the hour capped a 3-2 win for Standard Liege. Two weeks later in Belgium, Athlone again scored twice. Trouble was, Liege scored eight.

> *"What made the game harder was we had four or five injuries to main players. Even though we were league champions we had a tiny squad and financially things were threadbare. A lot of weeks players would play through the pain barrier and line out in our first eleven even though they weren't near fit. But that was the type of character we had. To win the title first time around was great but to do it two years later with just half the squad was an even bigger achievement."* – **Turlough O'Connor**

It was the Midlanders' last venture into Europe to date. A League Cup defeat to Drogheda in 1984 followed, then in 1987, after a poor season of which just three wins were achieved, Town was relegated into a First Division still in its infancy. Under former player Denis Clarke, Athlone made an immediate return and, despite losing seven of their 27 games, pipped Cobh Ramblers to the 1987/88 First Division title in their centenary year.

The 1983 Standard Liege v Athlone Programme

The nineties brought relegation from the Premier Division in 1991/92 and promotion back to it in 1993/94 as runners-up to Sligo Rovers. However the bipolar existence continued and in 1996 the club was relegated again. This time it came with one of the most important spot kicks since the one by Mr. Minnock in 1975, and it was that same fate from 12 yards and missed penalties from Adrian Carberry and David Dowling which ultimately saw Athlone lose 4-3 in the promotion/relegation play-off against Home Farm Everton. Michael O'Connor's side had been surprisingly beaten 2-0 in the first leg at Whitehall and were up against it at St. Mel's Park. Goals from Conor Frawley and the heroically named Michael Collins forced the game into extra time for Athlone, but those missed spot kicks ensured a Premier Division birth for a Dermot Keely Home Farm side who would then sell a young Richard Dunne to Everton. Ironically, Keely had managed Athlone Town just months previously.

> *"I had nothing against Athlone, but the minute I arrived I just knew it wasn't right and ended up leaving shortly after. I've only ever made that mistake once before and that was with Derry City, and I've managed a lot of clubs, so getting it wrong twice out of twelve isn't bad!"* – **Dermot Keely**

He also somehow managed four clubs that year – Dundalk, Finn Harps, Athlone and Home Farm! Likes a bit of variety does our Dermot.

There was a welcome League Cup campaign in 1999 that saw Athlone beat Galway, Drogheda, and Rockmount on the way to the showdown with Derry City on December 8. Unfortunately, the Candystripes were in unstoppable form and The Town went down 5-2 in the final.

The new millennium was welcomed with Bill Clinton popping into town, Westlife violating modern music and a clown who said all our computers would go tits up because of the Y2K bug. It also saw the men from St. Mel's hoping for a return to the promised land of Premier Division football.

There was a title charge in 2000/01 when, under Liam Buckley, Athlone pushed Monaghan United and eventual champions Dundalk for the First Division title, but had to be content with third place and a two-leg decider against the students of UCD. The midland outfit won the home leg 2-1, but saw the scores reversed in Belfield Park three days later. Extra time couldn't separate the sides so that meant penalties, which obviously meant more heartbreak! UCD prevailed 4-2 on spot kicks and it remains the closest Athlone Town has come to Premier Division football since. John Gill managed the club for a brief period in 2005 and has vivid memories of his time there.

> *"I remember my first weekend at the club I had a mutiny on my hands! Half the players were from Dublin and half Athlone. I had arranged that every second week we'd train in Dublin, only to find out the Town players weren't having it. I remember having to read the riot act before we finally settled on a suitable training ground in Mullingar, half-way between both. It was some start!"* – **John Gill**

Despite First Division bottom half finishes for the rest of the decade, The Town has created one of League of Ireland's most well-known cult heroes of the period in Rod De Khors. Despite his exotic sounding name, Rod is a Dubliner who had three different spells with Athlone Town and was so popular he even had a book written about him.

> *"The fans were great. I remember going for a drink locally after games with players like Val Kennan and Barry Murphy and everybody would be so friendly. I endeared myself to them on the final day of the 1994/95 season against Derry City. The game was 1-1 and in the final seconds when Derry got a corner. I was absolutely knackered and the goal-post was only holding me up when Paul Hegarty headed towards goal. Somehow I got my leg to it, poked it wide and the whistle blew for full-time, denying Derry the title."* – **Rod De Khors**

An infamous clash with Eddie Gormley in one particular game saw De Khors sent off for placing his head where he shouldn't. As he walked off the pitch the crowds sang, "Who Needs Cantona, We've got Rod De Khors" – the title of local journalist Kevin O Neill's book on the Dubliner.

The oldest club in the country said an emotional farewell to St. Mel's Park in 2006 with a final game at the old ground against Monaghan United on November 10. The spiritual home of Athlone football since 1929 had seen some truly memorable moments. A League of Ireland birth. Championship Glory. Italian aristocrats and that penalty. A time never forgotten by so many and owed to so few. The club have had to roll with the punches the last few years, with sparse attendances, poor league positions and a seemingly revolving door at the manager's office.

Old friends are best. Some of Athlone Town's best players are brought back as special guests for one of the last games played at St Mel's Park. (L-R): Denis Clarke, Turlough O'Connor, Jackie Quinn and the late Joe Gaffey. (photo credit: Westmeath Independent)

Like many League of Ireland clubs, before and after, those most common of words, "financial difficulty", led the club to host an emergency general meeting with supporters as fears of the club's financial plight were laid bare in 2008. A patron scheme was launched and the wolves were fought off from the door (along with the poor starving bank manager) and the threat to Ireland's oldest club went away. The one bright spot was of course the new state-of-the-art, Athlone Town Stadium in Lissywollen, which the club moved into in 2007, with Kilkenny City the first opposition on March 9 that season. The Town celebrated in style with a brace from David O'Dowd and one from Eric Lavine in a 3-0 win.

For almost a century and a quarter now the oldest club in the land has been with us. Had one Orlando Coote of Larkfield not placed an advert in the *Westmeath Independent* there wouldn't have been an Athlone side to draw against Castlerea on February 9, 1887 in its first game, or maybe not even a triumph in the Free State Cup in 1924. Has one advert ever created a life of 124 years? Me thinks not.

> *"I was in a pub in Athlone some years back with a friend of mine who used to be a bookie. He'd given me a tip from the newspaper, and I like my horses so put on my glasses to study the form. The second I did a voice from the other end of the bar said, 'It's a pity you didn't have them on against Milan' – all I could do was smile!"*
> – John Minnock

Ground Info

Built in 2007 as a replacement for St. Mel's Park, the Athlone Town Sports Stadium is a modern facility located in Lissywollen, just 900 meters from Athlone City Centre. Though it would be hard to compete with a heaving St. Mel's during its heyday, the ground has lots of advantages which come with a modern purpose-built stadium. Parking will never be a problem with spaces for 200 cars, and should Milan ever come to town again the Athlone Sports Centre next door could probably be used as an emergency car park. The ground has one main stand that houses just over 2,000 people and runs the length of the pitch. It's the first phase of a development which could see the capacity at the stadium rise to 8,000 over time.

Record Attendance

9,000 v AC Milan (UEFA Cup, October 22, 1975)

Cost

Adults: €10.00
Students: €5.00 (with ID)
Under-16s/OAPs: €5.00
Under-14s: Free with paying adult

Programme

€2.00 – and coming in at a euro less than the standard League of Ireland programme. The fact that each issue is in black and white means nothing to the average fan; it's all about substance over style. A few more contributors would have bulked it up nicely, but I do like that they have named their programme *All Tangled Up in Blue and Black*.

Rivals

Separated by a mere 40 minutes, Longford Town will always claim this honour, year in, year out! The clubs first locked horns at top flight level in the 1987/88 First Division season and have been regular visitors to each other's ground in the same division the last four seasons.

Mascot

Leo the Lion – it should be mandatory that every club has a nutcase in some oversized animal suit, running up and down the sidelines, getting the crowd going and waving his hands behind the goal when the opposition has a penalty! Athlone's offering to the world of mascots is Leo the Lion.

Food and Drink

The nearest bar to the ground is the Green Olive located in Ballymahon Road whilst the Shamrock Lodge Hotel is also used by some Athlone supporters. Not far from the ground just off the roundabout to the right you will find Centra with a Supermac's in it! Surely that's a first?

Club Shop

A spacious club shop can be found under the main stand. One section will do you soup, sandwiches and coffee whilst the programme stand houses some old memorabilia for the collector in you plus a couple of recent Athlone Town books are available as well, one of which is *When We Were Kings*, the story of Athlone's first triumph in the FAI Cup.

Websites

www.athlonetownfc.ie
www.irishfootienetwork.com (Athlone section can be found there)

Local Radio

Athlone Community Radio 88.4 FM
Midlands Radio 103 FM

The Match – Athlone Town v Monaghan United (First Division, May 14, 2011)

Athlone has one of the youngest squads in the League of Ireland and manager Mike Kerley has had to mould his side into one that competes quickly at this level. Monaghan was on a solid run of form under Roddy Collins and was boosted by an away support that stood and sang their way through the entire 90 minutes (I got the feeling the lads where down for the weekend on a session). The result was never really in doubt after Ryan Brennan's opener as United won comfortably 3-0.

Bohemian FC

Formed: 1890

Ground: Dalymount Park

Capacity: 3,750

Nickname: Bohs or Gypsies

"I got £12 sterling in coins thrown at me in Dalymount. When I went to Scotland for the return leg I got 10p! They were far more charitable over here!" – Bohemians' goalkeeper Dermot O'Neill on Glasgow Rangers fans after their 1984 UEFA Cup tie.

One of Ireland's oldest clubs, boasting a 121-year history, Bohemians was founded on Saturday, September 6, 1890. At the time Parnell was leader of the Irish Parliamentary Party, Kitty O'Shea got dumped by the hubby and the country wasn't too long out of a famine caused by the one sodding vegetable that we still eat to this very day! It took three years before they secured their first ground (on a site on which ironically Croke Park now stands) and given the grandiose title of the City and Surburban Racecourse and General Amusement grounds.

Because no true nationwide league was in effect at the time, the Gypsies had to be content with winning the Leinster Cup, which between 1894-1899 they did six times in a row. At the time, the Irish Football League consisted almost entirely of clubs from what is now Northern Ireland, though some southern clubs did play in the Irish Cup. Bohemians became the first club from the south to reach the final in 1895 where they played Linfield. Bohs scored once. Unfortunately, Linfield scored ten. They eventually joined the Irish League in 1903. By this stage the club moved into what would become the spiritual home of League of Ireland football – Dalymount Park.

Basically a vegetable patch was the humble origins for the ground, as in 1901 the club turned it from a bed of carrots, potatoes and turnips at the back of the Dalymount terraced houses on North Circular Road into a place that's seen countless memories and wonderful matches over the last 110 years. If walls could speak, what tales they would tell.

Bohemians clinched the 1908 IFA Cup, defeating Shelbourne 3-1 at Dalymount Park in the first cup final contested between two clubs south of the border. The formation of the Free State League in 1921 saw the Gypsies compete in its inaugural season, finishing runners up to champions St James' Gate.

The club's first League of Ireland title arrived three years later in 1924 seeing off Shelbourne by four points and winning 16 of their 18 games with Englishman Dave Roberts hitting 20 goals. There was a runners-up spot to fellow Dubs' Shamrock Rovers a year later, but the title came back to Phibsborough in both 1928 and 1930 with old rivals Shelbourne the runners-up on both occasions. The 1928 season was also the club's first league and cup double. Having lost just two games in the league, Bohs destroyed non-league Cobh Ramblers 7-0, St. James Gate 5-0 and Shelbourne 4-1 before goals from Jimmy White and Billy Dennis against Drumcondra gave Bohemians the Free State Cup in front of a 25,000 strong crowd on St. Patrick's Day, 1928.

The thirties might have seen the Great Depression in Europe, and prohibition in America (could you imagine drink being illegal here?), but Phibsborough's finest were still on a high no bottle of stout could give. Another league title was captured in 1933/34, followed by the highest scoring 90 minute Free State Cup final to date: a 4-3 victory over Dundalk in 1935 with Jimmy Menton scoring the quickest goal in the cup's history after just 55 seconds. By this stage Bohemians were coached by Enniscorthy-born Bill Lacey. The Wexford man had played over 200 games with Liverpool in two different spells, as well as lining out for their neighbours across in Goodison Park before return to Ireland.

There was one more league title in 1935/36 as they saw off the challenge of then reigning champions, Dolphin FC, and the club then became the second winners of the Dublin City Cup, a popular competition that ran for 40

Bohemians side that took on Cork FC in Dalymount on October 15, 1938
Back (L-R):*George Lax (Coach), Mick McDarby, Tommy Mallin, Kevin O'Flanagan,*
Bill Nolan, Joe O'Brien, Andy Maguire, Charlie Harris. Front (L-R): *Eddie Wall,*
John McNally, Billy Jordan, Frank Fullen, Kevin Kerr (photo credit: www.bohemians.ie)

consecutive seasons. It ended a highly successive period in the club's history. Players included Plev Ellis, Paddy Andrews, Fred Horlacher (who succumbed to pneumonia aged just 33), Mick and Paddy O'Kane, and Harry Cannon who won nine competitions with the club.

Jimmy Dunne then stepped in to coach Bohemians in the early forties but success completely eluded the Phibsborough side for the entire decade. Their amateur status hampered the club and they finished bottom in 1948, '49 and '50. The only bright spots were reaching the FAI Cup final in 1945, where Shamrock Rovers beat them 2-0, and two years later when they lost out to Cork United after a replay.

The fifties again proved a barren phase and the club ended that decade like the one before, finishing bottom, with the 1959/60 season a particular low point. Bohemians became the first League of Ireland side since Bray Unknowns in 1941/42 not to win a single game, finishing the season with just five draws and 15 goals. Being an amateur club at this time was extremely hard going and Bohemians suffered among a sea of professional clubs.

The arrival of Sean Thomas coincided with an upturn in the Gypsies' fortunes, and in 1964/65 Bohemians got involved in their first serious title race in almost 30 years, finishing third behind Shamrock Rovers and eventual champions Drumcondra, and a year later Thomas repeated the trick before going one closer to finish runners-up in 1966/67 behind Dundalk. A new set of heroes had emerged, among them people like Mick Martin, the prolific Turlough O'Connor and Tommy Kelly, the club's record appearance holder with 575 games to his name.

Thomas left and two awful seasons followed, however that all changed in February 1970 when the club changed its constitution to allow the signing of professional players. Immediately there was an influx that paid dividends. Players like Johnny Fullam, a main part of Shamrock Rovers amazing six-in-a-row FAI Cup triumphs, former St. Pat's stalwart Dinny Lowry and Tony O'Connell, three-time cup winner with Shamrock Rovers and officially the first player to sign professional forms with the club. A man who went on to initiate the first shirt sponsorship deal in Irish football (with his company Jodi), he became a life-president and was inducted into the club's Hall of Fame. Not bad for a man who played just 42 games for the Gypsies!

People eating flowers, banning bombs and the start of a sexual revolution ushered in the seventies, but in Dalymount there was a revolution of a different kind. With amateur status behind them, Thomas's men made an immediate impact by winning the FAI Cup just three months later. The campaign opened with a Tony O'Connell goal to beat Cork Celtic, whilst another one-goal victory was enough to see off Shelbourne a month later. Doing their best Arsenal impersonation, the Gypsies recorded yet another 1-0 win in the semi-finals against Dundalk, courtesy of Ben O'Sullivan, putting them within 90 minutes of their third FAI Cup. With an obvious home advantage in Dalymount, the Gypsies started as favourites against Sligo Rovers. However the Bit O'Red, playing in their first FAI Cup final since 1940, weren't going to make it easy. The first game ended in a scoreless deadlock as did the replay.

By this stage the Gypsies had played five games with a record 500 minutes of football in-between and still hadn't got their hands on the cup. Finally, on May 3, 1970, goals from Johnny Fullam and Tony O'Connell gave Bohemians a 2-1 victory – their first FAI Cup since the days of Paddy O'Kane, Billy Jordan and Paddy Andrews. Tommy Kelly was also a happy man: his Man of the Match award won him a £50 voucher!

"To see people crying in the stand and winning the cup as a professional club for the first time was such a huge thing for the supporters. Of the goal I remember the ball breaking nicely for myself, just ahead of David Pugh, allowing me to take it on and hammer it home. I moved into the business end of things soon after and my company's sponsorship deal with Bohemians in 1973 meant the club became the first in the entire British Isles to have a sponsor's logo on their shirts."
– Tony O'Connell

Bohemians – 1970 FAI Cup Champions Back (L-R): *W. Watson, B. Duffy, W. Harmon, P. Howlin, K. Kerr, H. Bussey, S. Moore, E. Kettle, N. Nolan* Centre (L-R): *G. Mooney (asst. Hon. treas.), A. McSwiney, F. Swan, D. Parkes, D, Lowry, J. Clarke, B. O'Sullivan, M. Kelly, T. Hamill, T. Whittle.* Front (L-R): *D. Maguire (asst. Hon. Sec.), R. McFetridge (Hon.Sec.), P. Dunne (trainer), J. Conway, J. Doran, J. Fullam, L. Rapple (Pres.), T. Kelly, R. Nolan, S.Thomas (manager), J. Dinan, G. Devlin (Hon. Treas.) (photo credit: www.bohemians.ie)*

Bridging that 35-year gap spurred the Gypsies on to a healthy fourth position in the league the next season in a year when Fran Swan became the first Bohemians player to score in Europe in the club's Cup Winners Cup defeat to Czech side TJ Gottwaldov, 4-3 over two legs.

Thomas's side got closer and closer each year to the League title. In 1971/72 they finished third behind Cork Hibernians and champions Waterford, whilst repeating the trick a year later in '72/73. Twelve months on they claimed a runners-up spot to Cork Celtic, their highest position since '66/67. Two of those campaigns garnered European football, both against German sides. In September 1972, FC Koln won 5-1 over two legs with Gerry Daly scoring – a year later he was signed by Manchester United – whilst the autumn of '74 saw the Gypsies ship four goals over both games without reply to Hamburg.

There was no denying the Dalymount Park posse in 1975. And it was a cakewalk. Now under the stewardship of Billy Young (who held the post for 16 years), Bohemians hit the front early in winter and were unstoppable. There was so much experience throughout the team: Mick Smyth, Tommy Kelly, Declan Ingoldsby, Johnny Fullam, Terry Flanagan, Turlough O'Connor and John Doran, now Bohemians General Manager. The club's first League of Ireland Championship since 1936 was wrapped up on March 3, 1975 with a Sean Sheehy goal at home to Athlone Town with three games to spare, and the club made it a double with League Cup success over Finn Harps.

"Terry Flanagan was a great strike partner to play with. Big, powerful and held the ball up exceptional well. Johnny Fullam was a leader on the pitch and of course Billy was an excellent manager. He never worried about the opposition as he was so tuned into getting the best out of his own players and we played with such flair under him. I don't think Billy really got the recognition he deserves in football." – Turlough O'Connor

Off on their travels the lads went again, this time playing in the European Cup. However it would be an experience still fresh in many players' and fans' minds as Bohemians drew Scottish giants Glasgow Rangers. The Glaswegians had just won their league under Jock Wallace to end Celtic's nine-in-a-row domination, and boasted Alex McDonald, Derek Johnstone, Sandy Jardine and John Greig in their ranks. Of all the 31 teams in the draw, the Scotsmen were the very last club Bohemians wanted to be paired against.

Rangers won the first leg 4-1, but the ugly shadow of sectarianism was never far away, coming to the fore during in an ill-tempered second leg in Dalymount Park with fighting on the terraces and in the streets. The game ended 1-1 and Wallace's men left in a hail of broken glass praying they'd never have to play in Dalymount again. How wrong that would prove!

Billy's Young's men had to be content with relinquishing their title to Dundalk the same year, but a second FAI Cup that decade was achieved in May 1976 with victory over Drogheda United with a Niall Shelley goal. It was proving beyond doubt the most successful spell in the club's history for many years, as power shifted from Milltown to Dalymount.

A Cup Winners Cup appearance in September '76 provided the Gypsies with their first win in Europe at the ninth attempt, when Danish club Esbjerg had their lights turned out (considering the first three letters of their name I just had to put that awful pun in). A 2-1 win at home was followed by Noel Mitten's strike in Denmark – a rare away win for an Irish team on foreign soil sealing a 3-1 aggregate win. The second round proved unfamiliar waters for Young's men, as it did for many an Irish club in that era, and Slask Wroclaw (sounds like a Polish rock band) won 4-0 on aggregate.

Normally, seeing a magpie in your backyard is a sure sign of getting flattened by a truck within about 20 seconds of laying eyes on the unlucky sods, but the Gypsies were happy to welcome one into theirs when Newcastle United came calling in the first round of the 1977/78 UEFA Cup after Bohemians had secured European football again. They were changing times at Newcastle.

Joe Harvey, who had brought the club the Fairs Cup, was sacked after 13 years and his replacement Gordon Lee followed suit. Richard Dinnis stepped

*The prolific Turlough O' Connor scores again against a helpless Dundalk
(photo credit: www.bohemians.ie)*

in as caretaker manager but his Newcastle side couldn't break down Bohemians at Dalymount in a 0-0 draw. They did, however, make up for this by scoring four without reply at St. James' Park.

Bohemians then won a tight league championship in April 1978. With rivals Shamrock Rovers, Drogheda, Waterford and Finn Harps all taking points off each other, it wasn't a surprise when Bohemians ended up drawing 10 of their games but crucially finishing two points ahead of Finn Harps with a 2-0 home win against Sligo Rovers to secure the 1977/78 championship. Scorer on the day who be Turlough O'Connor. His brace that afternoon made a total of 24 goals to set a new club record for goals in a season. It stayed firm until Glen Crowe surpassed it in 2001.

Europe beckoned again. After seeing off the challenge of AC Omonia, Dynamo Dresden arrived in Dublin for a European Cup last 16 tie on October 18, 1978. Again the Gypsies acquitted themselves well, holding the German champions scoreless, but the second leg proved a bridge too far and Dynamo got six lucky goals without reply.

Victory over hated rivals Shamrock Rovers (or, let's just say, "a side they're not fond of") in the 1979 League Cup final made up for losing their league title to Dundalk that year, and there was a trip abroad again, this time in the UEFA Cup and a creditable 2-0 defeat to Sporting Lisbon.

A frustrating period for Young's men followed. Despite finishing top four in the next four seasons, a runners-up spot to their old Southside pals Shamrock Rovers in 1984 was as good as it got in the league. The FAI Cup was an even bigger source of annoyance, particularly in 1982 and '83. Having played six games to get to the 1982 final, which included a massive four game semi-final duel with Dundalk (3-3, 0-0, 1-1 and finally 2-1), Bohemians ran out of juice in the final losing to a Brendan Storan goal, which gave Limerick the cup.

A year later Drogheda attempted the same run in the semi-finals, this time taking the Gypsies to three games before goals from Jackie Jameson, Barry Murphy and Paul Doolin finally saw Bohemians into the final. Their opponents, rather surprisingly, were Sligo Rovers. On a day so wet I expected Noah to pop by Dalymount Park with the ark, both sides served up one of the best cup finals in history, but despite leading at half-time through a Barry Murphy header, Bohemians conceded twice in the final half hour and lost out for the second year running.

The real shame of those finals was the magnificent Jackie Jameson walking away without a winner's medal. The gifted Dubliner played over 200 games for Bohs and scored 70 goals, yet never won a league or cup or got capped at full international level for his country.

Astonishingly, the club's three European appearances in the eighties all came against teams from Scotland. Rangers, Dundee and Aberdeen all came to Dalymount in 1984, '85 and '87 respectively and left without a win. Dundee drew 2-2 but won at Tannadice, and Aberdeen scraped through thanks to one goal at Pettordie, but it was the tie against Glasgow Rangers in the 1984/85 UEFA Cup that will be remembered – for right and wrong reasons.

Having battled each other on the field (and off it) in 1974, the last thing anyone wanted was a repeat of the previous trouble. Again, it was more than a football match. Ironically, Jock Wallace, the manager showered in broken glass on his last visit to Dublin, was now back in charge of Rangers! He had left the Scottish giants after three league titles in 1978, but returned to manage Rangers in 1983, literally weeks before the UEFA Cup draw was made! I'm sure the words "Jesus" and "Christ" passed his lips on hearing the draw.

Over 2,000 Rangers fans arrived in Dalymount to a sea of Celtic shirts and a Union Jack being burned. Bohs goalkeeper Dermot O'Neill stood in front of the away fans watching the action as missiles rained down on him.

> *"I actually got £12 in sterling coins thrown at me that night. I remember that because I counted it! When we went over to play in Scotland for the return leg I got just 10p. They were far more charitable over here!"*– **Dermot O'Neill** *(from Paul Keane's* **Gods vs. Mortals***)*

The game itself was enthralling. Ally McCoist had given Rangers an early lead, but Dave O'Brien's equaliser after 25 minutes soon levelled things. The

Glaswegians regained the lead less than three minutes later through McPherson, only for O'Brien to level again. A Bohs' side including the likes of Mick Shelley, Dave Connell, John Reynor and a 21-year-old Paul Doolin trying to keep his nerve among the madness won the first leg through a Gino Lawless strike on 51 minutes in front of a 12,000 strong crowd that evening at Dalymount.

> *"It was my first ever European game. Years earlier I'd been to Dalymount to see Newcastle play Bohemians in Europe; now I was on the field and playing against the likes of Davie Cooper, Dave McKinnon and a young Ally McCoist. When you're so young you don't really think about the history or any trouble off the field or even nerves, you just concentrate on the game."* – **Paul Doolin**

The second leg at Ibrox was one of the biggest "what might have beens" in League of Ireland history. Just like Dundalk in 1979 against Celtic, Bohemians came agonisingly close to knocking out one of the Old Firm giants. Dermot O'Neill and his defence stood firm in front of eleven men and 31,000 fans until the 84th minute when Craig Paterson's goal broke a nation's hearts (yes, even Shamrock Rovers' fans had wanted a Bohemians win), whilst Ian Redford's goal two minutes from time added more agony.

The nineties started with a new man at the helm. Having managed the club to two League of Ireland championships, two League Cups, and an FAI Cup triumph, Billy Young was sacked on November 9, 1989. Kilkenny manager and former Bohemians defender Eamon Gregg, who had shared in those triumphs under Billy, was drafted in as his replacement in 1990. The club finished the year sixth, and had an even poorer season in 1990/91.

Redemption came in the form of the club's fifth FAI Cup triumph in 1992, when Gregg's men saw off the challenges of non-league Bluebell, Dundalk, Shelbourne and First Division St. James' Gate to square up to Cork City in Lansdowne Road on May 10 that year. Noel O'Mahony's side had finished third, were in a rich vein of form and went on to win their first League of Ireland title within 12 months, however a Dave Tilson strike gave the Gypsies the Blue Riband that day. Bohs were actually denied a cup double that season when Derry City defeated them in the League Cup final 1-0. The victory led to the club's first Cup Winners Cup appearance since 1976, however Romanians Steaua Bucharest didn't particularly make it an enjoyable one, winning 4-0 on aggregate, though yet again the Gypsies went an eighth European game unbeaten at home.

A dramatic 1992/93 season saw Bohemians forced into a first three-way play-off with Shelbourne and Cork City to decide the destination of the league championship. Winning the league had been in the Gypsies' hands, but a defeat to Dundalk on a dramatic final day of the season forced them into the play-offs. It was dramatic for all the wrong reasons as Bohemians' game kicked off late after the most unreliable of Irish transportation, the bus, broke down on the way to Oriel Park.

Bohemians fell short in the play-offs and Eamonn Gregg never recovered. By November of that year, despite another trip into Europe (losing to Bordeaux) Gregg was sacked. Keeping the same trend he was replaced by another former Bohemians stalwart in Turlough O'Connor. The appointment made sense. As a manager O'Connor had led his native Athlone Town to two League of Ireland titles and replicated it at Dundalk before his Dalymount Park appointment in December 1993.

Bohemians qualified for Europe via the Inter-Toto Cup for the first time in 1995, but got little change from a group involving three Scandinavian clubs and the French side Bordeaux. Turlough's charges pushed fellow Dubliners St. Patrick's Athletic all the way in the league title race in 1995/96 before finishing second, and a year later donned the bridesmaid's outfit again, this time to Felix Healy's Derry City.

Russian giants Dynamo Minsk got the fright of their lives in the 1996/97 UEFA Cup preliminary round, scrapping through on an away goal at Dalymount. The Gypsies even had the tenacity to hold Dynamo scoreless on their home patch in the second leg, but it wasn't enough. A year later Ferencvaros accounted for Bohemians in the same tournament.

The loveable Roddy Collins then took over in 1998 and led Bohemians to the 2000 FAI Cup final only to fall to Shelbourne 1-0 in a replay. Despite an almost disastrous 1998/99 season, which saw Bohemians finish third last and only hold on to their Premier Division status in a promotion/relegation match with Cobh Ramblers, a feather in Roddy's cap during his three-year tenure was signing a 22-year-old striker from Clonsilla who went on to score over 110 goals in 180 games for the Gypsies (133 overall in his two spells) and put himself among the top ten goal scorers of all-time in this country. Only 18 years old, Glen Crowe's career looked promising when he signed professional forms for Wolves in 1995 having been spotted at Stella Maris, however his career stalled and after a handful of appearances and some loan moves he found himself back in Ireland. England's loss was Bohemians' gain as Crowe became the league-leading goal scorer for three seasons between 2000-2003.

The new millennium saw a period of dominance on the pitch at Dalymount Park, better than any in their history, however they've sailed close to the wind off of it. Under Collins an eighth league title, their first since 1977/78, was clinched in the most dramatic of circumstances in 2001. Having fought off a relegation battle in his first few months as manager, then bringing the Gypsies back into Europe, Collins also experienced a season just as dramatic but with mixed emotions.

It started with an astonishing defeat of former Cup Winners Cup champions Aberdeen in the UEFA Cup. Roddy had signed players like Dave Hill, Simon Webb, Trevor Molloy and the much loved Kevin Hunt, and Bohemians produced a huge shock by coming from behind at Pettodrie to beat the Don's 2-1 on their home turf with late goals from Shaun Maher and Trevor Molloy. The second leg saw the Scottish club win 1-0 at Dalymount, but Bohemians progressed on the away goals' rule. The next round pitted the Dubliners against German club Kaiserslautern, who boasted the talents of Youri Djorkaeff and a young Miroslav Klose. The Bundesliga side came to Dublin in September 2000 and made off with a 3-1 win. Game over? Not on your life!

Glen Crowe astonishingly scored early in the second leg in Germany and put the proverbial cat among the pigeons, but despite another effort being ruled offside the Dubliners couldn't come up with another goal that counted. However, the result will go down as one of the greatest away results in League of Ireland history.

> *"The result against Aberdeen gave us great momentum. We'd just become the first Irish team to get an away win against a Scottish Premier team. Despite losing at home to Kaiserslautern I always thought if we could score early out there we had a chance. After Glen did we had a perfectly good goal disallowed as well as their goalkeeper making a world class save so there was no doubt in my mind we could have won and gone through on away goals. The funny thing about it is we had two men sent off, both in the home legs against Aberdeen and Kaiserslautern, but not lost to either side when we had eleven men on the field!"* – **Roddy Collins**

It gave Collins' men the base for the season and the league title soon became a fight between Bohemians and Shelbourne. Going into the last day, the Gypsies (who created one of the most unbelievable comebacks in the league that year, coming from 4-1 down against Shamrock Rovers to win 6-4) needed to beat Kilkenny City away at Buckley Park and hope Shelbourne messed up at home to Cork City. Bohemians won with goals from Morrisson, Molloy, Rutherford and a brace from Crowe, and astonishingly an Ollie Cahill goal for Cork City at Tolka Park saw Shels' snatch defeat from the jaws of victory and hand the championship to Bohemians. A week later, the Gypsies completed a League and Cup double with Tony O'Connor's goal in a 1-0 win over Longford in the 2001 FAI Cup final.

> *"To support Bohemians as a kid, to walk by Dalymount hoping one day I'd play with them, to eventually achieve that and then manage the club to their first league title in 23 years and first double in 73 years felt amazing. It was a great achievement, not for me, for the club."* – **Roddy Collins**

It saw Bohemians compete for the first time in the Champions League format (not for Roddy as he was replaced by Pete Mahon), where after beating Estonian champions FC Levadia Tallinn the Black and Red stripes went out to Swedish outfit Halmstad. Mahon then left in December 2001, replaced by a young Stephen Kenny.

Six months earlier Kenny had watched his Longford side lose out to Bohemians in the FAI Cup final at Dalymount, and now he was managing the Dubliners. He didn't disappoint. Despite still only 32 years of age, Kenny led Bohemians to another League Championship in 2002/03 seeing off Shelbourne in the title race by four points. Again progress was made in Europe, beating the Belarus champions FC Bate before a second qualifying round defeat to Rosenborg.

> *"When I joined Bohemians they had about 28 full-time players – so much different to the part-time operation at Longford, so the first thing I needed to do was trim the squad back. We let go a bulk of players then added the likes of Paul Keegan, Ashley Bayes, Derek Coughlan and Bobby Ryan to name a few. We had a great attacking brand of football that season, Rutherford on one flank, Ryan on the other whilst Keegan and Crowe worked brilliantly up front. And the lads worked so hard so it was great to get a reward at the end of it all."* –**Stephen Kenny**

Defeats to FC Tallinn in the UEFA Cup and K.A.A. Gent in the Intertoto Cup soon followed in 2004 and 2005, whilst Gareth Farrelly and Sean Connor came and went in the managerial hot-seat after Kenny vacated it. Farrelly got Bohemians to a League Cup final, whilst Connor presided over a third place finish which got the Gypsies into Europe where they lost in 2008 to FK Riga.

The 2008 season also saw an absolute stroll to the League Championship. Under an equally young Pat Fenlon, Bohemians clinched the Premier Division title by a record 19 points, destroying all opposition, and then added the FAI Cup to the Dalymount trophy cabinet with a 4-2 penalty shoot-out win over Derry City in front of 10,000 in the RDS after the sides had drawn 2-2 in normal time.

Bohemians manager Pat Fenlon in deep thought (photo credit: Fergus McNally)

"Certainly there was pressure when I stepped into the Bohemians job. At Shelbourne injury had curtailed my playing career which eventually forced me into management when I was still young so the expectancy level when I took over at Tolka Park wouldn't have been as high as when I walked into Dalymount a couple of years later. Now I was an established manager who had produced trophies at Shels so obviously there was a need to succeed, especially as an ex-Bohs player. The club meant a lot to me. Strangely enough, one of my fondest memories at Bohs was actually a Leinster Senior Cup game from 1993; I captained an experimental side and scored the only goal of the game against Shamrock Rovers. Though I've had bigger successes it's the one that stands out as a player there." – **Pat Fenlon**

Red Bull Salzburg broke the hearts of everyone at Dalymount with a last gasp win in their 2009/10 Champions League fixture, but it was off-the-field problems that dominated proceedings. With the proposed sale of Dalymount Park to a property developer seemingly falling through, the need for improved finances was paramount. Still, Fenlon led Bohemians to consecutive titles for the first time in their history in 2009, beating off the challenge of Shamrock Rovers in the league championship as well as victory over First Division Waterford United in the EA Sports League Cup final with goals from Neale Fenn and a brace from Killian Brennan in a 3-1 win.

Despite the financial worry off the field, Bohemians unfortunately produced a performance no amount of money could make up for when they went out 4-1 to Welsh part-timers The New Saints in the second qualifying round of the Champions League in 2010. Fenlon pulled no punches, calling it an absolute disgrace.

Phibsborough's finest recovered enough to win the 2010 Setanta Cup thanks to Anto Murphy's first half strike against fellow Dubliners St. Patrick's Athletic, and brought last season's 2010 Airtricty championship to the last day, but a 3-2 defeat to Galway in the penultimate game of the season did untold damage. Having fought from going behind twice with goals from Paul Keegan and a Jason Byrne penalty, Bohemians disastrously conceded a 90th minute Jason Molloy goal to hand the advantage to their bitter rivals Shamrock Rovers

Setanta Cup Champions for the first time – 2009/10 (photo credit: Ian Anderson)

who had a vital points (but more importantly goal) difference going into the last game of the season. It was an edge they held on to, taking the title at the Carlisle Grounds in a 2-2 draw against Bray whilst Bohemians were beating Dundalk 3-1.

The 2011 season started with the "will they, wont they" scenario of everything from having unpaid players, dropping to the A Championship to seeing complete extinction, but Phibsborough's finest are still about and competing.

More importantly, they are still doing it on the hallowed turf of a ground that holds such nostalgia and strong memories within its walls, longer than any in our land – one which if lost the club and league would lose a piece of their identity. Even Shamrock Rovers fans might agree with that one!

> *"I remember signing Derek Swan from Glentoran in 1994. He was a snip at only £2,000. A year later the Glen's manager and chairman came down to Dalymount to have a look at us playing. We won 2-0 and their manager asked me, 'who was the small guy who scored both goals?' I said, 'Sure, that's Derek Swan, we signed him from you last season!' To which he replied, 'Christ, whatever you do don't tell the Chairman that's him!'"* – **Turlough O'Connor**

Did You Know?

The charismatic Brush Shiels was once on Bohs' books. "I signed with Bohs in 1964 having spent a little time training at Drumcondra. I remember Drums Chairman Sam Prole giving me my bus fare from Tolka Park. I suppose it was a bung of sorts! I managed to play a few times for the second string, and I'll always remember being in awe of Jimmy Conway. Jimmy was a fantastic right half, great feet, great composure, you name the cliché, and it fitted him. He's still the best I've seen at Bohs and in this league."

Ground Info

Whether you're the SKY TV generation or a seasoned campaigner who stood on the terraces to watch O'Connell and O'Connor in their prime, Dalymount Park is always worth a visit. The little green patch of Phibsborough arguably evokes more memories than any other football ground in the history of our little Republic – a ground that once held 48,000 for a match against the old enemy and hosted countless cup final classics. Crowds may have dwindled from the years when it looked like the whole country was crammed into the ground, but Dalymount is still a rite of passage for any League of Ireland supporter.

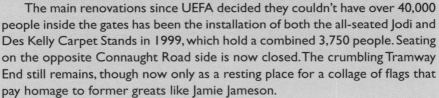

The main renovations since UEFA decided they couldn't have over 40,000 people inside the gates has been the installation of both the all-seated Jodi and Des Kelly Carpet Stands in 1999, which hold a combined 3,750 people. Seating on the opposite Connaught Road side is now closed. The crumbling Tramway End still remains, though now only as a resting place for a collage of flags that pay homage to former greats like Jamie Jameson.

Record Attendance

48,000 v England, May 19, 1957
League of Ireland – 45,000 v Shamrock Rovers (FAI Cup Final, April 22, 1945)

Cost

Adults: €15.00
Students/OAPs: €10.00
Under-12s: €5.00

Programme

€4.00 – and selling like hot cakes on my visit. Impressive in both content and layout with some good contributors. Will fill the half-time break without any problems and well worth the investment.

Rivals

Beyond any doubt – Shamrock Rovers. The clubs first met in 1915 in a Leinster Senior Cup fixture which Bohemians won 3-0, with Rovers first putting one over on the Gypsies in the semi-final of the 1921/22 Free State Cup. The Northsiders would have to watch Rovers dominate both league and cup, however Bohs' success after their switch to professional status in 1970 made them top dogs as the natural challenge to their Southside counterparts, and turned a minor rivalry into the classic, passionate derby you see before you today.

Mascot

On the night Bohemians had Dennis the Menace parading up and down the touchline before the game. Given that the mascot is modelled on a bully from a comic strip I'd use him in a more intimidating fashion – mind you, winding up Shamrock Rovers supporters before a local derby could result in kids seeing a cartoon figure being kicked to death in front of their eyes. Currently, the club is running a competition to rename him.

Food and Drink

Leo Burdock's have the contract for nosh inside the ground, and having shops littered throughout the capital you know exactly what you're going to get. I'm not a lover of curry chips, but when I saw a middle-aged man scoff one down in about 3.4 seconds then go back for more I made a beeline for the front of the queue.

There are three bars under the main Jodi Stand (the Phoenix Bar, the Jackie Jameson Bar and a Members Bar) which means you don't have to go too far for liquid refreshment. Outside the ground the nearest pub is the Bohemian on Phibsborough Road.

Club Shop

Located by the Jodi Stand and was doing a brisk trade. Bohemians' money problems have been well documented of late, but they won't go out of business for the lack of fans buying merchandise.

Websites

www.bohemians.ie – club website
www.thebohs.com – fans' forum

Local Radio

FM 104
Near 90.3 FM

The Match – Bohemians v Galway United (Premier Division, March 25, 2011)

Bohemians had a spate of injuries and fielded a slightly weakened side on the night, but that's not to take away from a great Galway United performance. The only goal of the game came on the hour after Karl Moore's cross was tucked past Barry Murphy by United's Joseph Yoffe to seal a win for the Tribesmen who were good value for their surprise three points.

Bray Wanderers

Formed: 1942
Ground: Carlisle Grounds
Capacity: 3,185
Nickname: The Seagulls

"After I scored the hat-trick in the cup final Pat Devlin told me he loved me. I still wake up in a cold sweat late at night at the awful thought of that!" – John Ryan

In all the foundations of League of Ireland clubs it's not really surprising that at least one of them could be traced back to an argument between the GAA and the "foreign sport". Bray Wanderers were those soldiers.

In a time when the country had been at war with itself (typical of us, gain independence then start a fight with each other), one thing was for certain – football or "soccer" was most definitely the evil foreign sport brought over by our nemesis across the water.

In 1922, a group of men from St. Kevin's, a local GAA club in Bray, not only left the association following a disagreement, but actually set up their own soccer team. In doing so they created a club still going strong almost 90 years later, though if you'd have told them soccer would be played at Croke Park and an English national anthem ringing out at a rugby match in the same venue they'd have had you sectioned.

Throwing themselves into the unknown (and possibly risking death by firing squad having switched to an English sport), the boys continued undaunted and formed Bray Wanderers. Entering themselves locally in the Sunday Alliance League Division 3, the club's first home ground was opposite Loreto Convent which is situated on Convent Road in the heart of the city. The club made quick progress and established themselves, working their way up to a runners-up spot in the Division 1 Sunday Alliance in 1928.

Their peers, of course, Bray Unknowns, were a well established League of Ireland side by this point. Entering the league in 1924, Unknowns had a moderately successful 19 seasons in the league, finishing fourth in 1936/37 whilst reaching the semi-finals of the Free State (or FAI) Cup in 1925, 1926 and 1940. However Unknowns played their first four seasons in Southside Dublin before moving to the Carlisle Grounds – currently, of course, the domain of Bray Wanderers.

The Carlisle Grounds can claim to be the FAI ground with the longest history as a sports venue. Opened in 1862 as the Bray Athletic Ground, it was renamed the Carlisle Cricket and Archery Ground later that year, in honour of the 7th Earl of Carlisle who performed the opening ceremony as Lord Lieutenant of Ireland. Later it was shortened to the Carlisle Grounds. Cricket and archery in the same ground? There's got to be a death in there somewhere.

Wanderers plugged away at the lower level, reliant on a dedicated handful of people like Andy O'Neill, Andy and Billy Hannon, Joe Dutton Sr, and the Fox brothers, Jack and Paddy, to keep the club running in testing times, with no money and pitches that on the odd time had the luxury of a blade of grass.

The club initially faded away but reformed in 1942, entering a much more competitive AUL League in 1943 – the same year Bray Unknowns folded. By the end of the decade, Wanderers, now well established in the Carlisle Grounds, had progressed to the AUL First Division (just losing out on the title to Rathfarnham) with players like Noel Dunne, Jack Scully, Owen Mullen and Lorcain O'Brien as part of the side that had brought Bray to their highest level of football to date.

National recognition came in 1951 when the club reached the FAI Junior Cup final. All roads led to Dalymount Park, where goals from Noel Dunne and Billy Devlin gave the Seagulls (an obvious nickname given their location) the cup over Drogheda United. Could they have foreseen a League of Ireland fixture between each other in later years?

In 1953/54 a double of an AUL title and another FAI Junior Cup was achieved, so there were no doubting Wanderers' credentials as a prominent junior football club. Bray's most noted player was of course one Alan Kelly Sr, who went on to play almost 450 games for Preston North End and got capped 47 times for his country.

Wanderers moved up to the Leinster Senior League in 1955 and by the end of the decade had added two Intermediate Cups to their ever impressive CV along with three Leinster Senior League titles in a row. There was also a first appearance in the FAI Cup against Longford in 1956. Having battled through the qualifying rounds, the Seagulls notched a 2-0 win against Longford Town, with goals from Jimmy Duggan and Jimmy Giles, and were denied a crack at Paddy Coad's magnificent Shamrock Rovers after they lost 1-0 in a replay to another non-league team – Workman's Club – in the next round.

The club reached the first round again in 1958 and '59, losing to Shelbourne and Chapelizod respectively. However there was a change in fortunes at the beginning of the sixties which was anything but swinging for the Seagulls. Despite having just completed three Leinster League titles and again reaching the first round of the FAI Cup (Sligo Rovers beating them 4-2), Bray withdrew from the Leinster Senior League partly due to lack of funds but also due to discontent with conditions in the league – and when you're complaining about conditions in an era when grass was a novelty you know things are bad!

It meant a return to the AUL and a halt to the great progress made. However all was not lost, and some familiar names from the past were directly responsible for the return of the Bray Wanderers seen today.

By 1973, ex-Republic of Ireland manager Mick Meagan and former Cork Hibernians' man Amby Fogarty had been co-managing Leinster Senior League outfit Bray Unknowns, but wanting to bring Wanderers back out of the doldrums they set about rectifying things. In changing their name from "Unknowns" to "Wanderers" Bray had a renewed life and in January of 1977 reached the first round of the FAI Cup for the first time since 1960, losing to Shelbourne 2-0.

The introduction of a new League of Ireland second tier in 1985 finally provided Bray Wanderers with the top flight status they craved, 43 years after they first kicked a ball around by the Loreto Convent. The First Division became the Premier Division and six new clubs competed in the inaugural 1985/86 League of Ireland First Division. Entering the league with fellow newcomers Cobh Ramblers, Derry City, EMFA, Monaghan United and Newcastle United, Bray, now managed by Pat Devlin, played their first game as a League of Ireland club on September 8, 1985 in a League Cup match against Dundalk. Jim Mahon had the honour of notching the Seagulls' first goal at the top level in the land, though pesky Dundalk took a point from the game. However beating a multi-talented Shamrock Rovers side, who won a league and cup double that season, in the very next game was especially gratifying with Mahon again on the scoresheet. The Seagulls went on to reach the quarter-finals of the League Cup (losing out to Home Farm 2-0) though loftier ambitions in the domestic league were rewarded that May.

It was hard to know how the club would react to that first season of League of Ireland football, but they need not have worried. With players like Des Kavanagh, Cormac Breslin, Dave O'Brien, Jim Mahon, Stephen Craig, Joe Lawless and "Chippy" Delvin, Devlin's side played their way to the top of the table, and a scoreless draw on March 2 at Ballybofey against Finn Harps gave Bray Wanderers the inaugural 1985/86 League of Ireland First Division championship, pipping Sligo Rovers by a point.

All set for the big time! Bray Wanderers 1985/86 squad – their first year in the League of Ireland (photo credit: Aidan O' Toole)

"It was a great experience. We were just a young bunch of lads playing for the badge and not money, without any real idea about how we'd do. We were playing to a great home support and travelling to places like Derry City who were pulling in close to 10,000 each home game. I learned so much that year, especially from players like Cormac Breslin. It was probably the only season he spent at the club but he taught me so much." – **Anthony "Bo" McKeever**

Wanderers only conceded 10 goals – a record that still stands today.

The step up in class didn't bother the lads in their first season in the top flight and reputations counted for nothing when you came to the Carlisle Grounds that year. Six wins and 17 points from their 22 games might not seem much, but Bray left four clubs underneath them to comfortably avoid relegation that 1986/87 season. However gravity kicked in 12 months later. The Seagulls got off to a poor start from which they never recovered and were relegated back to the First Division with Sligo Rovers, the side they had first come up with.

The turn of a new decade brought the fall of the Berlin Wall (and unfortunately David Hasslehoff singing on it the same night), a World Cup odyssey with an Irish baby boom to repopulate China and the gradual phasing out of the mullet (unless you live in my neighbourhood) and with it the start of a decade that saw Bray join an illustrious list of 23 previous teams before them in winning the Blue Riband of Irish football.

Little did anyone know when the campaign began against non-league opposition a week before St. Patrick's Day in 1990 that it would end in glorious sunshine and 30,000 people in Lansdowne Road – again against non-league opposition!

Oh, and *that* hat-trick.

> *"After scoring two I was fully aware by that point that Miah Dennehy had also hit a hat-trick against Waterford in 1972, but winning the game was all that counted. I remember Pat Devlin coming up to me after the game, looking me straight in the eyes and telling me he loved me. I often wake up in a cold sweat at night at that awful thought!"* – **John Ryan**

Bray took on Munster Senior League side Rockmount at home in the first round, comfortably winning 3-0. This put Pat Devlin's side into a last 16 meeting with Shelbourne at Tolka Park. A Brian Cosgrave goal managed to bring the game to a replay back at the Carlisle Grounds, where after 120 minutes without a net bulging once Bray clinched a quarter-final spot with a 4-1 win on penalties with Josh Moran the hero between the posts.

Home advantage, but more importantly a John Ryan strike, saw off Galway United in the next round, setting up a semi-final against the Candystripes of Derry City. The Premier Division Ulstermen were current cup holders under Jim McLaughlin and had added a continental flare to the league with players like Pascal Vaudequin, Nelson Da Silva and Owen De Gama, though it was only one player that truly worried Devlin.

Jonathan Speak scored 24 goals that season and the Bray manager had asked centre-half Mick Doohan to look after him (not in an Al Pacino way) but by half-time Bray's defence was about as much use as a chocolate fireguard with Speak causing mayhem. It called for drastic action.

> *"He had given us such a run-around in the first half that I was raging. But I had a plan! I turned around to John Holmes in the dug-out and said, 'At half-time, I'm going to take Mick by surprise, have a right go at him and then let on to punch him, to try get a reaction, you just make sure you stand in my way and stop me!' So in we went at the break, I had a go then made a run at Mick but slapped off the floor in front of him! Everybody just started laughing but it got the message across. We were a changed side after the break."* – **Pat Devlin**

> *"I wasn't a bit surprised as Pat was always going mental in the dressing room! You'd often see stuff thrown against the wall, but it seemed to get the right response from the players. He used to always say to me every year, 'I've signed a new full-back and he'll be taking your place.' And every year I saw them all off!"* – **Anthony "Bo" McKeever**

It had the desired effect. Wanderers turned the game on its head and goals from Reynolds and Smith put Bray through to the final.

> *"After the game Mick came up to me and said, 'Would you really have hit me?' to which I replied, 'Well I might just have.' He smiled and said, 'that's OK, I'd have hit you back!'"* – **Pat Devlin**

If Wanderers fans were pleasantly surprised to be in an FAI Cup final, you can be sure St. Francis supporters were stuck to the rafters in sheer delight. The non-leaguers made it past Kilkenny City, Cobh Ramblers, Newcastlewest (all away) before shocking Eamonn Gregg's Bohemians in the semi-final with a 1-0 victory.

Despite the fact that everyone outside the Carlisle Grounds was probably against them, when they walked out at Lansdowne on May 13, 1990, Wanderers made sure the non-leaguers wouldn't get the Roy of the Rovers ending and goals in the 20th, 60th and 81st minutes by an on-loan St. Patrick's striker made sure his name went down not only in Bray folklore but League of Ireland history.

> *"Brian Kerr had let me sign on loan to get some first team football at Bray and I really enjoyed the cup run. It may surprise many but we actually thought the pressure was off us in the final, despite St. Francis being a non-league side. Their win over Bohemians had shocked everyone and I think it made them a little cocky going into the game. We were lucky to have Pat as our manager. The professionalism he*

brought to Bray was second to none. Everything from our training methods to travelling two days before the game and getting suited and booted. I always maintained he was about ten years ahead of his time." – John Ryan

"With all respect to St Francis, I thought for the sake of League of Ireland football we had to win this game, but to be honest personally I was very confident we would. They never really troubled us that day." – Anthony "Bo" McKeever

The Bray Wanderers side that took on Turkish outfit Trabzonspor in the 1990/91 Cup Winners Cup Back (L-R): Adrian Cairns, Bo McKeever, John Ryan, Mick Doohan, Josh Moran, Alan Symth, Andy Lynch, Richie Parsons, Howie King Front (L-R): Dermot Judge (capt), Derek Corcoran, Martin Nugent, Colm Philips, Brian Cosgrave, Glen McCauley, Robert Murray. Mascot, Mark Devlin (photo credit: Vincent Kirwan)

For the first time Bray Wanderers got a chance to play in European competition. The excitement was palpable when the draw was made for the 1990/91 Cup Winners Cup. It placed the club into a tie against Turkish club Trabzonspor. A professional outfit who had won their national league no less than six times along with 12 different cups in all domestic competitions, it was a huge task for a part-time club still playing First Division football at the time.

But you can always call on good old fighting Irish spirit! Wanderers viewed it as an adventure but also gave the Turkish club something to chew on after the first leg in the Carlisle Grounds. A crowd of 5,000 watched Martin Nugent score the Seagulls' first goal in Europe in a drawn 1-1 game. Sadly, the European adventure ended two weeks later with Trabzonspor winning the home leg 2-0. If that was a tad annoying, the draw for the next round really pissed them off. Trabzonspor drew Barcelona.

Despite this, the season ended on a high with Bray winning promotion from the First Division, finishing three points behind champions Drogheda and a comfortable six ahead of third placed Cobh Ramblers. Premier Division status was maintained after finishing eighth in 1992, but the introduction of the ridiculous two tier league (which the Scottish Premier has been stupid enough to adopt these days) resulted in Wanderers being relegated a year later. OK, it didn't result in them being relegated as they finished bottom anyway but it was a balls of an idea from the start!

This led to a bipolar existence for the rest of the decade. Dumped back into the First Division, the team didn't respond and finished ninth in their first season back there, moderately improving to eighth in 1994/95. Promotion for a third time was achieved under Pat Devlin (interviewing the man is a nightmare as I couldn't get a serious answer of him for his cracking jokes and taking the piss!) in the 1995/96 season, going up as champions, but was followed by immediate relegation the next year.

Dusting themselves off from a painful 20 defeats that season, the club once again gained automatic promotion behind Waterford United in 1998, but it again only led to the minimum eight months in the Premier Division.

Since John Ryan's hat-trick at Lansdowne in 1990 the cups hadn't offered much solace outside of their ever changing league status. The best the League Cup could offer that decade was a semi-final placing in 1999, losing out to Derry City, whilst a low point of FAI Cup campaigns came in the shape of a 4-0 defeat at the Carlisle Grounds to non-league Fanad United in 1996. But there's always a good time coming, be it ever so far away, and things would change on May 20, 1999.

Despite Premier Division relegation, Wanderers became the first club to lose their top flight status and win the FAI Cup in the same season. It was also the first final since 1970 to take three games to decide. With Finn Harps the opponents, the first game was a hugely disappointing scoreless draw at Tolka Park, however the replay sparked to life with Jonathan Speak scoring for Harps just before the hour mark. Pat Devlin's men had to dig deep and Barry O'Connor popped up with three minutes left to send the game to extra time. Again the men from Donegal regained the lead in the first period, but Bray clawed the Northerners back with a Kieran "Tarzan" O'Brien goal from a rebounded Colm Tresson penalty with seconds left.

> *"I never expected Colm Tresson to miss it but followed it up anyway. To be honest, by the time Brian McKenna saved the kick I was already inside the area and when I slotted home the rebound I probably*

wasn't far from the penalty spot! It was then you got the feeling your name is on the cup." – **Kieran O'Brien**

Jason Byrne scores against Finn Harps in the second replay of the 1999 FAI Cup final
(photo credit: Micheal Tierney)

It was more of the same in the second replay. Finn Harps took the lead, but like a good old fashioned horror movie serial killer, Bray came back from the dead again, levelling through Jason Byrne, except this time Wanderers finally put the tie to bed with another strike from Byrne on 74 minutes to give the Seagulls their second FAI Cup.

It was a huge achievement, particularly for long-serving players like Maurice Farrell, who went on to make over 270 appearances in a 13-year spell with the club, and Alan Smith, Kieran O'Brien and of course Mick Doohan – the man almost flattened by Pat Devlin.

Despite starting the 1999/2000 season in the First Division, Bray had a European date with Swiss club Grasshoppers Zurich to keep. Just like their only other foray into Europe nine years earlier, it was a mammoth task for a side who started the season squeezing past Longford Town 1-0 in front of a couple of hundred die-hards to actually beat a professional Swiss outfit with 25 league championships to their name and Roy Hodgson as manager.

Hold up. Roy Hodgson as manager? Christ, maybe Bray should have beaten Grasshoppers! Nevertheless, a side with players like Turkish International Hakan Yakin and Swiss hitman Stephan Chapuisat won both legs 4-0 before going out to Newcastle United in the third round.

Anthony McKeever and Mick Doohan lift the 1999 FAI Cup
(photo credit: Micheal Tierney)

"It was my first European game so I was going to enjoy it, and though the task was daunting Pat was always a very good tactician, and for periods of the away leg we frustrated them. However it's the old adage of the last 20 minutes and we gave away late goals which killed us off. Physically you get tired but I think it's more mentally, especially if you're a defender trying to keep that level of concentration over 90 minutes against such a good side." – **Kieran O'Brien**

The season had a happy ending with promotion from the First Division (that opening day victory proving crucial as Bray pipped Longford by two points for the title) before an astonishing 2000/01 Premier Divsion season saw them finish fourth, winning 15 of their 33 games. However it wouldn't be Bray Wanderers if the decade didn't have a set of promotions and relegations. The new century was no different.

The year 2003 was an extremely strange one as it saw the club relegated from the Premier Division yet make the First Division play-offs the same calendar year. This was due to the switch from the tried and trusted September to April season in favour of summer soccer. The 2002/03 season started in July '02 and finished six months later in January, and then the 2003 season started that April, meaning that there were two football seasons in the one year. Only in Ireland (or perhaps America, where anything is possible). Eamon Zayed hit 19 goals that season (I mean year, no season, no year!) as the club lost in that play-off to Finn Harps.

A 2004 promotion gained Wanderers Premier Division status again, and this time for a healthy five seasons, mostly under Eddie Gormley before finishing last in 2009.

Things looked bleak, but just when you're ready to kick off against Salthill Devon and look nervously at the A Championship, up popped another Cork side to go bankrupt! The demise of Premier Division Cork City, who re-appeared as Cork City Foras that summer, automatically kept Bray in the top flight, a position which they still hold as they kicked off the 2011 season, though only after an amazing, heart-stopping sudden death penalty shoot out victory over First Division Monaghan United in the 2010 promotion/relegation play-off.

Bray survived an onslaught in the first leg at Gortakeegan, but stood firm only to fall behind in the last minute of extra-time at the Carlisle Grounds. Remarkably, a Jake Kelly goal and a sudden death missed penalty from Monaghan's Paul Whelan kept Devlin's men in the Premier Division.

> *"I never watch penalties, so to stand in our Portakabin that night at the Carlisle Grounds instead of the dug-out was nothing new for me. It's stood to me actually as we've won a few with me using that system! You could call it fate or luck, but basically it's down to one single thing . . .* [points to the sky and smiles] – Pat Devlin

If an amusement park is ever built in Bray it should definitely include a rollercoaster ride called "The Seagull" that mimics Bray Wanderers Football Club. Up and down, in and out, heart in mouth and always great value for money.

Ground Info

Located on Quinsborough Road in the heart of Bray, the Carlisle Grounds will actually be celebrating 150 years as a sports venue in 2012, having been first opened in 1862 as the Bray Athletic Ground. Wanderers' capacity is classed a shade under 3,200. The main stand holds just under 1,000 people with uncovered seating on the opposite Dart Side as well, and parking for 50-60 cars to the back of goal-facing Seapoint Road. There are also a collection of Portakabins (they are UEFA licenced) which, like the "Late Late Show", seems to have one for everyone in the audience – control room, hospitality, changing rooms, office and even First Aid. I suggested a lap-dance Portakabin to one member who laughed, but I'm sure walked away with an imaginary light bulb over his head!

Record Attendance

5,200 vs Bohemians (Premier Division, December 8, 2002)

Cost

Adults: €15.00
Children: €5.00
Concessions: €10.00

Programme

€3.00 – and if you like your stats then this one's for you. A lot more colour within the pages of *Wanderers Review* which I'm sure brings the printing costs up, but enough info for the anorak among you to stay happy whilst you sip your half time Bovril. Ah Bovril, remember that?

Rivals

UCD is the local derby however Bohemians have proved a bogey side over the years so the Gypsies are probably just as much a nuisance as the Students!

Mascot

It's a bit surreal when you pop to the toilet only to have a six foot seagull having a pee alongside you talking about the weather, but "Rocky" the club mascot seemed to pop up everywhere that night!

Food and Drink

Crowds can be sparse at Friday night league games but you'd still get a dedicated chipper holding the fort every weekend. However throw in a League Cup game on a Monday night and a battered sausage goes out the window. The club tuck shop stayed open; however an invite into the hospitality cabin along with a nice muffin saved the day! Outside the ground the Hibernia Inn on Marine Terrace is the popular choice for Bray Wanderers supporters for a pre/post match drink.

Club Shop

The club has a well supported online shop whilst at the ground you might find what you're looking for in "Rocky's Roost" – home of the Bray Wanderers Junior Supporters Club which I thought was a neat idea. Obviously there was a recruitment drive on as there were a few bodies floating about, whilst the mascot for the night played on the foosball table inside the hut, eagerly waiting to run out on to the Carlisle Grounds with his club captain.

Website

www.braywanderers.ie

Local Radio

East Coast Radio 103

The Match – Bray Wanderers v Drogheda United (EA Sports Cup, March 28, 2011)

From the word go I was convinced this cup tie was heading to penalties. It just smacked of it. Drogheda had brought a few down, though most seemed to be under18, which, considering it's a Monday night and an hour up the M50 to Drogheda, is slightly worrying. Do their parents know where they are? The game was won in typical fashion – on my only visit to the toilet – through a Shaun Skelly goal for the visitors.

(photo credit: Brendan Moran, Sportsfile)

Cork City

Formed: 1984
Ground: Turner's Cross
Capacity: 7,366
Nickname: The Rebel Army

"We'll still be happy if we lose. It's on the same time as the Beer Festival!"
– Cork City manager Noel O'Mahony before the UEFA Cup tie against
Bayern Munich

The chameleons of League of Ireland football. A club that's been represented with no less than eleven different versions, changed more times than a closet transvestite and 87 years after they were first represented by men more attune to camshafts and gearsticks, the City by the Lee still has a competing League of Ireland side to call its own.

A lot of research was done for this book. Some clubs' histories I could get through on a few cups of coffee and the right documents. Some needed a bit more delving with a wee drop of whiskey. Cork turned me into a full blown alcoholic. By the time I'd finished their chapter, Jack Daniels could have sponsored the entire publication, but to tell the story of those who graced the fields everywhere from Milltown to Market's Field I have to briefly include them now.

From Fordsons to Foras, the Leesiders have produced teams of great depth and quality. They've won honours, courted controversy, gone bust but risen from the flames, again and again. It's a common misconception to think the Leesiders are the only ones to have constantly changed names (Dublin clubs have made far more title changes throughout the years), however if ever the next resurrection of Cork football needs a crest may I suggest the phoenix?

Fordsons was the first club from the county. The car and tractor manufacturer was set up in the city in 1917 by Henry Ford, creating almost 3,000 jobs at a time Ireland was still under English rule. The club quickly coined the nickname "the Tractors" and played their home games at Ballinlough Road, reaching the 1924 Free State Cup final before losing out 1-0 to Athlone Town.

Spurred on by this, the club went one better two years later by defeating Shamrock Rovers 3-2 in the 1926 final having twice come from behind. Englishman Dave Roberts scored for the Cork club but it was a brace from Paddy Barry either side of that goal that gave the Fordsons their first major honour.

The club was the opposite side of the financial coin in League of Ireland terms as they never struggled for money. Healthy gate receipts and the sponsorship of good old Henry saw to that, however at the end of the 1929/30 season Fordsons were informed by the management of Henry Ford that they could continue as a factory team only and compete in local leagues. It was a blow considering that in their six-year tenure the club had reached two Free State Cup finals (winning one) and finished in the top four almost every season.

A name change was necessary and in 1930 Cork FC, originally nicknamed the "League of Nations" because of an over-reliance on foreign imports, was founded. The club didn't have the use of Fordsons Ballinlough ground, which was vacated by the motor company, so they became tenants at the Mardyke.

The team was full of Irish internationals. Charlie Dowdall, a league winner with St. James Gate in the inaugural League of Ireland season, became the first Cork FC player to be capped at international level in 1931 against Spain. Eight other players, including Billy Harrington, Tom Burke and goalkeeper Jim Foley, were also capped whilst playing for the club.

Two years later, another Leeside club thought it was time to get in on the act so Cork Bohemians, a club which had already won the Munster Senior Cup four times, were entered into the League of Ireland in the 1932/33 season.

Cork FC was the more successful of the clubs, winning the Free State Cup in 1934 by beating St. James Gate 2-1 with goals from Tim O'Keeffe and Jack Kelso. There were runners-up spots in the league in 1931/32 and 1933/34 whilst also reaching another Free State Cup final in 1936 losing to Shamrock Rovers.

As for Cork Bohemians? Things didn't quite work out the same! Having gained entry into the league following the expulsion of Waterford FC, Cork Bohs finished seventh in their first season, last in their second and, crippled with financial trouble, went bust after just two short seasons.

Cork FC then folded two years later in 1938 and were immediately replaced by the first version of what we see today – Cork City FC. This saw the shortest reign of a club from the city as despite boasting players like Irish internationals Jackie O'Driscoll, Tom Davis and Owen Madden the club folded after a disastrous 1938/39 season where only Waterford kept them off the bottom.

In 1940, the fifth Cork side to enter the league came in the shape of Cork United who played the final few fixtures of Cork City's ill-fated season. Keeping several players from the season before whilst adding new talent, United was a resounding success. For almost a decade the club boasted the talents of

Cork United – 1941 FAI Cup Champions Back (L-R): *M. Goold (MD), R. McCarthy, J. Clayton Love, W.E. Williams, W. O'Hare.* Middle (L-R): *H.R. Kenworthy, W. Little, J. McGowan, J. Foley, P. Duffy, J. O'Riordan, F. McGreevy, M. Lynch.* Seated (L-R): *S. Palmer, J. O'Reilly, R. MacFarlane, O. Madden (capt), L. O'Neill, S. McCarthy, F. Mullins.* Front: *J. Hooks, M. McKenna (photo credit: Plunkett Carter)*

players like former Huddersfield Town defender Bill Hayes, Tommy Moroney and Johnny McGowan, both later of West Ham United, the ever reliable Florrie Burke, Owen Madden, Seanie McCarthy and Fox Foley. Frank O'Farrell, who went on to manage Manchester United, also played for the club briefly. United was so dominant they won five League of Ireland titles in six seasons. Along with this United added two FAI Cups (1941, 1947) and two League of Ireland Shields.

Cork United regularly pulled in thousands for their games, but in October 1948 the club was voluntarily resolved bringing to an end an eight-year association with the league. But those rebels down south didn't leave a small thing like the liquidation of a soccer club get them down, so Cork Athletic was immediately formed!

Athletic won the League of Ireland title in their first complete season, 1949/50, finishing a point ahead of Drumcondra. A double was on, however Dublin club Transport killed off that dream. That 1950 FAI Cup final was the first to go to three games. Paddy O'Leary and Paddy Cronin scored in the initial game which finished 2-2, and the replay three days later also finished the same, this time with two Jackies (O'Reilly and Lennox) scoring, however Transport finished the job in the second replay 3-1.

The lads didn't get too downhearted and a Hugh Ross side featuring the great Noel Cantwell remedied this a year later, winning the League Championship and FAI Cup in 1950/51. They pipped Sligo Rovers by a point for the league title and defeated Shelbourne with a goal from Johnny Vaughan to complete the first double from a Cork side since Cork United in 1941.

A poor league season followed and in trying to retain the FAI Cup, Athletic was beaten 3-0 in the final by Dundalk after an initial 1-1 draw. It didn't help matters that just before that replay one of Athletic's directors had to face trial on an attempted murder charge with some of the club's officials and players even giving evidence! Even by Cork's standards and football history this was strange!

By then, fellow Cork club Evergreen United had entered the league in 1951, playing their home games at Turner's Cross. In 1953, both sides met in the first all-Cork FAI Cup final. It took a replay on a wet and miserable April 29th in Dalymount for Athletic to prevail 2-1 with goals from Raich Carter and Jackie Lennox.

"The town was absolutely abuzz in the lead up to the final. I worked as a carpenter in John Sisk's and every day I would get wound up by the Evergreen fans working with me – and I still get people getting on to me even now! But it was great banter. We had such wonderful players. People like Johnny Vaughan and Murty Broderick. Our big

signing of course was Raich. We were amateurs and he was on £50 a week, but he was great in that final." – **Former Cork Celtic player John Coughlan who played in the 1953 final**

After that cup final victory Athletic went into decline, though Manchester United and Celtic legend Jimmy Delaney managed the club to another cup final before they folded in 1957.

"Jimmy was magnificent. I played under him in the 1956 Cup final against Shamrock Rovers when both he and Jimmy Murphy scored, but it turned out to be an awful experience. We were 2-0 up with ten minutes left and Rovers still ended up beating us 3-2. I'll never forget Ronnie Nolan scoring in the last minute. It took me 15 years to get revenge when I won the league in 1971 with Cork Hibernians. But it was worth the wait." – **Former Cork Athletic player Donie Wallace**

Cork Hibernians in their debut season of 1958. Back (L-R): *Jimmy Redmond, Johnny Vaughan, Sean O'Brien, Patsy Dorgan, Peter Doolin, Jack O'Connor* Front (L-R): *Paul O'Donovan, George Clifford, Jackie Morley, Eddie Crossan, Liam O'Flynn (photo courtesy of Plunkett Carter (photographer unknown))*

Seven teams applied to take the place of Athletic (Cork Hibernians, Glasheen, Wembley, Cork Celtic, Bray Wanderers, Workmen's club and Chapelizod) with Cork Hibs winning the vacant league spot. Setting up shop initially at the Mardyke before moving to Flower Lodge, Hibernians lasted almost 20 years in the top flight with a 1970/71 League Championship and back-to-back FAI Cups in 1972 and 73 being the zenith of the club's lifespan.

Hibs enjoyed some truly memorable years with players to match. People like John Lawson, Tony Marsden, Carl Davenport, Sonny Sweeney, ex-Arsenal full-back Dave Bacuzzi, who managed the league championship winning side of '71, and Dave Wigginton – the all-time Hibernians top goalscorer with 73 strikes.

Oh, and I'm forgetting a wiry, young slip of a lad called Miah. Signed by manager Amby Fogarty in 1969, Miah Dennehy became a legend on Leeside, scoring a hat-trick in the 1972 FAI Cup final against Waterford FC, signing for Nottingham Forest for the huge sum of £20,000 in 1973 and standing for *Amhran Na bhFiann* in the green of his country 11 times.

Hibernians also reached the FAI Cup final in 1960 and '63, took home the League of Ireland Shield twice (1970, '73) and won the Blaxnit Cup beating Coleraine in the 1972 final before leaving the league in 1976.

Hey, who's the new boy? George Best (2nd from right in front) lines up for Cork Celtic during his brief stay in 1975 (photo courtesy of Irish Examiner)

Cork Celtic, who had joined the league in 1951 as Evergreen United but changed their name at the start of the 1959/60 season, enjoyed a 28 year residency before checking out in 1979. However in that time they captured a League of Ireland Shield in 1961, and finished bridesmaids in the FAI Cup three times before finally winning the League Championship in 1974. Many will remember the introduction of George Best as a short-term solution to a financial crisis a year later. Geoff Hurst played nine games, scored three goals and, strangest of all, former German international Uwe Seeler played for one game in 1978, scoring twice against Shamrock Rovers. I'm guessing the six that Rovers replied with made up his mind about staying!

At this stage another Cork club threw their hat into the ring. Albert Rovers were elected to the league in 1976 in place of Hibernians, lasting six seasons, but in true confusional Cork style changed their name three times! Albert Rovers was relaunched as Cork Albert, then lengthened to Cork Alberts, reached the 1978 League Cup final, and then changed to Cork United in 1979 which they stayed under until being expelled from the league in 1982. The following year marked the first season a Cork club did not compete in the league since 1924, and it stayed this way until the arrival of Cork City in 1984.

Elected to the league on July 1, 1984 and playing in Flower Lodge with Bobby Tambling as manager, Cork City played their first game under that moniker against Avondale United in the Munster Senior Cup winning 2-1. Tambling was replaced by Tony "Tucker" Allen after 13 games.

That first season saw Cork win ten games and finish ninth, however with four teams being relegated to the new First Division that year it meant City only survived by two points. If the first season was close, the second was even tighter than a duck's arse. This time only four goals kept Tony Allen's side up, their −21 goal difference slightly better than Shelbourne's −25.

There was a move to Turner's Cross in 1986 and some mid-table stability under Noel O'Mahony, however there was managerial musical chairs soon after as Eamon O'Keefe took charge of proceedings. O'Keefe, who had notched up almost 200 appearances in England between Everton, Wigan, Port Vale and Blackpool, delivered the club's first silverware in the shape of the 1987/88 League Cup. Coming out of a group with Waterford, EMFA, and fellow Rebel County members Cobh Ramblers, City then beat Limerick and St. Patrick's Athletic before facing off against Shamrock Rovers on October 21, 1987 in the League Cup final. A Kieran Myers goal 13 minutes from time in front of 3,500 at Turner's Cross saw the first national silverware residing by the River Lee since Cork Celtic's 1974 League Championship triumph. A year later, O'Keefe vacated the hot seat through a combination of poor results and dwindling attendances with Noel O'Mahony returning to manage the club.

A first FAI Cup final was reached in May 1989, however Derry City won to complete a treble of League, League Cup and FAI Cup victories that season. Crucially, however, it meant bringing European football to the club. Noel O'Mahony's side was placed in the Cup Winners Cup, however any romantic dream of a trip to Barcelona at the Nou Camp was replaced by a testicle-numbing trip to Russia and Torpedo Moscow. Torpedo had won their national league three times and the Soviet Cup a further six so there was no denying their pedigree. City went down 5-0 behind the Iron Curtain and lost to a single goal at home two weeks later to call a halt to their European campaign.

By the start of the nineties City was competing at the right end of the table and crowds were healthy and happy. A record breaking 24 game unbeaten run, starting on April Fool's Day, 1990 with a win against Athlone and ending on January 20, 1991 against Shamrock Rovers, was enough for Cork City to finish runners-up in the 1990/91 league championship losing just two games all season. Crucially, one of those was to Dundalk in front of 12,000 people at Turner's Cross, which effectively handed the title to the County Louth men.

The boys got ready to stock up on Duty Free again (probably an advantage on the Russian trip given the Muscovites fine taste in vodka), this time getting a plum draw against German footballing giants Bayern Munich.

> *"We were actually on tour playing in a prestigious tournament in China when word came through about Bayern Munich. It was great news to play one of Europe's finest clubs, so we were looking forward to it. Mind you, on that tour we were playing against the likes of Den Haag, the Polish B team and the Shanghai national side in front of 30,000 people each game. It was fantastic. I think people thought we were the national side as when we first stepped off the coach everybody wanted to know where Jack Charlton was!"* – **Dave Barry**

The game was switched to Musgrave Park, the home of rugby in Cork. Munich arrived with a world class pedigree and a world class mouth in Stephan Effenberg. The temperamental Munich player lined up against Cork City at Musgrave Park on September 18, 1991 and scored in a 1-1 draw. Infamously, he later gave German fans at the 1994 World Cup a clear view of his middle finger after being substituted by manager Berti Vogts. Berti may be five foot nothing but he didn't get the nickname "Der Terrier" for showing Yorkshire Terriers at Crufts and promptly sent the big midfielder packing from his national side.

Cork City celebrate winning the 1992/93 League of Ireland championship at the RDS.
(L-R): Anthony Buckley, Phil Harrington, John Caulfield, Dave Barry and Liam Murphy
(photo credit: Ray McManus/Sportsfile)

It was a special day for Cork, and in particular Dave Barry. The Cork Gaelic footballer doubled-jobbed for City when not winning All-Ireland titles and put City up 1-0 against Germany's most decorated club side that afternoon. O'Mahony's side had drawn Bayern at the right time as they were struggling badly in the Bundesliga with new manager Soren Lerby under pressure. The Corkmen then travelled to the Olympic Stadium for the second leg where two late goals by Bruno Labbadia and Christian Ziege in Bavaria finally finished off the Leesiders.

A climb that started in August '84 reached a high point in May 1993 when, after the most complicated three-way play-off system in the entire history of world football was finished, Noel O'Mahony's Cork City side became Premier Division champions for the first time in their short nine-year history.

On the last day of the 1992/93 league season Bohemians only needed a draw away to Dundalk to take the title, but on the way to the game at Oriel Park their bus broke down. Whilst the bus driver was up to his tits in oil, Cork was comfortably beating Limerick 3-0 and the third lover in this football ménage a trois, Shelbourne, won their game via a last minute Paul Doolin goal. So by the time Bohemians finally kicked off in Dundalk the equation was simple for Turlough O'Connor's men.

However Tom McNulty then earned the freedom of Cork City by scoring the only goal of the game and condemning Bohemians to defeat, thus making history with a three-way play-off between themselves, Shelbourne and Cork City. Four games were played by all three teams. Naturally, they all won one, drew two and lost one!

It was then decided the RDS Showgrounds would host two games as a neutral venue in the second round of play-off games. City, having beaten Bohemians 1-0 at Turner's Cross, was finally crowned League of Ireland champions on the April 25, 1993 with a pulsating 3-2 win over Shelbourne with goals from Pat Morley, Dave Barry and Paul Bannon.

Times were good, but Cork has never sailed in a calm sea, and ardent followers will always tell you choppy waters are never too far away. So it was vomit over the stern side when Noel O'Mahony announced his resignation soon after. It was also the season City played their football in a venue that sits as comfortable with City supporters now as a month-long dose of hemorrhoids. Bishopstown was supposed to be the shining light of Cork football, a way forward into the future, but it was beset with problems from the start. If Cork City was the Titanic, Bishopstown was its iceberg.

Even before the club's first game at the venue, a friendly against Glasgow Celtic, the County Council ruled that the stand had contravened planning regulations. The venue was also on the outskirts of the city at the time and badly served by buses, which particularly affected Northsiders. One bad winter at the ground highlighted the major drainage problems, and although a state-of-the-art system was installed, fans just didn't take to the stadium and stayed away. Rather bizarrely, about the only thing it did attract to the ground was fog as for some reason probably only known to Stephen Hawking, Bishoptown Stadium became a fog magnet! So now not only were the fans not coming to the games, the teams were having trouble finding the place. Let's just say there were a few cancellations!

Manager Damien Richardson guided the Leesiders into European action in the 1993/94 Champions League-beating Cwmbran Town before going out to Galatasaray. Richardson then resigned and Noel O'Mahony came out of retirement to lead Cork to a 1995 League Cup victory over Dundalk in his third and final term.

"I remember both European cup games for very different reasons. We knew it would be hostile when we played Galatasaray away but it really stunned me. I had collected a head injury prior to the match so wasn't starting the game but I remember having to use the first aid box to cover my head on coming out of the tunnel to shield myself from the missiles being thrown at me. The Cwmbran game at home how-

> *ever was a happier memory as I scored. Mind you, after the game I*
> *had to thumb a lift back all the way to Galway!"* – **Johnny Glynn**

City looked across the water for their next manager, appointing Northumberland-born Rob Hindmarch, a man who had made over 100 appearances at Roker Park for Sunderland, who took charge but only lasted a season. Sadly, Rob succumbed to Motor Neurone disease aged just 41 in 2002.

By this point Bishopstown was on life support. With the ground effectively pulling Cork City down the last game at the ill-fated ground was a 1-0 defeat to Derry City on January 21, 1996. The inevitable receiver was called in and City looked to be heading the same road as their former counterparts. If you'd been on the terraces of Flower Lodge or seen teams called Hibs, Celtic or Albert's, this has an all too familiar ring to it. Thankfully, they were saved by a consortium who took over the debts and assurances were made so that City could move back to Turner's Cross which they did a mere two weeks later. Relegation still looked on the cards, however Dave Barry steadied the good ship Corcaigh to secure their Premier Division status.

Back at the Cross, performances improved, crowds came back, hope sprung eternal. An Intertoto Cup place in 1997 saw the club play four games in a group containing the likes of Standard Liege, drawing three and losing just once whilst silverware arrived back on the Lee in the shape of a first FAI Cup win under the Cork City name tag. On May 16, 1998 Derek Coughlan wrote himself into City folklore with the only goal of the Cup final against Shelbourne in the replay at Dalymount Park.

It proved to be the highlight of Barry's managerial stint. Not that he stopped there. There was also a third League Cup final victory in the decade a short few months later in the 1998/99 season.

> *"Having seen the trials and tribulations of Hibernians and Celtic*
> *from the terraces as a boy it meant so much to win the cup as a*
> *manager with Cork City. Not only for bringing the club their first*
> *FAI Cup but also because I felt like I carried on a family tradition*
> *as my grandfather and great-grandfather had won it as well."*
> – **Dave Barry**

Barry's grandfather Bobby Buckle had indeed won the cup with Cork FC in 1934, emulating his father Roy Buckle with Fordsons in 1926.

The Leesiders took on Shamrock Rovers in that League Cup final over two legs. The first encounter at Tolka Park ended with Cork scoring both goals. Unfortunately, Noel Mooney put one of those in his own net, before Brian Barry-Murphy equalised. Noel Hartigan struck the only goal of the second leg the night before New Year's Eve to make sure it was a happy start to 1999.

The decade ended with some notches on the European bed-post with home leg victories over the Ukrainian side CSKA Kyiv, and more notably against high class IFK Gothenburg, though it wasn't enough to progress on either occasion.

The new century has seen Cork consistently play in Europe, consistently challenge and win honours, and consistently start again from scratch under another name. Players like George O'Callaghan, Michael Devine, Dan Murray and John O'Flynn came in, and former St. Patrick's Athletic boss Pat Dolan led Cork to the quarter-finals of the 2004 Intertoto Cup – the first time any League of Ireland club had reached the last eight in a European competition.

"It should be mandatory to spend two years in Cork! The city and club were fantastic. You don't have to convince Cork people to come out and support Cork City Football Club and they bring so much passion. I was blessed to experience the best two years of my life and I'm very proud of the team I built with Noel O'Connor. In my view it was the best side in the history of League of Ireland football and it changed the way English football viewed the league with so many of that team going on to play for Ireland and in the UK." – **Pat Dolan**

Despite finishing second in the league, Big Pat was gone that summer, replaced by a returning Damien Richardson, who delivered Cork City's second League of Ireland championship in 2005.

"When I returned to Cork it was really a case of unfinished business. I felt so guilty leaving in 1995, I just felt the chairman should have invested in the squad at the time and didn't so I left. What made it worse was that the supporters and people of Cork were behind me so when Brian Lennox approached me in 2004 to manage City I was only too happy to say yes." – **Damien Richardson**

It went to the wire, but in the best way possible (if you're a neutral as opposed to a Cork City fan with a nervous disposition.) On the last day of the season Cork met second place Derry City in a title showdown. The Leesiders entered the game a point behind having drawn with Shelbourne in the penultimate match, while Stephen Kenny's Derry was beating St. Patrick's, so it meant the November 18th showdown had the makings of a classic. The Turner's Cross faithful whipped up a storm, a crowd of 8,000 turned out and goals from John O'Flynn and Liam Kearney gave Richardson's men the title.

"That title win would rate as my finest achievement as a manager. I remember Kevin Doyle scoring in our first game away to Finn Harps and there wasn't a doubt in my mind we would win the league, even at that stage. It was a matter of keeping everyone focused. Kevin and Shane Long signed for Reading not long after and it tested us, but everyone stepped up to the plate. Denis Behan came in and done a great job, along with people like Roy O'Donovan, and John O'Flynn, but to be fair everyone was magnificent. Our captain Dan Murray was exemplary – a true leader when we took to the field. You couldn't get a better way to win a title – home to Derry, the last night of The Shed and a passionate crowd in your eardrums."
– **Damien Richardson**

The FAI Cup final two weeks later was widely expected to be the icing on the cake and a first League and Cup double for Cork City, but Drogheda had other plans and upset the form book to beat Damien Richardson's men 2-0.

A Champions League win over Cypriot opponents Apollon Limassol followed that summer, before defeat to Red Star Belgrade, but the capture of a second FAI Cup was confirmed on December 2, 2007 with Denis Behan's 60th minute goal against Longford in front of a crowd of just over 10,000 at the RDS.

Cork City Foras Co-op take to the field on March 12, 2010 against Waterford United – just weeks after it looked like League of Ireland football in the city was finished (photo credit: Blinkofaneye.ie)

Roy O'Donovan, the man who started that cup run with a penalty against Shelbourne in the first round, was sold for €500,000 to Sunderland, and a year later manager Alan Matthews brought the Leesiders to Setanta Cup glory, defeating Glentoran 2-1 with goals from Dan Murray and Liam Kearney in front of 5,500 at Turner's Cross.

But things then took a despairing turn for the worst. Winding-up orders, final deadlines, appeals and the infamous "bus-gate" scandal followed. It all came to a head when the club was denied a Premier Division licence despite having finished third in 2009 under Paul Doolin.

> *"Cork City was a fantastic club with a great history but of course everything was completely overshadowed at this stage by the administration. I'd left Drogheda in a similar situation so naturally it was terrible to see yet another club go into administration but by the end it was a complete disaster."* – **Paul Doolin**

Like another phoenix rising from the flames, rescue came not from a local sugar daddy or foreign investor, but from tried and trusted people – the fans. Cork City Foras Co-up went to bat for the Rebel County in 2010, starting from scratch in the First Division. Ironically, their first game at that level was against Derry City, another club that had been dissolved the year before.

Crowds and support have never been a problem in the Rebel County, and with Foras holding on to Turner's Cross over 4,400 people turned up to watch the eleventh reincarnation of Cork football play Waterford United in their first home game on March 12, 2010, and under Tommy Dunne they finished the season sixth.

In June last year the club bought rights to the name Cork City FC, and we wait with bated breath to see what happens next in the ever changing world of football in the Rebel County.

Ground Info

Though they've spent time in Flower Lodge and Bishopstown, Turner's Cross has more or less been the home of Cork City over the last 27 years now.

The ground actually originates as far back as the late 1800s when local rugby club Cork Constitution first became tenants there in 1897. Cork Celtic also used the ground during their League of Ireland tenure before Cork City took up residence in 1984.

It's a 7,366 all-seated stadium with a view for everyone in the house. Though the Donie Forde Stand is the main focal point in the ground (holding almost 2,000) it's not the biggest, as the St. Anne's Stand holds a massive 2,800, one of the biggest single stands in the league. The Derrynane Road End holds just over another 1,100 and there's no real need to ask where the rest of the supporters are housed – the Curragh Road stand.

Redeveloped in the middle of the last decade, the "Shed" End was one of the most renowned in the league, a last bastion to stands of the past where corrugated iron rattled to the sound of the Cork faithful within it. Health, safety and UEFA have dictated a more comfortable and fan-friendly stand these days, but it still contains the hardcore Cork fans who would gladly return to standing, shouting and the risk of being trampled on in a goal celebration in the name of Cork City.

Record Attendance

12,000 v Dundalk (Premier Division, April 21, 1991)

Cost

Adults: €10.00
Under-16s/OAPs: €5.00

Programme

€3.00 – and at 44 pages one of the biggest in the League. Of the grounds I've been to I've never seen as many empty programme boxes on a match day. Cork fans support their club in every way and thankfully for them they have a solid reading experience to boot. One article that surprised me came from Paul Barry – written entirely in Irish. How patriotic. Throwing in a couple of poems and articles from their opponents Mervue United makes *City Edition* well worth the money.

Rivals

Throughout generations it's changed. Clubs like Cork Hibernians and Cork Celtic would have classed Waterford as their main rivals in Munster, however Cork City fans tend to look towards Dublin clubs like Shamrock Rovers, Shelbourne or Bohemians.

Mascot

In keeping with the fan-friendly experience that clubs are actively adopting, Cork have "Corky – the Cheetah", a wild animal that constantly went round with his thumbs up and happy to stop at every corner of the ground and have kids pester him – whatever you're on Corky, I'll have some.

Food and Drink

The ground has two chippers, with pride of place going to Esther & Deirdre Delaney of Bob's Catering for the free hot dog and tea! There are also a couple of Tuck Shops there. Directly outside the ground the Horseshoe Inn on Curragh Road is one of the best pubs in Ireland for any fan. Great atmosphere, whilst the equally welcoming Evergreen Bar and Turner's Cross Tavern on Evergreen Road are worth a visit, as is the Beer Garden which kindly donates 50 cents of every beer sold on matchday to the club.

Club Shop

Located inside the Curragh Road End with friendly staff who tried to convince this Waterford man that a Cork City scarf would be the ideal purchase to keep me warm on the way home! They have a neck those Leesiders, but it's all done with a roguish glint and a smile!

Websites

www.corkcityfc.net/home
www.ccfcforum.com – online fans' forum

Local Radio

Red FM 104-106

The Match – Cork City FC v Mervue United (First Division, May 26, 2011)

Mervue had surprised a few before this visit to Turner's Cross, having won almost half of their eleven games to this fixture in late May, however Tommy Dunne's men never looked in trouble and quickly sealed the game with three first half goals from Graham Cummins, David O'Neill and Gearoid Morrissey – though it was a game Mervue goalkeeper Eoin Martin won't want to remember.

Derry City

Formed: **1928**
Ground: **Brandywell Stadium**
Capacity: **7,700**
Nickname: **The Candystripes**

"I banned my mother from watching me play as she always gave me too much abuse! The night we played Benfica she watched from our bedroom window on the Lone Moor Road overlooking the stadium." – Felix Healy

A unique club that's overcome unique adversity, Derry City's history differs from every other club in this book. Troubled times with little money will sound familiar, but never have the divisive subjects of politics and religion intruded so much on the green blades of grass as in the history of Ulster's second city.

The origins of the club came under the guise of Derry Celtic, who first competed in the Irish League in the 1900/01 season, playing their games at Celtic Park – Derry's GAA ground at present. That first season saw Celtic take just a single point from the ten games played, but there was a gradual improvement, finishing fourth in 1910.

However with relegation an issue in 1912, Derry Celtic had to avoid finishing in the bottom two. Nine points from 18 was never going to be enough and Derry would sink (yes, I'm ignoring the obvious Titanic pun; I had a great-granduncle on it!) along with Tritonville FC from Dublin into the relegation places. The club was then voted out of the league, by one vote, and never returned.

A world war, an Easter Rising, and the worst first sex-change operation (don't say I don't try to educate on the smaller details of history!) passed before Derry had another senior football team.

The foundation of a new Free State League in 1921 saw clubs like Bohemians and Shelbourne leave the Irish League up north, thus creating a new window of opportunity. Annoyed with no senior team and equally irate at the fact near neighbours Coleraine, with a mere quarter the population of Derry, had been elected to the Irish League in 1928, a group of fans got together to form a new club.

Settling on the name Derry City, they applied for membership of the Irish League but along with Crusaders and Brantwood FC had their applications turned down. In the case of the Belfast clubs, the league decided the teams weren't up to scratch, whilst in Derry's case the application was received two days after the deadline! Can you imagine the planning? "Right lads let's do a final recap. Team – check. Directors – check. Supporters – check. Application? Oh Christ, better post that!"

But they were nothing if not determined and a year later on May 31, 1929 Derry City finally entered the IFA at the expense of Belfast club Queens Island FC. The club had done well to get in when you think of the fate of the two clubs who had their application turned down with City the year before. Crusaders got so browned off they tried entry into the Scottish League, whilst in 2008 Brantwood gave up on the idea of getting elected – 80 years after first trying!

The club courted controversy in some circles by dropping the official title of the city – Londonderry – in their club name, but were granted permission to play in the Brandywell Stadium by the local corporation, thus beginning a love affair that is still going over 82 years later.

The first official match played by Derry City took place on August 22, 1929 where a crowd of 8,000 saw Derry lose to Gentoran 2-1, with former Dundalk coach Joe McCleery in charge. Despite finishing as league runners-up in 1932, McCleery parted company with the club when the board refused to let him pick the side!

Between 1932-40, Donegal-born Irish international Billy Gillespie, a man who made over 400 appearances for Sheffield United, was drafted in initially as player–manager (he insisted *he* pick the team and the board agreed!). Billy had brought a Sheffield United strip back with their traditional colours of red and white striped shirts and black shorts to replace Derry's white shirts – thus the "Candystripes" were born. Gillespie had an immediate impact, winning the City Cup twice and guiding the club to an IFA Cup final in 1936 and four consecutive runners-up spots in the league championship.

Under the tenure of Scotsman Willie Ross, Derry City won the IFA Cup in 1949 in front of 27,000 at Windsor Park against Glentoran, with goals from Hugh Colvan, Matt Doherty and Barney Cannon giving Derry a 3-1 win. Johnny Ferris at centre-half was the only local in the side. The victory was made more significant as outside-left Jimmy Kelly had been knocked out cold, was stretchered off, got the magic sponge treatment and returned 15 minutes later. What a man! These days it's a three-month stint in rehab and a five-book deal talking about the horrors of having to sniff smelling salts!

Jimmy is a true Derry City legend. Over a 20-year Derry career Bally-bofey-born Kelly was capped by both Ireland sides and scored some 380 goals. Not bad for a winger!

Inspired by former Glasgow Celtic outside-right Jimmy Delaney, Derry won the IFA cup again in a 1954 after a second replay with a goal from Con O'Neill. Over 93,000 people had attended all three games in Windsor Park, and though the Scotsman was instrumental it was goalkeeper Charlie Heffron's outstanding performances over the entire final that made him the real hero.

At centre-half that day was Willie Curran – the only local man in that side. Outstanding throughout the entire cup campaign of '54, he is now 80 years young and still sells the half-time draw tickets at the Brandywell.

In 1957 the club lost out to Glenavon in the final with a side that featured Barney Travers, a man constantly mentioned as one of the club's greatest players.

Derry went on to record their first cup double by winning both the IFA and Gold Cups in the 1963/64 season, thus qualifying for Europe for the first time entering a draw drum along with Europe's elite in the shape of the 1964/65 Cup Winners Cup. Derry drew Romanian giants Steaua Bucharest. Six League titles. Six National Cups. Six full internationals. Yep, it spelt trouble. Despite their best efforts Derry City went down 3-0 in the first leg and Bucharest added two more without reply at the Brandywell.

By this point Belfast native Jimmy McGeough had signed for the club and became part of a team with players like Eunan Blake, Dougie Wood, Jimbo Crossan, Johnny Mackenzie, Matt Doherty, Joe Wilson and Fay Coyle that tormented teams from Cliftonville to Coleraine, and saw Derry City take the Irish League championship for the first and only time in their history. And it was done in style, losing just twice all season. On April 17, 1965 captain Fay Coyle lifted the league championship trophy over his head in front of a

Derry City – IFA League champions, 1965 (photo credit: Derry Journal)

heaving Brandywell that had just been treated to a 5-1 hammering of Ards. Significantly, it had been masterminded by Willie Ross in his second tenure at the club. The Scotsman spent a combined 19 years in the hot-seat (he returned briefly in 1972 as well) winning a League, IFA Cup and Gold Cup in his time at the Brandywell.

Again City returned to Europe, this time in the 1965/66 European Cup. Drawing Norwegian opposition in FK Lyn, it represented a winnable tie for City. The first leg was an eight-goal thriller with Derry losing out 5-3 in Oslo, with Ronnie Wood claiming the club's first goal in Europe, quickly followed by Bobby Gilbert notching a brace. However a packed Brandywell in the return leg saw City hammer the Norwegians 5-1 with strikes from Crossan, Ronnie Wood, McGeough and two from Joey Wilson, thus becoming the first Irish league side to win a European tie over two legs.

Anderlecht were waiting in the next round, however politics, a word that seemed synonymous with life in Northern Ireland, was about to step in.

The Brandywell's base in the predominantly Nationalist Bogside area – an area that would see the worst of the Troubles at its height – was always divisive in the eyes of the IFA. For a predominantly Catholic club (though half the board were Protestant) in a mainly Protestant league it became a problem. It was one of the reasons the IFA decided to ban Derry City from playing their tie at home against Anderlecht (even though Anderlecht was happy to play there) instead insisting they play the tie in Belfast.

Derry didn't back down. In a show of defiance, the club stated if they couldn't play the home leg in the Brandywell, they would refuse to represent the Irish League in Europe. In the end, the Candystripes travelled to Belgium, got soundly walloped 9-0, and the second leg was never played in Belfast or the Brandywell. It was the start of the end. In September 1971 Ballymena United's bus was seized and burnt out by masked men outside the Brandywell and the club was forced to play their home games at neighbouring Coleraine – a 40 minute drive away. Support dwindled and the club found it harder and harder to make ends meet. By the end of 1972 Ulster's second city was without a Senior League club again.

Portadown FC then put a proposal that clubs should go back to playing football in the Brandywell. It proved to be the most controversial vote in Irish League history, and one which ultimately shaped Derry City's future. Along with Portadown, Derry, Bangor, Cliftonville and even Ballymena (whose bus had been torched the season before) voted in favour of the motion. Crusaders, Ards, Glenavon, Glentoran, Distillery and Linfield all voted against. Crucially, Coleraine, who had given Derry their Showgrounds stadium to play in whilst away from the Brandywell, abstained.

In 1913, one vote had brought about the demise of Derry Celtic. Almost 60 years later history ironically came back to repeat itself. Six votes against, five for with Coleraine abstaining meant the club had little choice but to withdraw from the league. Call it fate or coincidence, but it happened on Friday the 13th, 1972. It was the last of Derry City ever playing again in the Irish League. Forced to play in a local Saturday morning league just to keep the club alive, the club applied for Senior League status but was always turned down due to lack of support from other league sides. Dark days indeed.

But to gain what is worth having sometimes you have to lose everything. In 1984, a consortium that included Terry Harkin, Eamon McLaughlin, Tony O'Doherty and Eddie Mahon announced the formation of a club known as Derry FC and applied for admission to the League of Ireland. Meanwhile, Derry City, fed up with being constantly turned down by the Irish League, also sought admission with Fran Fields helping their cause. Eventually, it was decided to allow *one* Derry team into their newly-formed First Division of the league, so the consortium withdrew its application "in the interests of football" leaving the way clear for Derry City to take their place in the League of Ireland First Division to end a 13-year period without senior football in the city.

On September 8, 1985 over 9,000 people witnessed the rebirth of the club in its first official game south of the border – a League Cup tie against Home Farm with Terry Kelly captaining the Candystripes. Former Sunderland and Manchester City winger Dennis Tueart set up Barry McCreadie to score the club's first goal in a 3-1 win. Jim Crossan had the honour of managing on the day Derry brought an end to their wilderness years, though he didn't last the full season and was replaced by Noel King.

The Derry City team that lined up against Home Farm for that historic League Cup game in 1985. Back (L-R) *Jim Crossan, Eddie Mahon, "Tootie" McMullan, Eddie Seydak, Gary Jones, Martin Cassidy, Barry McCreadie, Terry Kelly, Tommy McBride, Eamon McLaughlin.* Front (L-R) *Philip Johnston, Liam Bonner, Tony O'Doherty, Liam McDermott, Kevin O'Neill (Jamie Mahon – Mascot) Dennis Tueart, Paul McGuinness, Herbie Wade (photo credit: Derry Journal)*

City soon became the main attraction. Along with Tueart at the club there was international flair in the shape of Brazilian Nelson Da Silva and South African striker Owen De Gama. Not long after French defender Pascal Vaudequin and Serbian hitman Alex Krstic joined, along with former Arsenal legend Alan Sunderland (though only for eight games) and Scotsman Stuart Gauld.

The League of Ireland Shield had been won in their first season (a 6-1 aggregate hammering of Longford Town) and a fourth place finish in the inaugural League of Ireland First Division had been achieved, but 1986/87 saw King's side produce an astonishing 16 wins from their 18 league fixtures (losing just once to UCD) to finish six points clear of Shelbourne to take the First Division title and a promotion that had looked inevitable from the club's first match in the League of Ireland.

Premier Division clubs weren't complaining either. From Sligo to St. Pat's, and Bray to Bohemians, Derry's die-hard supporters made sure there were more than an extra few quid going around the turnstiles of the cash-strapped clubs.

Hometown hero Jim McLaughlin, who had played for his beloved City in the fifties, took over from Noel King at the end of 1987, guiding them to a safe mid-table position in their first season among the republic's elite.

> *"I left Derry as a young boy in 1958 so it was obviously a delight to come back and be part of the club. Initially it was as a general manager but when Noel King left I stepped into the manager's job. To be honest I didn't feel any burden of pressure despite what I had achieved when I was at Dundalk and Shamrock Rovers. Derry were new to the League and didn't have the history and expectation those two clubs had. Nonetheless, it was still exciting."* – Jim McLaughlin

McLaughlin is an iconic League of Ireland figure. A man who brought astonishing success to Dundalk, winning three league titles and three FAI Cups, he carried on a proud tradition at Shamrock Rovers by winning three successive league championships and a brace of FAI Cups in a mere three years. Even by the Glenmalure club's high standards it was impressive.

With a comfortable league position secured, Derry went for the jugular in the FAI Cup dismissing St Josephs Boys, Bohemians, Home Farm and hammering Longford Town 6-2 over two legs, scoring 19 goals on the way to meeting Dundalk in the 1988 FAI Cup final. Central to that run was Jonathan Speak. The striker from the small Tyrone village of Sion Mills terrorised defences the length of the country, scoring 24 goals that season, with six coming in one game against Sligo Rovers.

> *"The funny thing about Jonathan was he hadn't the greatest physique, wasn't fast on his legs but could still score goals! And he was so reliable at it. On top of that he was one of the nicest people you could ever work with."* – Jim McLaughlin

Many expected the fairytale of life down south to continue that day, but John Cleary had other ideas and it was his hotly disputed penalty on 20 minutes that shattered that dream as Dundalk completed a league and cup double. However, it wasn't all bad. Though the Lilywhites had foiled McLaughlin's men, they had already helped Derry by winning the double. It meant the Candystripes were going back into Europe.

The 1988/89 Cup Winners Cup, Derry's first trip abroad for European competition since the ill-fated Anderlecht tie in 1965, wasn't a flight to sunny Spain or a lengthy coach and ferry ride to the middle of absolutely nowhere, but a short skip across the pond to the similarly green green grass of Wales and a first round tie against Cardiff City.

Derry held the Welshmen scoreless at the Brandywell but went down 4-0 at Ninian Park to end their involvement in Europe. They may have been beaten but on the bright side they could have draw Ukranian cup holders FC Metalist Kharkiv and taken four weeks to get back home.

An overhaul of the team, which included bringing in 20-year-old Finn Harps striker Liam Coyle and the experience of Shamrock Rovers stalwarts Mick Neville, Kevin Brady, Noel Larkin and a youthful Paul Doolin, saw Derry monopolise Irish football that same season.

It started with a 4-0 victory over Dundalk in the League Cup final in September 1988 to avenge the FAI Cup final defeat, and soon the Candystripes raced to the top of the league table. A final day victory over Cobh Ramblers with two Paul Doolin goals crowned Derry City as League of Ireland champions for the first time in their history, ironically finishing two points clear of McLaughlin's old club Dundalk.

A remarkable treble was completed with victory over Cork City in the FAI Cup final replay on May 7, 1989. Derry had hit 13 goals in five games to make the final, including a 4-1 aggregate win over Shamrock Rovers in a two-legged semi-final, but Cork City foiled the Candystripes in the first game at Dalymount Park.

A week later the same venue saw Felix Healy write his name into the club's history books by scoring the only goal of the replay to complete a domestic treble, something not achieved before or since.

"It was a great year. The League Cup was seen as a pre-season tournament of sorts at the time but Derry were drawing massive crowds and took it seriously. All of a sudden it became a competition. I remember the FAI Cup final goal as I hit it so quickly the ball had struck the net before I could even look up and see it!" – **Felix Healy**

"Although Derry was a new club to the League there was still expectation. The day Jim McLaughlin walked through the door it doubled. Here was a home town boy who'd done it all with Dundalk and Rovers so we were expected to do big things. To be honest it took us a while to click. I remember drawing 1-1 with Fanad United in the League Cup and to look at us you'd never have thought a treble was on! It took time for us gel." – **Paul Doolin**

Representing the Republic in Europe for the first time as champions, Derry drew a plum tie against Portuguese champions Benfica (who were then managed by Sven Goran Eriksson) in the 1989/90 European Cup. The excitement was fever pitch. The huge buzz that hadn't abated from their return to league

Derry City Captain Felix Healy shakes hands with the ref before the European Cup game against Benfica at the Brandywell (photo credit: Derry Journal)

football went into overdrive and on September 13, 1989, Derry supporters tore the roof off the Brandywell when Felix Healy walked his side out.

> *"To live on the Lone Moor Road behind the Brandywell and lead City out against a team that had once featured the great Eusebio was amazing. I had banned my mother from watching me as she always gave me abuse, but she watched from the top window of our house overlooking the ground while my dad popped over at half-time. It was surreal."* – **Felix Healy**

Despite conceding two goals in five minutes just after the hour, Paul Carlyle's 74th minute goal sent the home crowd ballistic, and although a 4-0 defeat followed in Lisbon, the fact that the players walked out to 65,000 in the magnificent Stadium of Light was not lost on supporters who'd been through the Troubles and the wilderness years when Saturday League football was the only option.

The nineties brought a domineering three League Cup victories in four years. In 1991, Limerick was put to the sword in the final 2-0, whilst the success in 1992 came at the expense of Dubliner Bohemians, under manager

Roy Coyle, with Jonathan Speak scoring the only goal of the game. The hot seat was then vacated by Coyle, but Tony O'Doherty would still mastermind the next League Cup victory – in December '93 against Shelbourne. What Shamrock Rovers had done in the FAI Cup throughout the '80s, Derry was replicating in the League Cup in the '90s.

There was a disappointing defeat in the 1994 FAI Cup final for the Candystripes, going down 1-0 to Sligo Rovers, but Felix Healy took up the baton and rectified it twelve months later, delivering the FAI Cup for the second time in the Candystripes' history. Working their way past Finn Harps, Home Farm and Dundalk, Healy's side then got involved in a three game semi-final marathon with the Red & Black stripes of Turlough O'Connor's Bohemians. The first of those games ended scoreless at Dalymount. Four days later it was deadlock again at the Brandywell and the tie was finally put to bed in the second replay, but only after extra-time with a goal from Paul McLaughlin and a brace from Peter Hutton finally settling the tie 3-2.

And the winner is Mrs Rogers from the Strand Road! Portugese legend Eusebio does the half-time draw during Derry's game against Benfica.

Having just missed out on the league title again that year, the Candystripes didn't want to be bridesmaids in another domestic competition and goals from

Peter Hutton and an all important Stuart Gauld penalty were enough to defeat Shelbourne in the 1995 FAI Cup final, clinching the Blue Riband of Irish football for the second time. A week earlier Gauld had missed a penalty against Athlone in St. Mel's Park, which would have given Derry the league championship, but he wasn't about to let lightening strike twice.

In the 1996/97 season, Healy primed the club for an assault on the league title. Taking off at a frantic pace, Derry stayed top almost all season. Bohemians tried their best to make the title race interesting, but long before Derry's 5-2 hammering of Bray at the Carlisle Grounds on the last day of the season the League of Ireland championship had been sown up.

> *"We really showed what we were made of that year. One game that sticks in my mind was a match against Dundalk. They were up for it big-time and we found ourselves 2-0 down after about ten minutes. But we didn't panic, dug deep and turned it around to win 4-2. It showed the character we had and it was probably the best team performance I'd ever been involved in in all my time at Derry."* – **Peter Hutton**

A massive ten points – the biggest title winning gap since Athlone Town in 1982/83 (only Shelbourne in 1999/2000 and Bohemians in 2008 also rate higher) – gave the Candystripes their second League of Ireland championship. Having progressed without too much bother in the FAI Cup, Ulster's second city was priming themselves for a double, but a stubborn Shelbourne side, who had drawn three times with Derry that league season, again proved unbeatable, taking the FAI Cup 2-0 to deny the Candystripes a double.

That September they boarded a plane, caught themselves a train and found themselves back in Europe again – this time facing Slovenian champions NK Maribor. Of course, by this stage the Champions League era had been ushered in, and the price for any Irish club, should they somehow get through two early rounds, would be a four-team group format with untold riches awaiting the benefactors. Unfortunately, Felix and the lads didn't get much time to dream, going down 3-0 on aggregate to the Slovenians who then went on to win their league title six times in a row.

A new millennium saw the club file for bankruptcy due to an unpaid bill, but glamour friendlies against Glasgow Celtic, Barcelona, Real Madrid and Manchester United saved the day. Opposition like that would have been more welcome at the Brandywell in European competition, but when you're knee deep in shit . . . The matter was resolved and there was a League Cup triumph in 2000 under Kevin Mahon. The former Derry player guided the Candystripes to a 5-2 hammering of his old club Athlone Town, before adding the third FAI Cup in the club's history in 2002 with victory over Shamrock Rovers in the infamous interim season.

Only in Ireland could you get two FAI Cup finals in the same year. Dundalk and Derry can both lay claims to the 2002 FAI Cup! Dundalk defeated Bohemians at Tolka Park 2-1 in April, whilst six months later on October 27 at the same venue, a Liam Coyle goal saw off Shamrock Rovers in front of 10,000 people to give Derry the very same cup!

For the first time in the club's League of Ireland history, Derry was embroiled in a relegation battle the following season. Coming to Waterford United on the final day of the 2003 season, Mahon's men needed a victory. Standing in their way were 11 men in blue managed by one of Derry's favourite sons – Jimmy McGeough. McGeough was to leave United after the game, however, after a disagreement with the board. Effectively, it was his last game as manager.

It was perversely attractive, made more so by the fact RTÉ had decided to show the game live. The Candystripes shaded the game 1-0 and then came through a local derby in the 2003 two-leg promotion/relegation play-off against local rivals Finn Harps, with Coyle again the hero with an extra-time winner after Mark Farren's early goal had been levelled by Harps forward Kevin McHugh (who went on to sign for Derry in 2006).

> *"It was possibly the biggest game in the club's history. If we lost, we went down and everybody knew Derry City would go bust. What made it harder was the fact our record on the road was very poor. Before the game I had to talk Ciaran Martyn into playing as he was injured. Thankfully, it turned out to be a blessing in disguise as he got the winner. I got back on the bus that day knowing the club had a chance of surviving."* – **Gavin Dykes**

With a collective sigh of relief, Derry returned to winning ways and an astonishing run in the League Cup over the last decade saw the Candystripes totally dominate the tournament. Yet again!

Between the last day of May 2005 right up until May 4, 2009 Derry went on a run of 17 unbeaten games in the competition to win four League Cups in a row. UCD was their first victim in the 2005 final, where goals from Alan Murphy and a Patrick McWalter own goal sealed Derry's sixth success in the tournament, this time under Stephen Kenny. A year later the Candystripes were at it again when Shelbourne were put to the sword in a dramatic penalty shoot-out at the Brandywell. The Candystripes had both Killian Brennan and goalkeeper David Forde sent off but still won 3-0 on penalties thanks to substitute goalkeeper Patrick Jennings (son of former Spurs and Arsenal great

Pat) literally saving the day for the Ulstermen. Under John Robertson, a three-in-a-row was captured in 2007 with a solitary Kevin McHugh goal defeating Bohemians, and incredibly a fourth straight victory in the tournament was sealed with the 6-1 mauling of Wexford Youths in 2008.

The run finally came to an end on May 4, 2009 in a second round 1-0 loss to Galway United. Nine victories since 1988 tell the story of Derry's dominance in the League Cup, and I haven't even touched on the two finals they lost in 1989 to Dundalk and 2002 to Limerick FC!

In 2006, Derry posted a highly impressive win over IFK Gothenburg in the first qualifying round of the 2006/07 UEFA Cup (winning both legs 1-0) before an absolute annihilation of Scottish newcomers Gretna away from home. That 5-1 win put to bed the myth that Scottish Football is light years ahead of us as the small but dedicated League of Ireland going public could afford a wry smile that night in a game that remains the highest away win by any Irish side in Europe.

> *"I remember the Scottish press and Rowan Alexander, the Gretna manager, being very dismissive of us before the game, but it turned out to be my most memorable night in Europe with Derry. If some of the goals that night had been scored in the English premiership people would still be going on about it."* – **Peter Hutton**

It led to a tie against Paris St. Germain, where after holding the French giants scoreless at home, Kenny's men bowed out 2-0 at the Park Des Princes on September 28, 2006 with over 2,000 Derry fans making the trip.

> *"I remember going to watch them play against Marseille in preparation for the tie. PSG are the biggest club in France, the only club in Paris – a city of about 10 million – and had Portugal's top-goalscorer Pauleta, a man who's scored more goals at international level than Eusebio and Ronaldo in their team yet we'd held them scoreless at home through a couple of great goal-line clearances and arguably should have had a penalty. We started well in the return leg but a set piece done us for the first goal and Pauleta's class finished us off afterwards, but it was a great experience, especially for the fans."* – **Stephen Kenny**

Just five short weeks later Derry won the 2006 FAI Cup in one of the most dramatic FAI Cup finals in history against St. Pat's in the last match played at the old Lansdowne Road. A terrible wet, windy, don't-put-the-dog-out night saw the Candystripes come from behind three times thanks to Mark Farren, Clive Delaney and Peter Hutton before an unfortunate Stephen Brennan handed Derry City the cup with his own goal.

> *"It was an amazing season. To win both domestic cups, play six games in Europe and then lose the league championship on goal difference! We were so unfortunate in the League. We went into the last three games against Waterford, St. Patrick's and Cork knowing we had to win them, which we did, all 1-0 with Mark Farran scoring all three goals. It was a huge effort and a blow to fail to make a clean sweep of trophies by a mere few goals."* – **Stephen Kenny**

Despite finishing runners-up in that 2006 Premier Division race, Derry got an unlikely call up to the Champions League courtesy of Shelbourne going belly up, and that summer Armenian outfit FC Pyunik came calling to Ulster's second city, nipping away with a scoreless draw at the Brandywell before finishing off John Robertson's side.

Robertson left soon after and a returning Stephen Kenny brought Derry to the 2008 FAI Cup final where, despite two Sammy Morrow goals in normal time, the Candystripes lost out on penalties against Bohemians with missed spot kicks from Kevin Deery and Ruaidhri Higgins.

Another European campaign followed with victory over Skonto Riga in the Europa League to help Irish clubs move even further up the coefficient rankings (we currently stand 29th of 53 teams), before CSKA Sofia ended any further progress in the third qualifying round.

But the good times stopped rolling. Faced with mounting debts and a participation agreement with the FAI breached, the unthinkable happened and Derry was dissolved in 2009. It has become an all too familiar scene in League of Ireland football (Cork went the same way that year as well) but thankfully over 82 years of history was saved when the club re-founded in January 2010 with a new board, new chairman and a new lease of life, albeit in the First Division, where they had started on their introduction to League of Ireland football in 1985.

They didn't waste much time as the much decorated Stephen Kenny took the minimum eight months to get Derry City back up by way of the 2010 First Division title, and this year the Red and White stripes kicked off again among the elite in the Premier Division.

A unique club, brought up in unique times and overcoming unique adversity. It nice to have the town they love so well still with us.

> *"Being from the North would always be an issue with some supporters and some players endured a few hardships because of where we were from. You tried to take it in your stride. The funniest would*

be when we played against Rovers in a game at the RDS. Paul Mooney was getting a lot of stick from the crowd when an orange was thrown at him on the field. It didn't faze him at all; he simply picked it up, took a bite and lobbed it back to the guy who threw it."
– Peter Hutton

Peter Hutton leads Derry City out with St. Patrick's Athletic captain Colm Foley for the 2006 FAI Cup final – the last soccer game to be played at Lansdowne Road (photo credit: David Maher/Sportsfile)

Did You Know?

Sammy Curran got the club's first hat-trick agaisnt Portadown in the 1929/30 season. They still lost the game 6-5!

Ground Info

The Brandywell has been home to the Candy-stripes of Derry City for almost 84 years now. Only Bohemians at Dalymount have a longer home ground residency. Located on Lone Moor Road in the heart of the Bogside, City's famous old stadium is a ground of character and reeks of nostalgia. It's been testament to times good and bad, and evokes many memories, but still remains the heartbeat of the club. Genera-tions have passed through its turnstiles and it's unthinkable of seeing the Red & White stripes that Jimmy Delaney famously adopt-ed running out to play football on any other pitch than the blades of grass at the Brandywell.

The Main Stand inside the ground runs pitch length and holds 2,460 whilst the opposite stand on the Lone Moor Road holds a further 300. It's often referred to as the Glentoran Stand as part of the structure was actually given to them from Glentoran Football Club in 1955 and brought piece by piece down to Derry. There is an uncovered seating area to its left which seats a further 200 and terracing on the Brandywell Road End.

Despite a track running around the ground it doesn't stifle the atmos-phere at all, and the Brandywell faithful in full flow can be quite a sight.

Record Attendance

9,800 v Finn Harps (FAI Cup, February 23, 1986). In 1998 a Derry City Select which included David Ginola played against a Mick McCarthy Ireland XI in a benefit game for victims of the Omagh Bombing with a crowd reported in the region of 10,000.

Cost

Adults: £13.00 (Stand), £11.00 (ground)
Students/OAPs: £10.00 (Stand), £9.00 (ground)
Children Under-16: £5.00
Children Under-12: Free in terraces with adult

Programme

Not only is it easily one of the top three publications in the league, but at £2.00 it's cheaper than programmes half its size (and yes, I'm taking the euro conversion into account). I actually think the lads are selling themselves short! People like Brian Dunleavy, Mick McBride and former player Eddie Mahon write some great articles. It's quite opinionated and doesn't shy from speaking its mind – what you see is what you get.

Rivals

Finn Harps lie 29 miles to the west and is one of those rarities – a local derby between two clubs in different countries. The fixture has attracted big crowds in past decades, however most Derry City fans look south towards Tallaght and Shamrock Rovers now as the team they love duelling with most.

Mascot

He comes and goes, but R. Mucker is still walking out with the Candystripes to *Teenage Kicks* by the Undertones at the Brandywell most Friday nights.

Food and Drink

Two local chip vans regularly serve the masses at the Showground End. It's also the first ground where I've been able to get a Hawaiian burger! The closest bar is Mailey's on Lecky Road, whilst the Brandywell Inn, Mary B's or the Oakgrove in Bishops Street are all popular with the City faithful. A more recent addition is the Derry City Social Club located in Crawford Square, which is well worth a visit.

Club Shop

The Candystripes' store will stick out in its red and white stripes the minute you enter the ground and have very helpful staff.

Websites

www.derrycityfc.net
www.derrycitychat.com

Local Radio

BBC Radio Foyle 93.1
Drive 105.3 FM

The Match – Derry City v Shamrock Rovers (Airtricity League, Premier Division, July 8, 2011)

Having driven from Waterford I needed a sleep . . . which is exactly what the first twenty minutes of the game unexpectedly gave me, but the second half between these old foes was easily the best 45 minutes of my 21 ground journey and a great advert for League of Ireland football. Derry should have been ahead long before Daniel Lafferty's free-kick was fumbled by Rovers goalkeeper Alan McManus to gift City the lead.

Rovers pressed for the rest of the game, with Derry goalkeeper Gerard Doherty producing two unbelievable saves to keep his side ahead with the last ten minutes of the game end to end before the referee blew for full time and the roof disappeared off the main stand!

Drogheda United

Formed:	1919
Ground:	Hunky Dorys Park
Capacity:	3,302
Nickname:	The Drogs

**"The best player I ever played with was Ronnie Whelan who was, in my eyes, a superstar. He was the type of player who knew what was happening all over the field. It just seemed to me he had eyes in the back of his head."
– Former Drogheda AFC player Liam Cullen**

Despite forming in 1919, Drogheda United only entered the top tier of Irish football in 1975. Why? Well the Boynesiders' story is a tale of two clubs. One founded the year the first shots were fired in the War of Independence, the other a few months after Gay Byrne first walked out to present the *Late Late Show*. One became a successful non-league club, the other a League of Ireland team reaching the FAI Cup final. After years as separate entities, the two were joined together 36 years ago and have been living with each other, in sickness and in health, ever since.

A man of true courage and value was responsible for the foundation of Drogheda United. Jack Lougheed had been knee-deep in muddy trenches fighting in World War I, one of many from a local soccer team called Centaurs who answered the call to fight for the Allies against the German army and their friends (which included the sneaky Bulgarians who hopped into bed with them again in 1939) and returned the only one alive.

At one point a club called Drogheda FC had been playing in the local Junior and District League, but with the British Empire about to loosen its grip on us in 1919, Lougheed, along with his friend Tom Monks, entered a team called Drogheda United into the Dundalk and District league, playing their games at Magdalene Park, just off Patrick Street in the town.

There they won the local title in 1921, before moving on to the Leinster League soon after. There was a change of playing fields in 1927 to a small ground on Windmill Road they called United Park – home of Drogheda United this present day.

Players of the day included Christy Finnegan, Henry and George Somerville, the Dwyers – Gerry, John, Joe and Paddy – Tom and Alfie Monks with the most famous being Tommy Breen, a man who went on to play for Manchester United and became a dual internationalist with both Ireland (IFA) and the Republic.

United formed a minor team that in 1935 reached both the Leinster and Free State Minor Cup finals but came away second best in both. A year later they won the Leinster Minor Cup beating a Home Farm side that had included names like Manchester United legend Jackie Carey, Arsenal inside-left Kevin O'Flanagan and Mick O'Flanagan who played for both the Republic and the Irish rugby side.

In the 1939/40 season, as the Second World War raged (and those Bulgarians now helping out Hitler) United reached the first of four FAI Junior Cups, losing to Drumcondra. Two years later they were back, only this time to be beaten by Distillery. The lads tried again a season later – and were denied by the Costal Defence of Cork, and to rub salts into an already open wound Drogheda went on to create a little piece of unwanted history when in 1951 Bray Wanderers beat them, making them the first club to reach four Junior Cup finals and not win any. There were a couple of Leinster Cups in-between, but try telling that to poor Dessie Fagan – the only man who unfortunately collected all four losers' medals! He did however go on to collect a total of 26 medals for Drogheda and passed on a happy man having lived to see his beloved Drogs finally win the League of Ireland title in 2007.

Pushed on by Paddy Reilly, a huge driving force behind the club at the time, a move to the Athletic Union League followed. Even at that level thousands were turning out regularly when they played against League of Ireland reserve sides like Shamrock Rovers and Bohemians.

Local priest Fr. Kevin Connolly had a direct role in the Drogs ending up in the League of Ireland. In 1958, as part of the Lourdes Athletic Club, the local cleric sought out a plot of land, struck a deal with its owners (getting a 75 year lease at £35 and 8 schillings per year) and Drogheda Corporation (who charged £25 over 150 years!) and built a new stadium which the priest was determined would accommodate all sports.

> *"I don't believe that there is a single person who had a more positive impact on the good fortunes of Drogheda than Fr. Connolly. What an absolute dynamo he was. After St. Patrick's and St. Bridget's schools were moved to Bothar Brugha, Fr. Connolly took them under his wing. He was responsible for getting football boots from, I think, Donagheys shoe factory, for all attending St. Patrick's who were interested in playing football. We'd play a match with our new boots, take them home, clean and polish them and then bring them to school the next day for inspection – believe me, if they were not shining, you were in big trouble. Nothing was too small for Fr. Connolly."* – **Liam Cullen**

Having approached Drogheda United about moving into the facility and been politely refused, Connolly set up a new soccer team, Drogheda Association Football Club, which was entered in the Leinster Senior League Division II. Whilst Connolly's vision bore fruit almost straight away with Drogheda AFC doing well in the league and FAI Junior Cup, Drogheda United, who had seen a mass exodus of players out the door to play with AFC, were struggling big-time in the AUL. The polite refusal to join forces seemed a bad call and the decision not to throw all the eggs in one basket looked worse on June 22, 1963.

The expansion of the League of Ireland to twelve teams in the 1963/64 season saw Drogheda AFC receive the first preference votes of all ten League of Ireland clubs, and gained entry to the league for the upcoming season. The club's first game in the top flight was just what the doctor ordered – a local derby against Dundalk in the League of Ireland Shield at Oriel Park.

Mick McElroy had the privilege of scoring the first goal in senior soccer for the club in a pulsating game that the Boynesiders lost 4-3. It's also worth pointing out that at the time they were managed by Peter Farrell, a player who will forever be cherished in this country for scoring in the famous 2-0 win over England at Goodison Park in 1949 – the first time England had been beaten on their own soil by a non-UK side. The club also boasted the talents of Arthur Brady, Paddy Byrne, Mick McGrath, Willie McCrory and Johnny Campbell who hit the club's first hat-trick that year.

Drogheda getting ready to play Shamrock Rovers in the 1964 League of Ireland Shield
– their first season in the league (photo credit: Connolly Collection/Sportsfile)

The historic first home league game at the Lourdes Stadium against Cork Hibs on November 10, 1963 ended in a 2-2 draw. Mick Elroy notched again, as did Eddie Nesbitt – but in the wrong goal – and Drogheda played most of the game with ten men after Paddy Byrne had been creamed in a tackle! For you kids out there, these were the days of no substitutes.

The Drogs went on to finish tenth that season, picking up five wins along the way and having the satisfaction of seeing two more illustrious clubs, Waterford and Bohemians, finish beneath them. They also made their first FAI Cup appearance that year as a league club, beating non-league Cork side Glasheen before going out to Drumcondra in the next round.

The second season, however, proved a hard ride. Waterford man Mick Lynch had been brought in as player/coach but it proved the wrong move. Hopes had been high for the season but from the start it was anything but. Down 2-0 in the first eight minutes of their first league game against Cork Hibs, a losing streak then followed, and in one game against Drumcondra, Mick's surname seemed very apt to describing the scene at Lourdes Stadium that day.

"Drumcondra scored a last minute winner, however some of the Drogheda players had seen Mr. McConkey the linesman raise his flag then quickly put it down. This would lead to bedlam. The problem was referee Mr. O' Leary lived on the East Wall Road, a stone throw from Drumcondra's home ground – Tolka Park and linesman

McConkey was a former Drums' player! Lynch lost his cool and got sent off, the crowd then got incensed and somehow the officials made it to the dressing room alive. The crowd waited for almost a half hour outside in an attempt to have a 'discussion' with the officials. It was clear they wanted to 'Lynch' somebody." – taken from **Drogheda United: The Story So Far** *by Tom Reilly*

Thankfully, the club didn't have to apply for re-election due to an all important win against Shelbourne, but the club could have adopted Bob Dylan's *A Hard Rain's a-Gonna Fall* for the next twelve months.

If the '64/65 season had required the odd shot of whiskey for the committee and supporters to get through, the following one could have seen a heap of drunks roaming around outside Lourdes Stadium as things got decidedly worse. Former Dundalk defender Alf Girvan was brought in, but Drogheda only succeeded in doing worse, finishing the season bottom of the table with five points and one win to their name. Only Bohemians in the 1959/60 season had a worse point and goals tally since the end of World War II.

The one bright spark of the season was Theo Dunne. The former Shelbourne man became coach of the club (they really didn't do managers back in the day) at the tender age of 28. Bringing in players like James Kenna from Shamrock Rovers, Leo O'Reilly from Dundalk, and Eddie Cowzer from Drumcondra, and both Cruise brothers, Pat and Brian, Drogheda survived the dreaded re-election vote and went on to the semi-finals of the FAI Cup in 1967 and also avoided finishing bottom.

"I remember playing in that semi-final against St. Pat's. We'd shocked everyone by getting there in the first place as Bohemians were odds-on favourites to beat us the round before but we were magnificent and won 2-0. We had a great team – players like Leo O'Reilly, Paddy Martin, Donal Culligan, Ronnie Whelan Sr. and of course Theo Dunne looking after us. I remember skimming the bar that day and the ball going straight into a huge flag that said 'Drogheda for Europe' behind the goal." – Tommy Byrne

"I played with many great footballers and the vast majority of those that played with Drogheda were certainly much better equipped to play the game than I was! A lot of them were from Dublin and playing football from the time they left the cradle. The best I ever played with was Ronnie Whelan who was, in my eyes, a superstar. He was the type of player who knew what was happening all over the field and it literally seemed like he had eyes in the back of his head." – Liam Cullen

Drogheda AFC in 1968 Back row (L-R): *Ronnie Whelan, Dougie Boucher, Joe Colwell, Frank McEwan, Noel Ennis, Tony Swan.* Front row (L-R): *Brian Tyrell, Joe Wilson, Ray Keogh, Theo Dunne, Tommy Pullen, Arthus Fitzsimons, player/manager (photo credit: Gerry Malocca/ Tom Reilly)*

The 1971 season proved to be one of the most dramatic in the club's history. In a league championship that started poorly and became an uphill battle, the men in Claret and Blue, now managed by Mick Meagan, made it all the way to both the League of Ireland Shield and FAI Cup finals.

The former Everton defender and Republic of Ireland manager first guided the Boynesiders to the League of Ireland Shield final that October but fell at the last hurdle. Getting hammered 5-0 in the final was bad enough . . . the fact that it was done by Dundalk made it twice as bad.

For a side that finished in an almost customary bottom half of the league position, nobody outside Lourdes Stadium took too much notice when Drogheda won 3-0 away to non-league Transport in the first round of the Blue Riband of Irish football that year, but a 5-2 hammering of Shamrock Rovers, a side that had won six of the last seven FAI Cups, made people sit up and take notice. The last week of March saw Meagan's side draw 0-0 with Cork Hibernians, but a week later at Tolka Park a David Shawcross penalty and an extra-time Frank McEwan winner (and a special mention to Meagan himself who played the game with a broken nose!) put the Boynesiders into the 1971 FAI Cup final.

Limerick provided the opposition on Sunday, April 16. Both sides had few chances in a tight affair so it was no surprise that it went to a replay. Three days later however there would be one clear winner. A double from Hugh Hamilton and a Dave Barrett goal gave Limerick their first FAI Cup victory, leaving the Claret and Blue empty handed.

This gained the Drogs entry into the Blaxnit Cup – a cross-border competition between Irish League clubs and their Republican counterparts that was used at the time to ease political tension in the North. A semi-final fixture between Drogheda and Linfield resulted in a win for the Belfast club, but not before a notorious incident where one fan got hold of a Union Jack in the second leg at Lourdes Stadium and set it alight.

Sectarianism was a big problem in a divided Ireland. The Troubles were at their height. The McGurks Bar bombing took 15 lives that December, the highest death toll from a single incident during the period, and even the great Jimmy Hasty, truly a one-off gifted footballer who briefly played for Drogheda, lost his life during the period for being Catholic.

In 1975 Drogheda AFC and Drogheda United finally formed to become Drogheda United FC. It made sense on both parts. United was still struggling in the AUL whilst League of Ireland AFC still didn't own Lourdes Stadium and saw United Park as a good little football ground.

"I remember in the '75/76 season we played Finn Harps in Ballybofey and were beaten 7-0. The following season, we played them in Ballybofey again . . . and this time the result was 7-1 . . . to us! What a turn around. Unfortunately, this was part of our problem at Drogheda. We were capable of excellent performances, but also some awful ones. On another occasion in '75/76 we were being beaten 3-0 by Waterford at half time at home, yet we came out in the second half and scored 6 goals to win 6-3, and I got a hat trick that day!"
– **Cathal Muckian**

In 1976 the newly formed Drogheda United FC reached their second FAI Cup final. Cork Hibs almost wrecked the dream at the first hurdle. It took an astonishing four games and 420 minutes of football before goals from Brendan Tully and two from Cathal Muckian, who went on to a stellar career with Dundalk, finally saw off the Leesiders. Further victories over St. Pat's and Finn Harps put the County Louth club into their second FAI Cup final. After taking six games just to get there, Jimmy McAlinden's men finally ran out of steam in the final and were beaten in Dalymount 1-0 by Bohemians on April 18, 1976.

Three top three finishes saw out the decade with Cathal Muckian scoring 21 goals in 1977/78 and winning an Irish cap under John Giles. The end of the decade also saw the departure of Jerome Clarke who from 1968-80 had given twelve magnificent years to the club before joining neighbours Dundalk. Ironically, he actually replaced Giles in the same 1978 friendly against Poland in which Muckian won his only Irish cap.

Drogheda United line up before the 1976 FAI Cup final at Dalymount Park.
(L-R): Gene McKenna, Cathal Muckian, Martin Donnelly, Damien Byrne, Brendan Tully,
George O'Halloran, Jerome Clarke, Tony Brunton, Willie Roche, Junior Campbell,
Denis Stephens, Leo Byrne and Ray McGuigan (photo credit: Larry McQuillan)

Mid-table mediocrity followed until 1982/83 when Drogheda finished runners-up to Athlone Town in the league championship. Ray Treacy had started that season as manager, having had a big impetus into the club since 1980, but Tony Macken filled his departed seat midway through the season and led Drogheda to their highest ever league placing. Athlone, to be truthful, had a massive 16 point gap, but finishing second meant one thing – Europe.

The Boynesiders first round tie in the 1983/84 UEFA Cup turned out to be the stuff of dreams – and nightmares. A dream draw against Tottenham Hotspur that packed United Park with a side containing Hoddle, Crooks, Mabbutt and the man who never seemed to wear shinguards, Tony Galvin, but there was always the nightmare scenario of an absolute annihilation. On September 14, 1983, £20,000 came through the turnstiles only to see the Drogs get absolutely murdered. Mark Falco and Gary Mabbutt chipped in with a couple each in a 6-0 win, whilst the second leg was worse as eight goals were shipped at White Hart Lane for an aggregate score of 14-0.

A year later, however, the club finally won its first piece of silverware with a 3-1 win over Athlone Town in the 1984 League Cup final. That came after topping their league group, putting one over on Bohemians in the semi-final on penalties, then securing their first senior silverware with a brace from Paddy Dillion and one from Gel Martin.

The scene at the end April 1985 was a stark contrast. Despite manager Tony Macken delivering their first silverware, the former Derby County man couldn't keep United out of the bottom four and after a poor year that saw just seven wins from 33 games the Boynesiders were relegated into the new First Division for 1985/86. They spent three seasons trying to climb back out before Synan Braddish took the Boynesiders up as First Division champions in 1988/89, and in doing so gave the club their first league championship, albeit a league lower than they wanted.

Alas, their first season back to the Premier Division in four seasons didn't go to plan and by the penultimate game United was returning to the First Division. Determined not to spend another few seasons in mid-table mediocrity, the Boynesiders made an immediate winning return with players like John Toal, Richie Kelly, John Gill, Robbie Horgan, Dusty Flanagan and both Geoghegan brothers – Stephen and Declan – to bounce straight back up as First Division champions in 1991 under Liam Brien.

"As a player the two league titles were undoubtedly my best moments on the field. I always look back on that time fondly. I've played football with a lot of different players through the years but if you asked me who the best was I'd have to say Stephen Geoghegan. He was an outstanding footballer." – **John Gill**

Four crazy seasons of promotion and relegation followed during an insane second half of the nineties. There was relegation once more in 1994, but yet again an immediate return as runners-up to UCD in 1995. That brief hiatus from the First Division lasted the minimum 12 months as the club lost its Premier Division status by a point to Athlone Town on the last day of the 1995/96 season. Even the presence of the great Jim McLaughlin, who had brought them up the season before, couldn't stop the club from losing at home on the last day of the season to Sligo Rovers, which cost them their Premier Division status.

"What I enjoyed most about Drogheda was working with the club's chairman Vincent Hoey. He was an absolute gentleman when I was there and wanted so much for the club to do well. You always want people like that running a club and Vincent was probably the best Chairman I've ever had." – **Jim McLaughlin**

But the yo-yo continued. Promotion yet again in 1996/97, relegation from the Premier Division in '97/98. This was followed by a third First Division championship under Martin Lawlor and then automatic relegation the very next season! In fact, in the history of the League of Ireland, no club has gone up and down more times than Drogheda United.

The new millennium brought another First Division title. Having been relegated from the Premier Division in 2000, Harry McCue led the Drogs to the 2001/02 First Division championship title, winning it on the final day of the season with a Shaun Gallagher goal away to Sligo Rovers. Declan O'Brien also chipped in with 19 goals that season. Then something strange happened. Drogheda managed to stay up. Twice!

The Boynsiders avoided relegation on the last day of the 2002/03 season by way of a pulsating promotion/relegation play-off with Galway United (they had been 2-0 down from the first leg but beat the Tribesmen 3-2 with ten men after extra-time at United Park), then managed to avoided the drop again in the interim season of 2003, this time through Gary Cronin's and Declan O'Brien's goals in a last home game win against Bohemians that guaranteed Premier Division survival whilst making a balls of Bohemians' chances of clinching the title.

Thirty years after the amalgamation of both Drogheda clubs, United then won the Blue Riband of Irish football by taking the 2005 FAI Cup on December 4th in Lansdowne Road under Paul Doolin. Victories over Limerick, Dundalk and Bohemians brought United to the semi-finals stage against Bray Wanderers where goals from O'Brien and Sandvliet on a cold October afternoon in the Wee County in front of 4,500 carried them through to their first FAI Cup final since 1976. Despite being the underdogs in that final to a double-chasing Cork City side, Doolin's men settled better. The opening goal on 52 minutes from Gavin Whelan (the nephew of Ronnie Whelan) made the hearts of the Boyneside support among the 24,000 at Lansdowne beat a bit quicker and Declan O'Brien made sure there would be no injury time chewing of nails or novenas offered up when he put the tie to bed with eight minutes left.

> *It's important when you win to win magnanimously. The first thing I did when we won was to go into the Cork dressing room and I said to them, 'Look lads, I know what it's like to lose, and for years and years we struggled. I share this moment with you and know you will be successful again'. There has to be a winner and a loser in cup competitions. You have to think of the losers because it could be you tomorrow."* – **Former Drogheda Chairman Vincent Hoey (from** *DUFC: A Claret and Blue History* **by Brian Whelan).**

Finn Harps and Sligo Rovers during the 1980/81 season. All players pictured had a connection with Harps. L-R: Liam Harbison, Tony Fagan (partially hidden by hand), Chris Rutherford, Joe McGrory, Paddy Sheridan, Mick Ferry and goalkeeper Gerry Murray
(photo courtesy of Bartley Ramsey)

Slight advantage to Rovers here considering Bohemians started the game with a headless player!
(photo credit: Eddie Lennon)

Cork City fans in no doubt how they will do in 2011
(photo credit: Tony Tobin)

One man and his dog – Paul Roche celebrates winning the 1984 FAI Cup for UCD
(photo courtesy of UCD AFC)

Bohemians famous Tramway End under snow
(photo credit: Pete O Doherty)

The legendary Paddy Coad
(photo credit: Irish Press)

Bohemians take on Waterford at Dalymount, 1950

Sligo Rovers – 2010 FAI Cup Champions
(photo credit: Keith O' Dywer)

Longford Town FC has a long association with the aid agency GOAL. The club has donated jerseys that are now worn as far afield as Calcutta, India, and Uganda. This pic shows the red and black being worn in Darfur, Sudan (photo credit: Tiernan Dolan)

Drogheda goalkeeper Sean O'Brien makes a save during the local derby against Dundalk, 1963
(photo credit: Drogheda Independent)

Galway's Derek O'Brien tries but fails with a bicycle kick against St. Patrick's
(photo credit: Andy McDonnell)

Limerick fans crowd the streets after the club's first FAI Cup success in 1971 (photo courtesy of Aidan Corr)

Johnny Matthews in action for Waterford against Drogheda, February 1968 (photo courtesy of Johnny Matthews)

Rocky takes a rest. Bray's mascot needs a breather during Wanderers game against Drogheda United (photo credit: the author)

Kevin Murray heads away for the Blues in Waterford's opening game of the 2011 season against Athlone Town (photo credit: Sean Dempsey)

Alex Krstic (Derry) takes on Tom McConville of Finn Harps from the 1986/87 season (photo credit: Derry Journal)

The goal that wasn't. An amazing snap of Dundalk goalkeeper Walter Durkan grabbing the ball from inside his goal before scooping it back into play against St. Patrick's in 1952. Amazingly, the goal wasn't given (photo credit: Malachy Bellew/Irish Independent).

Crowd trouble during the 1986 FAI Cup semi-final between Waterford and St. Pat's at Inchicore. Cork officials John Spillane and Sean Ware are escorted by Gardaí to the dressing rooms after bringing a temporary halt to the match (photo courtesy of Irish Examiner).

It started the most successful period in the club's history, a surreal journey that brought the Boynesiders to domestic glory, cross-border cups and wonderful European nights. A gravy train that continued, well . . . for a couple of years anyway.

A second trip into Europe beckoned with a UEFA Cup first round game against Helsinki. Still on a high from the cup success, United took out the Finnish club by beating them 3-1 in extra time in the second leg played at Dalymount. Central to that victory was a Graham Gartland header and two Damien Lynch penalties.

The spot kick from 12 yards played a big part in what came next. This led to an astonishing game against another Scandinavian side – IK Start. The Norwegian club had already won their National league twice and had Norwegian international Ole Martin Arst in its ranks and was managed by former Liverpool player Stig Inge Bjornebye. Drogheda went down 1-0 in the first leg that August, but a late Eamon Zayed header back at Dalymount (despite the change in venue the atmosphere was cracking) brought the tie to extra-time.

When that didn't sort anything out, penalties were called for. After each side had put away their first five, they went to sudden death, and then when everyone had successfully scored, they went round again. Something had to give, and ironically it was one of the best strikers of a ball, Graham Gartland, who missed the crucial penalty as the Norwegians scraped through 11-10 on spot-kicks.

Cup success, however, wasn't far around the corner. In only the second running of the competition, Drogheda became the first League of Ireland side to win the Setanta Cup in 2006, defeating Cork City in the final courtesy of Mark Leech's extra-time goal. Having been beaten in the previous FAI Cup final, it's safe to say the Leesiders were sick of the sight of Doolin's men.

Another trip into Europe via the UEFA Cup followed in 2007, taking out Libertas of San Marino before Swedish club Helsingborg proved too hot to handle.

The good times kept rolling. A successful defence of the Setanta Cup followed in a dramatic penalty shoot-out at Windsor Park on May 12, 2007. In that North v South clash Damien Lynch had missed a penalty in normal time but thanks to Tony Grant's equalizer, and successful spot-kicks from Grant, Stephen Bradley, Shane Robinson and Stuart Byrne, not forgetting the heroics of Miko Vilmunen saving Linfield's last two spot kicks, the Boynesiders retained the cup.

By now the league had started and Doolin's men signalled their intention for a first League of Ireland title, going unbeaten in their first ten games to go top. A healthy five point lead opened up and on October 20th a last minute

Guy Bates' strike at United Park against Cork City was enough to clinch the 2007 League of Ireland championship for Drogheda United – the first in their history.

> *"It had been building for a while with the success we had previously. We'd become the first club to retain the Setanta Cup and the first to win it in the same year as a league championship, so that felt special. When I'd come to the club from managing UCD the facilities weren't anywhere near as good so it was the first thing I wanted to sort, but the Drogheda board understood completely what needed to be done to compete and we made changes. It was a fantastic time to be part of the club."* – **Paul Doolin**

> *"I came into the side with about half the season gone having been playing in Belgium. I played my part and was delighted the goal that won the title wasn't a tap in as I struck it from about twenty yards but to be honest there was such a sense of relief about it all. We'd been trying to wrap up the league for a few weeks, so it was more a feeling of 'Thank Christ' then anything else!"* – **Guy Bates**

Guy Bates starts the celebrations (photo credit: Eimear Taaffe)

The Champions League campaign saw Estonian champs Levedia Tallinn come calling in July where United had to come from behind and win 2-1 with goals from Ollie Cahill and Kudozovic. Knowing one goal could knock them out, Graham Gartland scored the winner a week later in Tallinn to give an aggregate 3-1 win.

League of Ireland Champions 2007
(photo credit: Eimear Taaffe)

This progression brought them to the second qualifying round where United gave Russian giants Dynamo Kiev the fright of their lives. Kiev has a huge European pedigree. They were European Cup Winners Cup champions in 1975 and '86, Champions League semi-finalists in 1999 and regulars at the group stage ever since. At home their record of 22 national league and cups stands up better than most on the continent. And that's only talking about when they were part of Russia! Since the break up of the Soviet Union and entering the Ukrainian League a further 22 league and cup titles have been added.

Having travelled to Dublin (Dalymount, yet again) and coming away with a 2-1 win there was nothing of real evidence to suggest Drogheda could overturn Dynamo in their own backyard. However the Boynesiders came within the metal frame of a post from creating one of the biggest shocks in Champions League history. Despite going behind twice, goals from Shane Robinson and Graham Gartland levelled the game at 2-2. Astonishingly, but for an Adam Hughes guilt-edged miss and Shane Robinson's late effort cracking a post United would have gone through on away goals!

> *"To put things into context, Kiev had just signed a player for €7 million. We were a side who had recently been part-time and second bottom of the League of Ireland! But on the night we finished fitter, stronger and had two great chances to finish them off. It honestly wouldn't have been a surprise to me had we knocked them out. The real killer for us was losing the first leg at Dalymount."* – **Paul Doolin**

The 2008 season was very different however. Financial troubles plagued the club and Drogheda went into examinership that October, suffered a ten point deduction, lost Paul Doolin and the bulk of the squad and of course faced liquidation. One minute you're the width of a post from getting into a play-off for the group stages of the Champions League, the next there's a mass exodus and 79 years of history floating down the tubes. A fine line between character building and soul destroying.

Chairman Vincent Hoey and the fans gathered ranks, raising enough money to pay off some immediate debts, but possibly the biggest victory in the club's history came not on the playing field with eleven men but in a courtroom in the hands of a man in a wig. In January 2009, a judge ruled in favour of not letting the club go into extinction and a huge sigh of relief (complete with customary tears of joy) emanated around the ground now named after a packet of crisps!

It's been a rocky road ever since. Drogheda finished bottom of the Premier Division in 2010 but the demise of Sporting Fingal and the granting of a Premier licence in February this year saw the Boynesiders, now managed by former player Mick Cooke in a last minute switch from Monaghan (thanks Mick, I had to change about three pages!), kick off the 2011 season against UCD.

They've got a fight on their hands this year to stay up, but if it's anything like Jack Lougheed's spirit down in the trenches in World War I then they might just do it.

Ground Info

Hunky Dorys Park is situated on Windmill Road just off the North Road and a stone throw from Our Lady of Lourdes Hospital. It's in a built up area, but there's a small amount of parking at the ground as well as the car park at Lourdes Hospital. Inside the ground the main stand on the O'Raghallagh GAA side can accommodate 2,128 people, having been redeveloped from terracing in 2010, whilst the Windmill Road Stand will keep a further 374 people dry should the Irish weather take hold. There is one further covered terrace on the same side holding 800 away fans whilst the Clubhouse hospitality room also offers a great vantage point to watch the game.

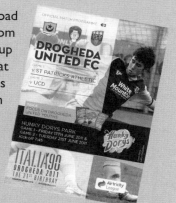

There's a wee bit of rust around and it needs more than one lick of paint but it only adds to the charm of a ground now called Hunky Dorys Park after the crisp-making magnates who sponsored it.

Record Attendance

6,000 v Aston Villa (Friendly, 1994)

Cost

Adults: €10.00
OAPs/Students: €7.00
Children (under 14): €5.00
Adult and Two Children (under14): €15.00

Programme

€2.00 – It's cheaper in price than almost all the other programmes in the country with the look and sheen of something that should be more expensive (it's all in colour) which must drive up the printing costs. Brian Whelan, author of the excellent *Claret & Blue Army* book on Drogheda writes for the programme so that's reason enough to buy it.

Rivals

Dundalk.

Mascot

Disappointed there wasn't a man in a giant furry animal suit leading the Claret & Blues out on my visit. Although the club doesn't have one you just know there's some die-hard fan dying to dress up as a piece of wildlife and wind up the opposition every Friday night.

Food and Drink

There is hot food available on both sides of the ground and if you're looking for a drink after the game you won't have to travel more than one minute's walk. The Windmill House is directly outside the ground on the Windmill Road side, or Mother Hughes Pub on North Road, but both are popular with local Drogheda supporters. The Hunky Dorys taste the same up there but they do a crisp (had to say it) pint of Budweiser!

Club Shop

Located at the club office in Windmill Road or online. Drogheda is the same as virtually every League of Ireland club now and utilises a new online shop at the club website to sell everything from match tickets to replica kits and pink hoodies for women!

Websites

www.droghedaunited.ie
www.superdrogs.freeforums.org

Local Radio

LMFM 95.8

The Match – Drogheda United v UCD (EA Sports Cup, April 25, 2011)

Yet again another few trips to the toilet cost me a couple of goals here. UCD took the lead via Samir Belhout whilst I was in the loo, and Darragh McNamara's equaliser 15 minutes later was also a victim of poor bladder control on my behalf. The Bank Holiday crowd got something further to cheer about when United took the lead just before half-time via Brian Gannon's head, but two second half goals from Robbie Creevy and a late, late Michael Leahy goal (much to the annoyance of a prophet of doom Drogs supporter alongside me who had seen it coming from the first minute of the game) gave the Students a win I felt they deserved.

Dundalk FC

Formed: 1903
Ground: Oriel Park
Capacity: 3,700
Nickname: The Lilywhites

" **People still ask me how I missed that chance against Celtic in the European Cup. I just tell them I had money on them!"**
– Tommy McConville

Cu Chulainn was never a man to be messed with, slaughtering a dog when he was a kid, leading an army as a teen, killing his own son, and tying himself to a rock so he could die on his feet. He never led this country. Brian Cowen did. Go figure.

Our mythological hero is synonymous with the town of Dundalk and in many ways its football club has also fought over the years in the heat of battle to achieve success (without committing homicide), which in 2011 sees the club in fantastic shape both on and off the field.

The Lilywhites, who have been proudly representing the Wee County in League of Ireland circles for 108 years now, began life as Dundalk GNR (named after Great Northern Railway) in 1903.

They began with football in the Dundalk & District League, progressing to the Leinster Senior League before gaining entry to the League of Ireland at the expense of Pioneers FC in 1926, playing their first game against Cork side Fordsons on August 21 with Joey Quinn scoring the club's first league goal in a 2-1 loss.

Despite only winning three of their 18 games that fledgling season, Dundalk managed to avoid finishing last (Brideville took that honour) and recorded a gate of £156 (around 5,000 people) in one game against Shelbourne.

The GNR fell off the club's name in 1930 and three seasons later Dundalk, with players like Eddie Carroll, Ben Lewis, Gerry McCourt and 29 goal striker John Smith, clinched the 1932/33 League of Ireland title, beating Shamrock Rovers into second place with the loss of just two games.

Cup Finalists and League Runners–up, 1930–31
(*photo from* The History of Dundalk: The First 100 Years, *by Jim Murphy*)

Joe Sayers hit a massive 43 goals in the 1935/36 season, a year that saw the club move from the Athletic grounds to their current home of Oriel Park.

The forties started with Ireland being accidentally bombed by a clown in Germany, the rationing of gas, and little money to go around; however, it was also the decade the Lilywhites first took home what is now the FAI Cup.

The 1942 cup campaign started with a 2-1 win over non-league Dubliners Distillery, and ended with a first cup triumph over Cork United at Dalymount Park in April that year. Seeing off Shelbourne with goals from Artie Kelly and

Noel Lavery in the next round, and then beating Shamrock Rovers in a replay with Kelly again notching the winner, Dundalk took to the field on April 26, 1942 in front of a crowd of 34,400 to take on Cork United.

United was the strongest team in Ireland at that point. With Florrie Burke, Bill Hayes and Jack O'Reilly (who were all capped for Ireland), they had already won a double a year earlier and, having defended that league title again in 1942, the Leeside club was after a "double double". However the Lilywhites forgot to read the script and stunned Cork, coming from behind with goals from the ever reliable Artie Kelly (2) and Johnny Lavery to win 3-1.

Dundalk's next success in the competition came after World War II in 1949 when the club won their second FAI Cup. This time it came at the expense of Shelbourne. Ronnie Henderson scored in every round as Dundalk captured the Blue Riband with a 3-0 win. In the entire cup run only three men scored the 11 goals it took to win it – Henderson, Jack Walsh and Danny McElhinney.

The fifties started with victory for the first time in the Leinster Senior Cup, but the biggest success the Oriel Park club had that decade was the capture of the 1952 FAI Cup. Ten years on from surprising Cork United in 1942, Dundalk again denied a Cork side the cup, this time Cork Athletic. It was a wild ride to the final. One that shouldn't have lasted beyond the first round.

In an astonishing game against St. Patrick's Athletic, Pat's all-time highest goalscorer Shay Gibbons scored two goals in a minute, but Dundalk still won 3-2! With the game delicately poised at 2-2, Saints winger Jack Breen scored a perfectly good goal through a crowded goalmouth. Unfortunately, Mr. Evans, the English referee, couldn't see what was going on and missed Dundalk goalkeeper Walter Durkan grabbing the ball from *two feet* inside his own goal, just before he scooped it back into play! Astonishingly, the goal wasn't given (mainly because the ref had been knocked to the ground by Dundalk's Jackie McCourt); the Lilywhites then scored a third and all hell broke loose.

In the semi-finals Dundalk came from behind twice again, scoring a last minute equalizer through Fergus Moloney against Waterford, before finally seeing them off 6-4 in the highest scoring semi-final replay in FAI Cup history. In the final on April 20, 1952 it yet again took a Houdini act with a late equalizer against Cork from Joe Martin, so by the time the replay rolled around the engraver could have scribbled the name of Dundalk on the famous old cup before the game. Sure enough, fate took hold and the Lilywhites beat Cork Athletic 3-0 in the final to win their third FAI Cup.

The club finished bottom of the table for the first time during a very poor 1953/54 season, but whatever they were doing wrong in terms of the league, they certainly had a taste for the 90 minute winner-takes-all cut and thrust of the cup.

Again this came to the fore in 1958 when Dundalk beat Shamrock Rovers with a single Hughie Gannon goal to capture the FAI Cup without even conceding a goal in the entire campaign, and defeating the legendary "Coad's Colts" side put together by Paddy Coad which included players like Liam Tuohy, Paddy Ambrose and Gerry Mackey.

A full 30 years separated the Lilywhite's first two League titles, but in 1963 that gap was bridged when Dundalk won the 1962/63 league championship. Surprisingly, both rivals Waterford and Drumcondra won more games than the Oriel Park outfit but finished joint second. It took a strange combination of results and a lot of novenas offered up by the Oriel Park faithful in order for the Lilywhites to actually take the title.

1958 FAI Cup Winners – Back (L-R): *Peader Halpin, Jim Malone, Jack Flanagan, Joe McGrath (Sec.), Jack Kieran (Chairman)* Middle (L-R): *Peter Kieran, Jimmy Devlin, Dr. Niall McGahon, Tommy Kerr, Johnny Robinson, Hughie Gannon, Ted McNeill, Joe Ralph, Ken Finn, Eugene Hoey, George Ware, B. O'H Kennedy, Gerry McCourt (trainer)* Front (L-R): *Niall McGahon, Vincent Gilmore, Shay Noonan (capt), George Toner, Leo McDonagh (photo courtesy of Jim Murphy)*

A last day draw against Bohemians, where the entire Wee County seemed to descend on Dalymount, seemed to have ruined the Lilywhites' chances only for all three teams beneath them to somehow make a mess of their last couple of games and hand the title to Dundalk!

This of course meant Europe and the club drew FC Zurich in their first European Cup tie. Despite losing 3-0 at home, Dundalk managed a brilliant 2-1 away victory, going out 4-2 on aggregate to a talented Swiss side that would go all the way to the semi-finals before losing to Real Madrid.

Central to everything good about the club at this point was a one-armed man by the name of Jimmy Hasty. One of the most remarkable players not only at Dundalk but of his era, Jimmy may have had the handicap of just one arm but that didn't stop thousands piling into grounds all over Ireland each week to watch him play. To say he was a one off is putting it mildly. He used what should have been a handicap to his advantage, often cutely leaning his stump on the shoulders of defenders knowing full well a referee would be slightly reluctant to give a free-kick against him! He topped Dundalk's goal scoring charts in 1962/63 with 18 goals, and almost doubled that to an astonishing 35 strikes in 1963/64.

Unfortunately, there was a tragic end to one of the country's most talented players when he was shot dead by the Protestant Action Group as he walked to work along Brougham Street in Belfast in 1974. In real life, it was just an alias for the UVF to avoid taking responsibility for the killing. Hasty was an innocent victim of a far from innocent time.

The sixties saw an even bigger upsurge in football in the country and some truly legendary sides came to the fore during the decade – Shamrock Rovers all conquering six in a row; Waterford's maundering Blues, and a brilliant Drumcondra side that first won a tie for us in Europe. Naturally, the Lilywhites were going to create their own little niche and 1966/67 saw Dundalk's most successful season to date. By winning a treble of the League, Shield and Top 4 Cup, Alan Fox's side left their name in club folklore. They also created a record for ten straight wins in a league season, which to date hasn't been bettered.

That third League of Ireland title was won convincingly, with seven points to spare over rivals Bohemians, whilst the Shield was taken at the expense of St. Patrick's. The Top 4 Cup (a tournament played between, hmmm, do I really have to explain this one?) was won after a replay 2-1 again against Bohemians. Sean Thomas' side must truly have been sick of the sight of Dundalk that season!

That summer Dundalk was drawn out of a bag in the European Cup against Bulgarian champions Vasas FC. The tie was technically still alive after Dundalk lost 1-0 at Oriel Park, however when the lads went behind the "Iron Curtain" it was most certainly curtains as the home side ran out 8-1 winners. A further trip into Europe in 1968/69 saw Dundalk beat FC Utrecht in the Inter Cities Fairs Cup before going out to Glasgow Rangers 9-1 on aggregate. Liverpool unfortunately improved on this in 1969/70 beating Dundalk 14-0 over two legs; mind you, I'm sure at least eleven of them were poor refereeing decisions!

Things started brightly in the seventies with a League of Ireland Shield victory over their rivals down the road, Drogheda, in a 5-0 final hammering,

*The legendary Jimmy Hasty wins the Supporters' Club "Player of the Year"
award in 1965 (photo credit: Jim Murphy)*

however league-wise the club was stuck in a rut. Mid-table for most of the decade, things looked a little stagnant until the arrival of Jim McLaughlin.

The Derry native ushered in the start of an all-conquering era which saw Dundalk win three league titles, three FAI Cups and two League Cups to make the Lilywhites the most dominant force in Irish football.

> *"I arrived in November 1974 as player-manager. The biggest shock was being told there was absolutely no money for anyone. I had no idea what was going on around me. All I wanted to do was train my players, put my mark on them and treat them the way I'd been lucky enough to have been treated as a player. In a way ignorance was bliss! So I went to Derry and signed Seanie McLoughlin, then Seamus McDowell. I then coaxed Brian McConville out of retirement and brought Sean Sheehy in from Bohs. It made the nucleus of our team and I built from there."* – **Jim McLaughlin**

The 1975/76 league title charge started and ended with Jimmy Dainty. The Birmingham native scored the only goal of the game on the opening day of the season at St. Mel's Park against Athlone Town, and was the last man to notch a goal in Dundalk's final game of the season away to Sligo Rovers.

In between, Dundalk stayed well clear of the pack and the celebrations started in the penultimate game against Cork Hibs when 5,000 people saw Jim McLaughlin accept the Bass League Trophy after a single goal from Terry Flanagan and a Man of the Match performance from the ever dependable Alan Spavin brought home the fourth league title in Dundalk's history. There were so many stars for the club in that period: Seamus McDowell, Jackie McManus, Sean Sheehy, Tommy McConville, Richie Blackmore and Sean McLoughlin to name but a few.

Dundalk welcomed PSV Eindhoven to Oriel Park in the 1976/77 European Cup campaign. The Dutch giants had just won a double in their home land and boasted the most famous twins in football – Willie and Rene Vander Kerkhof. McLaughlin's side didn't care for reputation and in an attack of bravery (or suicide) Dundalk went at the Dutch champions. Within 60 seconds Jimmy Dainty drove a thunderbolt just wide of the post before Seamie McDowell pounced on some sloppy Dutch defending to drive home from twenty yards. The roof then went missing on Oriel Park. When the absolute mayhem (from a crowd who paid £7,700) died down, Kees Rijvers' side gained control of the game, equalising in the second period as the game finished level.

Being slightly annoyed at the Irish club's temerity to actually take the lead against them in the first leg, PSV made no mistake in the second, convincingly winning 6-0 with Rene Vander Kerhof scoring four (mind you, he could be just robbing a hat-trick on his brother, who knows?)

In May of '77 the FAI Cup stopped off again for a year in the Wee County after Dundalk beat a battle-weary Limerick (who'd taken three games in the semi-final to shake off Drogheda), with Terry Flanagan notching twice in the final. Frank Devlin played a pivotal part of Dundalk's success that year, finishing top goal scorer.

In 1978 a League Cup was clinched on penalties against Cork Alberts (it seems as if every one of the 11 versions of a Cork club must have lost to the Lilywhites in a cup final) as success continued to flow. It was a glorious time to be at Oriel, a glorious time to support Dundalk. And a bad time to be on the other side of the pitch, though Hadjuk Split put paid to the Lilywhites in Europe that season.

Just when the Dundalk faithful thought it couldn't get better than league titles, FAI Cups and nights in Europe, McLaughlin's men decided to do it all in one season and 1978/79 saw Dundalk bring home the first double in their history. Although only three members of the 1976 championship winning league side remained (McConville, Blackmore and Dainty), McLaughlin had added Dermot Keely, Paddy Dunning and Martin Lawlor.

The club was unstoppable, mainly due to the strike partnership of Hilary Carlyle and Cathan Muckian, who notched 27 goals between them. Then there was Pop Flanagan, Sean Byrne and Martin's brother Mick in midfield, but the side, arguably the greatest to ever represent the club, could also count on names like Brendan Muckian, Vincent McKenna, Willie Crawley, Phil Fitzgerald, Kevin Mahon, Liam Devine and Frank O'Neill to contribute as well.

Shamrock Rovers were taken out at Milltown on the opening day and the club only lost three times that season. The winning of the league came in a dreary, bleak Flower Lodge in front of less than 100 supporters in a 3-0 win over a troubled Cork Celtic side, who then bowed out of League of Ireland football for eternity. The double was completed with a 2-0 win over Waterford in the FAI Cup final, with goals from Sean Byrne and Hilary Carlyle at Dalymount on April 22, 1979.

> *"I loved playing with Hilary at Dundalk as the man was an absolute nightmare to play against when I was with St. Pat's! He was so tough I had to book the hospital bed before I took to the field. There was always something broken, normally my nose! So at Dundalk it was nice to be on his side!"* – **Dermot Keely**

And off on their travels in Europe the Lilywhites went again. When League of Ireland clubs went abroad the words "moral victory" were never too far behind. After all, it was understandable as they were part-time clubs in a country where football wasn't even the most popular sport. However the club from the Wee County came within inches of shattering that well worn phrase one night in October 1979. By coming heartbreakingly close to beating Glasgow Celtic in the European Cup, McLaughlin's Dundalk side missed out on a quarter-final berth in the biggest club competition in the world.

The Lilywhites had travelled to Parkhead full of confidence, having disposed of Linfield and then Hibernians of Malta in early rounds. The first round tie against Northern Ireland champions Linfield brought out the very worst in sectarianism. It was a time when Republican and Loyalist tensions were raw. Derry City had withdrawn from the IFA league because of clubs being unwilling to travel to the Republican area around the Brandywell, so when the teams met trouble would spill out on to the terraces with football again becoming an unwilling witness.

"I never expected anything like that. I had left Derry when I was only 17 so was far removed from anything political. I was too young to know anything really, so to be involved in a match like that and the scenes at Oriel Park was such a shock for me." – **Jim McLaughlin**

To both clubs' credit, they have actively worked together over the years to put past troubles behind them and now have a great relationship which includes social events between both clubs and their supporters the last few seasons.

Having seen off Linfield 2-0 in a second leg held in Holland (Linfield was stripped of home advantage) and then Maltese club Hibernians, Dundalk drew Billy McNeil's Glasgow Celtic – at that point the Scottish champions and a side that between 1966-74 had won nine league titles in a row.

The Glaswegians giants boasted quality the like of Bobby Lennox, George McCluskey, Roy Aitken and the late Tommy Burns, however on October 24, 1979 Dundalk proved anything but willing fall guys at Parkhead. Despite going a goal down to Ronnie McDonald after only four minutes, and falling 2-0 behind on the half hour after George McCluskey beat Blackmore, Dundalk native Cathal Muckian made it 2-1 within a minute of Celtic's second goal. Normal serviced seemed to have resumed when Tommy Burns restored the two goal advantage just 60 seconds later, making it three goals in three minutes, but Dubliner Mick Lawlor's goal on 68 minutes meant Billy McNeill couldn't rest easy in bed that night.

The second leg has gone down in both Dundalk and League of Ireland folklore. Anyone who witnessed the game has probably replayed every single second in their head at one time or another. But none more than one Tommy McConville. For it was the Dundalk defender who was presented with the chance of sending the 1967 European Cup champions out that night at a heaving Oriel Park, but his effort two minutes from time goes down as one of the all-time "what might have been moments".

"We had a few chances to win alright. Everyone seems to remember my miss though! I was playing right full and was coming in on the back post with just a couple of minutes left. As the ball came in it got a slight touch off a Celtic defender so I threw myself at the cross as it was going away from me, but I hit the side netting. Even now people ask me how I missed it. I just tell them I had money on Celtic!"
- **Tommy McConville**

A gate totalling a massive £38,000 watched that draw at Oriel Park. Domestically, the ground was an absolute fortress at this point and the stadium by Castletown River in County Louth became a ninety minute death for many a club in the late '70s.

Despite finishing runners-up to Limerick in 1980, the Lilywhites entered Europe again, this time drawing Portuguese giants Porto in the UEFA Cup. Mick Fairclough, a man who'd been written off as a player at the tender age of 22 after an injury whilst playing with Huddersfield Town, made his European debut in that first leg at the Stadium of Light, where all the home side had to show was a 15th minute goal as the archetypical "backs to the wall" performance was again pulled out by a part-time Irish side in Europe.

Two weeks later McLaughlin's eleven gave it both barrels at home and only excellent goalkeeping from Porto's number one denied John Archibold, Mick Fairclough and Brian Duff. The game finished scoreless and Porto breathed a collective sigh of relief. Dundalk was out.

In 1981 another bridesmaid bouquet was handed out for finishing runners up again, this time to Athlone, but the FAI Cup found its way back to the Oriel Park trophy cabinet for the second time in three years, this time with a 2-0 win over Sligo Rovers with goals from John Archbold and Mick Fairlough. And to complete a cup double Dundalk also won the League Cup beating Galway Rovers (as they were called then) on penalties.

The 1981/82 Cup Winners Cup threw up a trip to the land of volcanic eruptions (boy how we remembered that!) as Icelandic side Fram Reykjavik beat Dundalk in a first round, first leg game. However a comfortable 4-0 win back at Oriel saw the club lock horns with English FA Cup winners Tottenham Hotspur in the next round.

A crowd of 18,000 scrummed into Oriel Park on October 21 (where in the name of Christ did they fit them?) to see Gareth Crooks put the White Hart Lane outfit up 1-0 only for Fairclough to equalise later on. When it was over former Irish international Tony Galvin knew they'd been in a match.

> *"We were told they would be tough as our manager Keith Berkinshaw had warned us. They had done really well and were an outstanding team in Ireland , and although we were expecting a hard game you still go, 'OK, it'll be tough, but we'll be fine'. So I think we were really taken by surprise."* – **Tony Galvin, taken from Paul Keane's** *Gods vs. Mortals*

It set up an interesting second leg which the Londoners couldn't take for granted, though ultimately another Gareth Crooks' goal killed the tie off at White Hart Lane.

The purple patch continued in 1982 under the Derry native with a third League of Ireland title, seeing off John Giles' Shamrock Rovers by four points with an impressive 20 victories in 30 games against a Rovers side desperate to end a barren run of 18 years stretching back to 1964 for their last League of Ireland title (ironically pipping Dundalk to the title that year).

Of all Dundalk's trips into Europe, arguably the club they would have hand-picked each year would have been Liverpool. The Merseyside giants set the standard for every other club to follow at the time, and came to town in the autumn of '82 having agreed to play the first leg at Oriel Park, running out 4-1 winners though they could only manage one at Anfield in the second leg.

Jim McLaughlin vacated the hot seat in 1985, replaced by Turlough O'Connor who managed a 1986 League Cup final victory over Shamrock Rovers and then a European night against Ajax in '87 (losing 6-0 on aggregate) before delivering a league and cup double in 1988.

O'Connor had pedigree long before taking the Dundalk job. As a player he had won both league and cup with Bohemians before stepping into management and leading Athlone Town to two League of Ireland championships. There was no one more capable of filling McLaughlin's shoes.

> *"There was certainly more pressure when I took over at Dundalk. When I first took charge of Athlone Town there was no real expectation that we would scale the heights we did so it came as a pleasant surprise to a lot of people. But it was different scenario at Oriel Park. I knew the history, league titles and cups so I had a lot to live up to."*
> **– Turlough O'Connor**

By now players like Alan O' Neill, Gino Lawless, Terry Eviston and top scorer that season Dessie Gorman were playing for the Lilywhites and the 1987/88 championship was clinched on the final day in a classic showdown against Brian Kerr's second place St. Patrick's Athletic.

In a tense, tight final 90 minutes of the 33 game league season, Dessie Gorman's header just before half-time was enough to secure a 1-1 draw and the point needed to clinch the title. The cup campaign saw wins over Sligo, Bray, Cork and Pat's before a Johnny Cleary penalty on May 1, 1988 was enough to defeat Derry City at Dalymount in the FAI Cup final to complete the double. Jim McLaughlin was in the opposing dugout.

> *"That cup final gave me one of my funniest moments at the club as I'll always remember Johnny Cleary's celebration after the penalty. He struck it away so calmly and then ran to celebrate with the fans behind the goal. Unfortunately, when he looked up into the stand in front of him it was full of thousands of supporters in Red & White. It took him a few seconds to realise they were Derry fans before he turned back to the certain circle with some choice words ringing in his ears!"* **– Turlough O'Connor**

Dundalk's goalkeeper Alan O'Neill and Barry Kehoe celebrate winning the 1988 FAI Cup against Derry City at Dalymount Park (photo credit: Ray McManus/Sportsfile)

A defeat to Red Star Belgrade ended Europe early that season, but a glorious decade was brought to a close on November 9, 1989 with a penalty shoot-out victory over Derry City in the League Cup final. God these Dundalk fans are spoiled!

The nineties saw two more League of Ireland titles and a loss in a 1993 FAI Cup final to Shelbourne. In 1990/91, Peter Hanrahan hit 20 goals in a season that saw the Lilywhites pip Cork City by two points to the league championship (they lost to Kispest Honved 3-1 in the European Cup) whilst Dermot Keely then delivered Dundalk's ninth and so far last League of Ireland title in the 1994/95 season. Despite having players like Mick Doohan, Stephen Kelly, Eddie Van Boxtel, Anto Whelan and Ken De Mange, Dundalk had been unfancied and all but dismissed by the press that season, leading Captain James Coll to comment after lifting the league trophy, "If you want to know who the best team were this season lads check the final fucking league table!"

The club entered dire financial straits in 1994 and a rescue package formed by Dundalk AFC Interim Ltd was launched to deal with mounting debts as the tide turned.

The club had to rely on a promotion/relegation play-off victory against Waterford United under ex-Cardiff boss Eddie May in 1997 and enticing Jim

McLaughlin out of retirement to co-manage with Tommy Connolly a year later. Faced with mounting bills, board cutbacks and the release of key players, Dundalk eventually lost its 73 year top flight status in 1999. A run of eight depressing straight losses in the last ten games condemned the Lilywhites to relegation to the First Division for the first time. There would be no quick fix the season after.

Their first game in First Division football brought defeat against St. Francis – a club only in their fourth league season that had only won two of its 36 games the season before. Defeat against Longford in the League Cup followed, and then a loss against a 10-man Limerick side who came from 1-0 down. Let's just say it was a depressing time to be a Dundalk fan. The club finally steadied themselves to end the season fourth.

However they soon began to adapt to their environment. A season later the club formed a co-op to continue to tackle their financial situation, Martin Murray was unveiled as manager and the Lilywhites returned to the Premier Division courtesy of a May Day win over nearest rivals Drogheda to clinch the 2000/01 First Division title. Martin Reilly notched the winner, one of his 20 goals that season, the highest total since Peter Hanrahan in Dundalk's championship 1990/91 season. Their return to the top flight lasted exactly eight months.

A poor league season saw Dundalk finish third last and a return to First Division football, but not before Martin Murray's side became only the second Premier Division club in history to be relegated and win the FAI Cup in the same season. It started with an unassuming draw at home to Galway United and ended with a 2-1 victory over Bohemians on April 7, 2002. The Lilywhites didn't make it easy on themselves getting to the final.

After beating Galway in a replay, they just pipped newly promoted Kilkenny City before going on the road again to beat Finn Harps in a replay at Ballybofey. The semi-final saw a 4-0 hammering of Shamrock Rovers at Oriel Park, and then a 5,000 strong Black & White army converged on Tolka Park the first week in April to see two Gary Haylock goals either side of the break beat Stephen Kenny's Bohemians to give Dundalk their ninth FAI Cup. The Bradford-born striker was pivotal to the Lilywhites that season and collected his fifth winner's medal in the competition. It helped ease the pain of the relegation that year.

European competition in 2002/03 came in a Uefa Cup tie against Croatian Cup winners Varteks. The less said about it the better. The lads lost 9-0 on aggregate. Things would get worse before getting better.

In 2003 Dundalk posted their lowest ever League of Ireland placing by finishing tenth in the First Division, and it wasn't until the arrival of John Gill that things finally got motoring. In 2006 the former Dublin City manager guided the Lilywhites to a promotion/relegation play-off win against Waterford United which should have guaranteed promotion.

Then came controversy. With the FAI bringing in the new procedure of licensing clubs each season, the Lilywhites lost out on their perceived Premier Division place to Galway United who took the 12th and final licence (Dundalk was 13th in the grading) and in the end had to settle for another season in the First Division. The irony of Galway finishing below them in that 2006 promotion season was not lost on them.

There was an appeal. There was a protest. There was a fan with a can of petrol and a match at Merrion Square. Strange days indeed.

> *"I actually lost my first four games in charge and was under severe pressure. And the fans let me know it! But we won our fifth and went 27 games unbeaten, so to have turned it around, win the play-off game against Waterford only for that debacle to happen at the end of the season made it very hard to take. It was a disgrace what happened to us."* – John Gill

Promotion finally came under Gill in 2008, taking the title by one point from a chasing Shelbourne. It was a campaign that went to the very last kick of the ball. Dundalk had been playing catch-up to Shels and coming into the final game of the season were trailing the Dubliners by a point. Dundalk went to Kildare County and promptly won 6-1. Shelbourne only needed a home victory against Limerick but slipped up in the 92nd minute when Colin Scanlon unwittingly became the toast of Dundalk with his late equalizer for Limerick to give the Lilywhites the title.

Gill left almost immediately but under former Bohemians manager Sean Connor, Dundalk posted an extremely strong 2009 season, finishing fifth and qualifying for Europe. An amazing Europa League tie with Grevenmacher of Luxembourg followed in last season's Europa League as a result. Going 2-0 up in the away first leg, and then having to rely on a late own goal just to salvage an amazing 3-3 draw, the Lilywhites just about did enough at home with goals from Neil Fenn and Fahrudin Kuduzovic to see off Grevenmacher despite their injury time consolation. A step up in qualifying rounds meant a step up in class, and unfortunately CSKA Sofia in the next round, where Dundalk lost 8-0 over the 180 minutes.

Since then Ian Foster has been in charge, bringing them to sixth in 2010, and the Lilywhites have again posted a strong start to the 2011 season.

After seven years outside the top flight Dundalk finally celebrate a return to the Premier Division with the 2008 First Division championship (photo credit: Andy McDonnell)

I'm pretty sure Cu Chuliann would be happy with the spirit his fellow warriors are showing at Oriel Park these days, though I don't think they'll need to slaughter dogs or murder any armies on the field of play any time soon.

Maybe a victory of Drogheda United would suffice!

Ground Info

Oriel Park is just right of the main Garda station on Carrick Road. You need not worry about directions – just follow the floodlight pylons which dominate the skyline around the area.

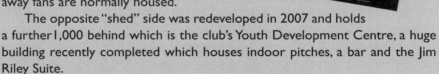

Oriel Park has been around since 1919 but the ground has undergone an overhaul in recent times and is now all-seated. The main stand is an 1,100 all-seater and boasts three bars (the Lilywhite Lounge, Enda McGill Suite and a Sponsors' Bar). There is also uncovered seating either side of the stand where away fans are normally housed.

The opposite "shed" side was redeveloped in 2007 and holds a further 1,000 behind which is the club's Youth Development Centre, a huge building recently completed which houses indoor pitches, a bar and the Jim Riley Suite.

Record Attendance

21,000 v Glasgow Celtic (October 24, 1979)

Cost

Adults: €20.00 (stand); €15.00 (ground)
Children: €5.00
The club has category B matches where stand tickets come down in price to €17.00 and ground tickets to €12.00.

Programme

€3.00 – and one of the best in Ireland. A continuous award winner, there's enough to keep you happy before, during and after the game. Well laid out with a good section on the visiting team, their players and when Dundalk has duelled with them before. There's also a well researched retro piece each week from Jim Murphy, author of *Dundalk FC: The First 100 years*.

Rivals

Though Drogheda United would be the most logical, and indeed there is a rivalry, those of an older generation will point towards Shamrock Rovers and Bohemians. The fact that the Drogheda game was a Category B match this year says a lot.

Mascot

Lily the Panda gets them going at Oriel Park.

Food and Drink

There were two chippys inside the ground, plus a coffee bar which was spread out like a little picnic area for some reason! It delivered the goods though. The nearest bar to the ground is Kennedys on the Carrick Road, just a couple of minutes from Oriel Park. Classy name, classy place!

Club Shop

Located inside the Main Stand.

Websites

www.dundalkfc.com – official site
www.orielweb.com – fans' forum

Local Radio

Dundalk101 FM
Worth a listen alone for the hilarious commentary of John Murphy. An ex-Dundalk player himself, he's extremely funny and brilliantly biased. Quote of the night from the Dundalk v Glentoran game I attended: "And the referee has given a penalty to Glentoran! I didn't see it myself but it was a disgraceful decision."

The Match – Dundalk v Glentoran (Setanta Cup, Quarter-Final, second leg, March 21, 2011)

There was a time when this fixture would invoke memories of bigotry, sectarianism and the odd burning of a tri-colour or union jack. Thankfully, times have changed and though there was a police presence (hats off to them for being so numerous and efficient) the game went off without any trouble. That's not to say there wasn't the odd Green, White & Gold or Red Hand of Ulster!

The game itself was a real cup tie. The Lillywhites had been 1-0 up from the first leg, but Glentoran played their part, even missing a penalty, before Matthews Burrows levelled from the spot. A beautiful move involving Keith Ward and Mark Quigley set up Ross Gaynor to slot home in the last ten minutes to clinch the tie on aggregate for Dundalk.

Finn Harps

Formed: 1954
Ground: Finn Park
Capacity: 4,800
Nickname: The Harps

"Lads, if it's actually possible, go out and enjoy yourself for the second half." – Patsy McGowan to his players at half-time against Derby County in the UEFA Cup. The lads were 9-0 down at the time!

If you had the princely sum of 4 shillings and happened to be in the Donegal town of Ballybofey one Autumn Sunday in 1969, you could have witnessed a little bit of history. You'd have seen ten goals going past a side making their League of Ireland debut, and wondered how in the name of Christ are this lot going to survive – but 42 years later Finn Harps have done just that. Not only have they survived and prospered, they've entertained and won a few trophies along the way.

Harps were formed in 1954, but spent a long time as a Junior League club in Donegal before gaining entry to the League of Ireland. At the time, they competed in the eastern area of the Donegal League playing their first competitive game against Kildrum Rangers at Finn Park in October that year in a match they lost 4-2.

Cup competitions in Letterkenny and Lifford offered the lads a bit of scope each year, but Harps lived in the shadow of the two main Junior League clubs in Donegal – Swilly Rovers and Buncrana Hearts. Rovers proved their metal outside of the county and province by winning the FAI Junior Cup in both 1962 and 1967, whilst Buncrana had won numerous titles in Donegal. However the arrival of Patsy McGowan and Fran Fields saw a shift in power and the rise of Finn Harps from local league to top flight football.

They first came to national prominence by winning the 1968 FAI Junior Cup against Telephones United (yes, that's their real name – God the puns I could think of!). A step up to the FAI Intermediate Cup followed, and then McGowan and Fields thought the timing was right to give the League of Ireland a crack and applied for membership.

"For years Donegal had been a hot bed of soccer. Everyone knew it, especially with teams like Swilly Rovers having won the FAI Junior Cup twice, so there wasn't a doubt that the public and players were there for it. I was confident of us stepping up to the League of Ireland but also doing well in it. Mind you, when we made our application one reporter described us as 'a club out of the bog with a set of goalposts and a couple of players'." – **Patsy McGowan**

Patsy McGowan and Richie Kelly canvased clubs throughout Dublin, Dundalk and Drogheda looking for their support, but there were also applications from Dubliners' Home Farm, a club with a solid Junior League reputation, and midlanders Athlone Town, who had already played League of Ireland football in the 1920s and won two Junior Cups since.

With five Dublin clubs already plying their trade in the league, Home Farm eventually missed out and Finn Harps, along with a returning Athlone Town, became members of the League of Ireland for the 1969/70 season.

The club's first offical game in the top flight was in the highly popular Dublin City Cup on August 17, 1969, however the Donegal club's introduction was a tad harsh! Lining out against a Shamrock Rovers side who had won six FAI Cups in a row, and contained the likes of Mick Leech, Frank O'Neill, Pat Courtney, Tommy Kinsella and Mick Smyth, Harps were absolutely destroyed 10-2. There might well have been a few League of Ireland directors who thought "Jesus Christ" to themselves and wondered had they made a cock-up by approving their application?

"I vividly remember after being beaten 10-2 we were told by all the press that we wouldn't last a season. I replied in the press conference by saying, 'Not only will we last the season boys, we'll be in Europe in four years'. There was an uproar of laughter in the room but I said,

'I'll put the smile on the other side of your faces'. And that's exactly what I did!" – **Patsy McGowan**

As it turns out, Patsy McGowan and the boys did just fine. Amazingly, after the Rovers loss Finn Harps went undefeated at home until the very last home game and came away a very creditable seventh of fourteen teams that season, winning 10, losing 10 and drawing the remaining six. On February 11 that year Harps played their first FAI Cup tie as a league club, drawing at home to Dundalk before losing 4-0 in the replay.

Brian Wright scores Finn Harps' first goal in League of Ireland football against Shamrock Rovers (photo credit: Derry Journal)

However it took only two more seasons for the club to make their first real impact, winning the Dublin City Cup in 1971/72 by defeating Cork Hibernians 1-0 in the final with a goal from Brendan Bradley, a man who went on to become a true great of Irish football with a massive 235 goals, the leading goal scorer in League of Ireland history.

"I remember scoring the first hat-trick for Finn Harps in the league. It came against Athlone Town and what made it even more special was RTÉ were showing the game that night on television. They had a wee sports programme on Sundays that showed the odd match so it was a big thing for us. Straight after the game myself and Patsy drove to Longford just in time to see it." – **Brendan Bradley**

There was an almighty scrap with Waterford under Patsy McGowan before finishing runners-up in the 1972/73 championship, however it got Finn Harps into Europe for the first time. Waterford had dominated League of Ireland football from the mid-sixties but McGowan's men cared little for reputation, and with players like Gerry Murray, Terry Harkin, Joe Nicholl, Jim Smith and of course Mr. Bradley in the side Harps severely tested Shay Brennan's Blues

The Finn Harps team that took on Aberdeen in the 1973 UEFA Cup
Back (L-R): *Declan McDowell, Charlie Ferry, Declan Forbes, Jim Sheridan,*
Brendan Bradley, Jim McDermott, Joe Harper, Donal O'Doherty.
Front (L-R): *Jim Smith, Tony O'Doherty, Terry Harkin, Gerry Murray, Peter Hutton,*
Joe Nicholl, Paddy McGrory (photo credit: Derry Journal)

that season. McGowan's men won nine of their first ten games and kept on the Blues coat-tails with both sides meeting in the penultimate game of the season at Finn Park. A point that afternoon would have been enough for the Suirsiders to clinch the title, but Harps were determined to make things go right to the wire.

The full range of Irish weather was on show (rain, sleet, snow, then rain again) and a biting wind flown in especially from the North Pole as Harps came from behind with goals from Bradley, Nicholl and Smith in a 3-2 win. As brave an effort as it was, McGowan's men (who beat Limerick in that last game) had to settle for second spot as Waterford made no mistake against a weakened Cork Hibernians side to take their sixth title in eight years. However from playing Junior League football less than a decade ago, Finn Harps had secured a place in Europe – just as Patsy predicted.

This led to absolute fever pitch in the small town of Ballybofey as that summer Finn Harps were paired with Scottish club Aberdeen in the UEFA Cup. On September 19, 1973 Terry Harkin became the first Finn Harps player to score in Europe in a 4-1 defeat to The Dons at Pettordie, whilst despite losing the second leg 3-1 Harkin also got the plaudits for notching Harps' first home goal in Europe.

"We performed quite well up there. Of course it was a big step up for
us and produced a lot of excitement around the town, but I treated it

as another match. By that stage I had played international football for Northern Ireland and was 33 so the tie itself didn't faze me but I was delighted to score in both legs." – **Terry Harkin**

A 4-1 win at home to Home Farm in mid-February of 1974 started Patsy McGowan's men on the road to Finn Harps' first, and so far only, FAI Cup win. By this stage the club was a well established top half team and would have fancied their chances. Charlie Ferry denied Bohemians at Dalymount in the next round, and continued a one-man mission by finishing off the Dubliners at Finn Park 2-0 in the replay, scoring one from a corner, something he managed two times that season!

A 5-0 annihilation of Athlone Town followed in the semi-finals before the Ballybofey men strode out on April 21 against St. Patrick's Athletic in the 1974 FAI Cup final. A turnout of 14,000 in Dalymount saw the Donegal club strike the front within two minutes from a Charlie Ferry goal, and a brace from Brendan Bradley spectacularly secured the FAI Cup for the first time in the club's history and completed a massive assendancy through the ranks.

Mass celebrations and bonfires on the Donegal Road in Ballyshannon awaited the team on their arrival home. It was a huge achievement and vindication for Fran Fields and Patsy McGowan, whilst also a great moment for Gerry Murray – the only hometown Ballybofey boy on the side.

"It was my proudest moment. I do remember the honour of playing in Europe against Aberdeen (and the novelty of my first time on a plane). I also remembered scoring six in one game against Sligo Rovers but the two goals in that final were far more important. That cup run gave me one of the funniest moments in my career. I remember we played Athlone in the semi-final at Oriel Park and whilst my back was to their goal I heard the crowd cheer for no reason. I turned around to see Town's goalkeeper, Mick O'Brien, climbing up the net from behind then jumping down on the crossbar, smashing it into pieces! They were 2-0 down so it was an attempt to get the game called off! Mick only suceeded in getting himself sent off. The funniest thing was he'd done the exact same thing the week before at our place as well!" – **Brendan Bradley**

"I recall we weren't particularly nervous, though there was much hype around Donegal about the game itself. I was working in a small town called Dromod in Leitrim at the time and was fair removed from the build-up which was a good thing. Pat's were favourites going into the game, but I wasn't anything but confident and when you've got a guy like Brendan Bradley in the side you always have a

chance. There was wire fencing in Dalymount that day but it was sod all help trying to keep the Donegal contingent from getting on the field after the final whistle. I always remember one poor security guy and his alsatian dog trying to keep them off the pitch . He just totally got swamped!" – **Jim Sheridan**

"It was hearbreaking for me. The biggest game of my career and I missed it after picking up an injury, ironically against St. Pat's just two weeks previous. That really effected me as I'd played in every game up to the final. I was heartbroken." – **Terry Harkin**

Yet again their was huge excitement that summer as Finn Harps drew Bursaspor in the Cup Winners Cup. The Turkish side were themselves only playing league football over a decade and little was known about them. Mc-Gowan's men travelled to Turkey for the first leg, losing 4-2 (Ferry and Bradley scoring) but managed a creditable scoreless draw at home. Prices had gone up from 4 schillings in 1969 to a massive £1.00 to get in and £1.50 to sit in the stand!

Successive League Cup final defeats in 1974 and '75 kept the Donegal club's domestic profile high, and for such a young side Harps were regularly making trips into Europe (and I don't mean on a ferry to do Christmas shopping in Fishguard). Again there was a title push in 1975/76, and in fact at one stage Harps were going so well in both league and cup it looked like there might have been a double on, however Dundalk lost only one game in the league all season and took the league championship by four points, whilst a 1-0 defeat in the semi-finals to Drogheda finished off the FAI Cup dream.

The prolific Brendan Bradley – with 235 goals, the highest goal scorer in the history of League of Ireland football (photo credit: Derry Journal)

But the runners-up spot again meant European football where Harps drew Derby County in the UEFA Cup. The English club had won two First Division championships in the seventies, boasted name like McFarland, Nish, Hector and Gemmill, so County goalkeeper Graham Mossley probably thought he'd be lucky to get about five minutes action during both ties. I think he got about six seconds. Derby . . . well, let's just say they won. But I suppose for the record it was a 16-1 aggregate score, though I must point out that Derby's goalkeeper statistically only kept one more clean sheet than Gerry Murray, Finn Harps' man between the posts.

> *"It was 9-0 at half-time. If ever I wanted a big hole to open in the ground and swallow me up, this was it! You can imagine it, here we were losing by nine and I still had another 45 minutes to go! I always maintained everything they done that day hit the net – good or bad."*
> – **Gerry Murray from *The Finn Harps Story* by Bartley Ramsey**

> *"It was a real eye-opener for us. I mean their team was full of internationals. Their centre-half pairing was Roy McParland and Colin Todd. They had Leighton James on the wing, Archie Gemill in the middle then players like Charlie George and Kevin Hector up front. What made matters worse for us was the fact it rained heavily and the surface on the Baseball Ground, which was fast anyway, was made twice as bad for us. Poor Gerry Murray must have thought he was in a coconut shy with everything that was coming at him!"*
> – **Jim Sheridan**

Everton dished out a beating over two legs, again in the UEFA Cup in the 1978/79 competition, though Harps saw out the decade finishing in a healthy sixth place.

If the seventies were the heyday of the club with warm fuzzy nostalgic moments and memories for those of a certain age, the eighties were anything but. Despite a semi-final appearance in the 1981 FAI Cup, Harps struggled in the league and were relegated for the first time in their history in the 1984/85 season, finishing second last with six wins from 30 games. It was a challenging time economically as well, and the huge crowds of the previous two decades had long since dwindled. Strikes were rife, half our wages criminally went in tax whilst one man stocked up on silk shirts and bought the odd island.

Despite relegation and the sacking of Patsy McGowan (Bobby Toland took over as caretaker), Finn Harps did manage to reach the 1985 League Cup final. It was an impressive run to get there as well, topping a group of Galway, Longford and Sligo Rovers before Jimmy McGroarty's goal knocked out a fancied Dundalk side in the semi-final. Fran Fields was also President of the

Finn Harps take on Waterford United in the 1985 League Cup final.
Back row (L-R): *Fran Fields, Eddie McGinley, Stephen McNutt, Declan McIntyre,*
Paul McNutt, Charlies McGeever, Oisin Harkin, Sean Ferry
Front row (L-R): *Con McLaughlin, Liam McDermott, Jimmy McGroarty,*
Ian Arkwright, Sean Boyle, Danny Kelly (photo credit: Derry Journal)

FAI at the time, though it would have pained him to present the League Cup to Waterford at Kilcohan Park, as despite an Ian Arkwright goal, Harps went down 2-1 in the final that March.

Former Manchester City winger Paul Simpson played on loan for Finn Harps that year, though one of the club's biggest assets was Con McLaughlin – the first Donegal man to score 100 goals in the League of Ireland.

> *"At the time it was every Donegal boy's dream to play with Harps. I made my debut under Eunan 'Busty' Blake and scored on my debut in a win against Cork Alberts in Flower Lodge. The club still had the likes of Tony O'Doherty and Charlie Ferry playing and they helped me settle. Mind you, I remember being a raw young player when Dermot Keely got me sent off in one game against Dundalk, kicking him in my naviete in front of the ref after he'd been kicking me behind his back for most of the game before that!"* – **Con McLaughlin**

In theory, the drop in league meant a "bigger fish in small pond", but in 1987 the club unwittingly went down in EMFA's history when they became their victims in the final of the First Division Shield. It was the year of Harps' worst ever FAI Cup result at Finn Park, a 6-1 defeat to Waterford United.

Tom McConville was sacked in 1987 to make way for Chris Rutherford, but Harps could only manage a fourth place finish at best in the next three seasons with a 7-0 hammering by neighbours Derry City a particular low point. John O'Neill then had a go in the hot seat but it took the return of Patsy McGowan before there was even a sniff at the Premier Division. That came in 1993/94 when McGowan brought his side into a promotion/relegation play-off with Cobh Ramblers. Despite winning the first leg through a John Gerard McGettigan goal, the Cork side ran out easy winners 3-0 in the return leg.

A year later there was an even bigger kick in the nuts. Again the Bally-bofey club clinched a play-off spot in the First Division, and this time tackled Premier Division also-rans Athlone Town. Hopes were high but after two games and 180 minutes, and even more extra-time, both teams had failed to hit the back of the onion bag. It went to penalties with Sean Barrett being the luckless man who missed the fatal spot kick in a 5-3 defeat, however there was a bit of a Luis Suarez moment during the game when Brian Lafferty had been sent off for handling an Athlone effort on the line, only for the resulting spot kick to be missed.

Finally, in 1996, over a decade after they'd lost their top flight status, Dermot Keely managed to position the club that crucial one place higher and achieve promotion from the First Division, finishing runners up to Bray Wanderers but a crucial three points higher than Home Farm Everton in third.

The Finn Park outfit managed to hold on to their top flight status that year, launched a five year development plan at a cost of £745,000 to the club, and the ageless Jonathan Speak notched his 100th League of Ireland goal. Signed in 1995 for £14,000 from Ballymena United, Speak is a legend in not only Harps' history but the League of Ireland's as well. His 17 goals during the 1995/96 season had helped Finn Harps gain promotion, and a further 14 back in the top flight by the former Derry City hitman meant the club avoided relegation.

There was success in the Irish News Cup in 1999 and the club just missed out on an Intertoto Cup place by a point, but it still proved a season of what might have been after Charlie McGeever's men lost to Bray Wanderers after 300 minutes and three ties in the 1998/99 FAI Cup final.

The campaign had started unconvincingly with a scoreless draw at home to non-league Belgrove before McGeever's men ran out 6-0 winners in the replay. Harps were taken to a replay again in the next round before Donal O'Brien's goal saw off Cork City. The lads continued to make life hard on themselves in the quarter-finals, drawing with Kilkenny City 2-2 before the Cats were thrown out of the competition and fined £2,500 for not showing up for the replay due to a chronic shortage of players.

Despite the disadvantage of no neutral ground in the semi-final, Finn Harps travelled to Galway United's Terryland Park and beat the Tribesmen with goals from Jonathan Speak and Tom Mohan to set up a date with Bray Wanderers on May 9, 1999.

Twice the Ballybofey club were tantalizing close to capturing only their second FAI Cup. The final ended in a dour scoreless deadlock but the replay was anything but. In that game Speak scored early in the second half only to see Wanderers equalise with three minutes left. Tom Mohan again gave Harps one hand on the trophy in extra time, but a penalty was then awarded to Bray with just seconds remaining. And you really know it's not going to be your day when Harps goalkeeper Brian McKenna saves Colm Tresson's shot, but the rebound is bundled back in by Kieran O'Brien.

The unlucky 1999 FAI Cup final squad that lost out to Bray over three games.
(photo credit: Derry Journal)

"My inital reaction was how could Kieran O'Brien be so close to me, as he was practically alongside me when I made my way up from the dive! I looked at the video at home later and O'Brien had encroached so much that he was almost level with Colm Tresson when he took the penalty!" – **Brian McKenna**, *The Finn Harps Story*

"After the second game we were physically and mentally drained. We'd gone ahead and missed so many chances to kill the game off. We absolutely threw it away. I remember playing that night only because of pain-killing injections so the third game just proved too much, not just for me but for all of us." – **Gavin Dykes**

More heartbreak followed. In 2001 Finn Harps was relegated from the Premier Division. Gavin Dykes had resigned as manager that January leaving Jonathan Speak to pick up the pieces. With a weekly budget of around £2,500 to run his squad for the season (try working with that, Mr. Mancini), Speak still guided Finn Harps to the promotion/relegation play-off game in 2002, where despite a Kevin McHugh hat-trick in the second leg against Premier Division Longford Town, the Ballybofey outfit still lost 6-5 on penalties.

A year later they suffered again, but this time twice in the same calendar year. Despite winning the First Division Cup (a competition everyone completely forgets about – mind you, so did I until I looked it up), Harps lost out again in the play-offs, this time to Galway United 2-1 on aggregate, but because of the move to summer soccer it meant a second season in 2003 – not that it stopped the pain as this time local rivals Derry City made sure there was no return to Premier Division football at the same stage.

The ugly world of finance reared it unwanted head soon after as the club found itself in debt to the tune of almost €250,000, but managed to solider on in the face of worrying adversity. Finally, in 2004 Finn Harps managed to place another cup in the Finn Park trophy cabinet and removed unwanted codwebs! This came in the shape of their first First Division league championship.

Noel King had started the season in charge of the Ballybofey outfit but left after six weeks. Former Derryman Felix Healy took over the mantle and by bringing in players like Anthony Gorman and Ian Rossiter, whilst holding on to the irreplaceable Kevin McHugh, Healy turned what could have been a transitional period into a 2004 First Division championship title, pipping UCD by a point with McHugh scoring 26 times that season.

Since then there's been relegation from the Premier Division in 2005, promotion back to it via a play-off victory against Waterford United in 2007, an FAI Cup game the same year where 5,000 saw Harps lose to Derry City at Finn Park in the local derby, and a drop out of the top flight again in recent seasons. In between, Jonathan Minnock broke Jim Sheridan's all time appearance record of 395, and Harps kicked off their 32nd season of unbroken football in the League of Ireland this March in a draw against Limerick at Finn Park with Kevin McHugh among the goal scorers.

Ground Info

From whatever direction you arrive at Finn Park in Ballybofey you'll have passed by some of the most magnificent scenery in Ireland. The Blue Stack Mountains alone are enough to make even the longest journey worth it (trust me, I drove from Waterford!). It's on the banks of the River Finn that you'll find Finn Park, home of Finn Harps Football Club for well over the last 50 years.

The Main Stand on the Navenny Street side is part terrace, part seated (300 seats) whilst the Chestnut Road side is home to the "Town End" terrace. Only three sides of Finn Park remain open; the "River Bank End" was closed some time ago, and Finn Park is in need of a lick of paint. However there's no need to run out to the local DIY store as in 2013 the club will relocate just down the road to Stranorlar and a new purpose-built 6,600 all-seated stadium which is already under construction. For parking around the ground look no further than the Navenny Car Park which will hold up to 300 cars.

Record Attendance

8,000 v Celtic (Friendly, May 18, 1983)

Cost

Adults: €10.00
OAPs: € 8.00
Students: €5.00;
Children Under-12: €3.00

Programme

€3.00 – Bartley Ramsey, author of *The Finn Harps Story,* is one of the con-tributors to the home programme, which in itself is good enough reason to make a purchase. Editor Joe Doherty works on a tiny budget but is helped with contributions from people like Aidan McNelis who helps run the club's excellent website.

Rivals

At 55 miles down the road, logistically, Sligo Rovers had been the nearest Finn Harps had for a "derby" game of sorts for years, but that all changed when the Candystripes of Derry entered the League of Ireland in 1985 and gave Finn Harps a real local derby they could get their teeth into. The first few meet-ings between the two sides at this level caught the imagination and cemented the rivalry, and although the sides operate on a different end of the scale at present, Harps will hope to be in the same division as Derry when they kick off at Stranorlar in 2013.

Mascot

Harper the Dog runs out to the Finn Harp faithful every Saturday night. Actually, he is only a pup yet. Born in March 2009, Harper was designed by the National School Children in Donegal and was unveiled to the Harps fans at the beginning of the 2009 season.

Food and Drink

A mobile chipper provides hot food inside the ground and trust me, when it's Finn Park on a November night in Donegal you'll be thankful of that hot tea inside you. Heeneys Bar and the flamboyantly named Barcelona Bar on Glenfinn Street are where the majority of Finn Harps fans can be found, whilst Bonners bar and the Villa Rose hotel are good supporters of the club.

Club Shop

Located on entry to the ground from the Chestnut Road side.

Websites

www.finnharps.com
www.irishfootnetwork.com (Harps have a fans' forum here)

Local Radio

Finn Harps Radio
http://www.ustream.tv/channel/finn-harps-radio
Live commentary of every away game is provided.

The Match – Finn Harps v Waterford United (Airtricity League, First Division, June 11, 2011)

Finn Harps is a long way to come for most supporters not to get a result, and when you've travelled four hours from Waterford only to go away empty handed it's a particularly hard kick in the nuts.

Harps under the management team of Felix Healy and Peter Hutton gained all three points, typically through the ever reliable Kevin McHugh. The northerners weren't exactly overflowing with confidence, having made a poor start to the season, however this was a Waterford side that had just lost manager Stephen Henderson and was trying to regroup.

Despite an increasingly subdued second half, Seamus Long could have grabbed the Suirsiders a last gasp point only for Harps goalkeeper, Ciaran Gallagher, to bring off a Schmeichel-like save from his effort and leave the Blues fans heading for a fine selection of local pubs. Driving back was never an option!

Galway United

Formed: 1937
Ground: Terryland Park
Capacity: 5,000
Nickname: The Tribesmen

"Denis Bonner was so good you could leave him on his own at the back and Paul McGee was a great striker – mind you, he's had more clubs than Jack Nicklaus." – Eamon Deacy

The Corrib may have looked pretty tempting to fans of Galway United on February 14, 2011. Faced with the Valentine's Day heartache of demotion to the footballing wilderness of the A Championship due to the failure to obtain a top flight licence, some supporters could have been forgiven for skipping the box of chocs and annual visit to the florists in favour of ending it all. Talk of a massive obituary column in the local press, however, was premature as five days later the Tribesmen won an appeal, got granted a Premier Division licence and clinched their biggest battle to date without a ball being kicked.

They've been around the block for almost 75 years now, initially achieving most of their early success at Junior League level, but since 1976 have been representing the county proudly though the biggest league title in the land still eludes them.

Where the Corrib meets Galway Bay you'll find the former fishing village of Claddagh. It's this area that saw the formation of a team called Galway Rovers in 1937, who plied their trade in the local Galway and District League and played their home games at South Park. At that time the nearest provincial town playing top flight football was Sligo Rovers (who won the Free State League the same year as Galway's foundation), but the majority of clubs playing League of Ireland were from Dublin – seven of the other eleven teams that year came from the capital.

The West may have been awake and crying out for a team but it was still over four decades before any football club was coming near Galway Bay for anything other than a session and maybe some oysters. Eventually there was a move to Terryland Park, a ground that's been the traditional heartbeat of the Tribesmen for several decades now. Having chased the elusive dream of League of Ireland football for years a major stepping stone was Galway Rovers' inclusion into the 1976/77 League Cup. The club gained entry into the league format in a group that involved Athlone Town, Sligo Rovers and Finn Harps.

This of course meant the club's first game at top flight level which took place on September 5, 1976 against Athlone Town in Group A. Strangely, all three current Galway clubs in the league have made their top flight debuts against Athlone Town, with all three failing to score against them, though Galway faired best holding the midlanders to a scoreless draw in this game.

The league cup campaign featured another draw (Eamon Deacy scoring the club's first goal at League of Ireland level in a 1-1 draw with Finn Harps), before a defeat to Sligo ended any further progression.But it had set the ball in motion and after 39 years as a non-league club Galway finally got their chance to join the League of Ireland in 1977.

For the first time in the league's history the First Division was extended to 16 teams and Rovers' application was accepted along with Thurles Town, thus bringing League of Ireland football to the county for the first time. It took the lads time to find their feet. Managed by Amby Fogarty, Rovers earned their first points before they even scored a goal. An opening day scoreless draw against St. Patrick's Athletic on August 28 marked their league debut but it took until October and five games in for Rovers to actually score their first goal. When the first goal and win came, predictably the opposition was fellow newcomers Thurles Town.

It set the tone for a long hard season. Fogarty's side had players like Tommy Lally, Eamon Deacy, Tony and Tommy Murphy and Micko Nolan that year, and despite only winning three times during the league campaign the

The Galway Rovers team that lined out for the club's first League of Ireland game, against St. Pat's in 1977. Back row (L-R): *Kieran Sciasa, Tommy Murphy, Jimmy Cummins, Tony Murphy, Kieran McDaid, Eugene Corley.* Front Row (L-R): *Gerry Curran, Jimmy Duffy, Shay Doyle, Eamon Deacy (Capt.), Fran Brennan and Frank Devlin (photo credit: Connaught Tribune)*

Tribesmen avoided finishing bottom and did not have to worry about any nasty re-election issues.

> *"It was very special being part of that team. Sure we knew what we were up against and we took a few hammerings but it didn't seem to matter to us. We were all young local lads representing Galway. We didn't mind getting beaten – we were always good losers in Galway!"*
> – **Eamon Deacy**

Their position didn't change in 1978/79, though bottom-placed Cork Celtic folded, and gradually a slow improvement saw the club leaving a bit of light between themselves and the dark hole at the bottom. Quite unexpectedly, a League Cup run in 1981 gave the Maroon Army their first taste of a national domestic final when John Herrick's side fought their way past Finn Harps, Athlone and Thurles Town, where a winner from John "Mags" Mannion in that semi-final saw Galway reach the 1981 League Cup final.

The opposition was a Dundalk side in the greatest purple patch of the club's history under Jim McLaughlin, but that didn't deter Galway and the two-legged affair was still delicately poised after the New Year's Day meeting at Terryland Park which ended scoreless, with a healthy £4,000 paying crowd to boot.

Despite being clear favourites, the Lilywhites couldn't put the Connaught men to bed in normal time of the second leg, but had more success from the penalty spot where the tie was eventually settled on spot-kicks to kill off the fairytale ending for the Tribesmen and their followers. It was particularly hard on goalkeeper Tom Lally.

> *"I had actually saved four penalties in the shoot out and missed one myself, before Paddy Dunning came up to take his for Dundalk. I didn't move, stayed central and stopped it but the referee ordered a re-take. I wouldn't mind but it was the only penalty I actually didn't move an inch for! That would have won us the cup. I then remember George Quinlavin's missed penalty. It was a powerful penalty al-right- it took off out of Oriel Park and probably landed somewhere in the Phoenix Park later that night."* – Tom Lally

Just four years into their League of Ireland infancy it was still an impressive achievement.

A change in name arrived soon after as "Rovers" was dropped in favour of "United" with which they started the 1982/83 season, however there was also a deepening financial problem at the club that year with mounting debts.

The cost of running a League of Ireland club had become a huge strain, but the involvement of local businessmen Joe Hanley and Mattie Greaney saved the day. The board had been cleared out and with Hanley as chairman, Greaney as treasurer and a more slim-lined board, a debt of just over £40,000 (or half of Rio Ferdinand's wage just to be more annoying!) was dealt with and a crisis avoided.

A first top half finish arrived in 1985 under Tom Lally and it continued to be a season of firsts with a final appearance in the FAI Cup. At the start of February non-league Avondale United were beaten 4-0 in Cork in an FAI Cup run that continued with an impressive 4-1 defeat of Shelbourne in a replay. The semi-final pitted United's width against a strong Limerick side that had finished eight points better than Lally's men in the league, but strikes from Martin McDonald and Johnny Glynn earned United a draw in a pulsat-ing semi-final at Tolka Park before John Mannion scored the winner in a St. Mel's Park replay to guarantee Galway United a place in the 1985 FAI Cup final.

> *"I remember the first game at Tolka well. Limerick had just won the Hurling League Championship the same afternoon and were giv-*

ing us a bit of stick when we were 2-1 down with only a couple of minutes left. 'We've won in the hurling now we're going to win the football!' Thankfully Johnny Glynn proved them wrong!" – Tommy Shields (Galway United supporter and club FAI Delegate)

"It was a great result. At one point in that semi-final against Limerick at Tolka Park we were 2-0 down and struggling badly but we showed great character to dig deep and come back then to win the replay. It gave us some quiet confidence going into the final." – Tom Lally

Again the Tribesmen came up against a club smack bang in the middle of a hot winning streak, and again that pesky Jim McLaughlin was at the helm. Under the Derryman, Shamrock Rovers had won two consecutive league titles, and boasted players like Mick Neville, Dermot Keely and Kevin Brady, so the odds were stacked against the Galwegians once again. It was close, but the failure to score for a second domestic cup final proved crucial as the Hoops, courtesy of a Noel Larkin goal, collected the trophy. As much as the travelling Maroon Army cursed the men from Glenmalure that day, there was also a wry smile on the bus back to Eyre Square. Shamrock Rovers' league and cup double meant one crucial thing for Galway United – Europe.

"We didn't really know what to expect at the start of the season but we had a young, competitive side with a lot of local players, so there was always a chance in the cup, and we beat some good sides before losing in the final. Europe was exciting. We were lucky to have added to the squad with players like Richie Blackmore and Paul McGee. I think a common problem at the time with a lot of clubs was the fact the league ended in April and Europe started three months later and the squad you finished the season with could be completely different to the one you start with in Europe." –Tony Mannion

A host of lucrative teams awaited in the Cup Winners Cup draw for Galway that boiling summer of 1985 (that's right, we had three days of sun, so that's classed as a scorcher). Benfica, Celtic or Sampordia could have come out of the bag. In the end it was Danish cup winners Lyngby that provided the opposition for Tony Mannion's side.

The club's historic first competitive game on the continent took place in the National Stadium in Copenhagen on September 18, 1985 when a solitary goal for the home team was all that separated the sides, and this after John Mannion had been sent off. The home tie (switched to the Galway Sportsgrounds) saw a bumper crowd on October 2 with historic first goals in Europe from Paul Murphy and Dennis Bonner. Unfortunately, the Danes scored three down at the other end ending Galway's participation in the cup.

> *"I think Lyngby were shell-shocked by our performance up there. They never expected us to play so well. Crucially in the return leg we had a few injuries, Eamon Deacy was out and John suspended and so we lacked a little strength in depth for that game." –* **Tony Mannion**

By that stage the Tribesmen were a different side to the perennial strugglers of years gone by. Tony Mannion was in charge of a solid team with the likes of Paul Magee, Kevin Cassidy, Ricky O'Flaherty and of course Eamonn "Chic" Deacy. A healthy start to the season boosted confidence in the League Cup and having won four of their five group games, the Tribesmen then took out Sligo Rovers in a penalty shoot-out and Home Farm in a five goal thriller to reach their second League Cup final. Their opponents? The team that had beaten them in the first one – Dundalk.

However this time Galway weren't the new kids on the block. There was plenty of experience behind them, and crucially United were also the form team in the league so goals that day from Denis Bonner (brother of Packie) and the ever reliable Paul McGee were enough to clinch Galway United's first domestic trophy at the top level in the Republic.

By the Spring of 1986 Galway was riding high in the league, had gone sixteen games without a loss, and remained unbeaten at home when league leaders Shamrock Rovers came to town in early March. With just six games of the 1985/86 season left, and the Tribesmen hovering menacingly in second place, it was billed as a title decider at Terryland Park. A huge crowd turned out, however a truly awful first half-hour destroyed any hope Galway had as three goals were hammered past Richie Blackmore, and despite pulling one back the Dubliners ran out comfortable 3-1 winners.

> *"We went into the game having to play three games in a week – Rovers, Bohs and Dundalk after an earlier Bohemians game was called off and rescheduled. Effectively that killed off our challenge, it just became hard to get the momentum going again after the Rovers defeat but to put it in context we were a provincial club, unbeaten in the league to that point having had a real go at winning a League of Ireland championship. As I said earlier, a bit more strength in depth and who knows?" –* **Tony Mannion**

> *"The three games in such a short space of time really took it out of us and they were three really good sides at that. Sure it was very disap-*

*pointing but we'd done extremely well to put ourselves in that posi-
tion in the first place." –* **Paul McGee**

Two more defeats followed to Bohemians and Dundalk and it looked like
a place in Europe might even be snatched from them, but a last day defeat of
Limerick 3-0 at Terryland Park saw Galway United qualify for Europe for the
second season in a row.

This time Dutch club Groningen proved the opposition, however a bigger
battle had to be won off the field first. Having been granted permission to
play in the predominantly GAA-based Galway Sportsgrounds the year before,
UEFA now insisted the lack of facilities at the ground deemed the second leg
of the tie against Groningen could not be played there. A typical stand-off
ensued as United threw themselves on the mercy of the GAA before a local
pitch in Carraroe, a local Gaeltacht village, sorted the argument.

It didn't matter much in football terms when United came back from Holland having been hammered 5-1 (mind you, Galway was level at the break)
and it seemed a pity that after the club's efforts to actually get the game staged,
which led them to a small Irish-speaking village on GAA turf, only 3,000
turned up in wet, miserable typical Irish conditions to see the Dutch club
win 3-1, though the home crowd at least saw the visitor's net bulge via Paul
Murphy's goal. The day had a lovely innocence about it. Local kids were used
as ball-boys, the Mayor of Carraroe met the teams before the game and officials from both sides enjoyed the corporate facilities – on the back of a lorry
which had been reversed in along the sideline.

> *"To be honest, I didn't really worry about where the home leg was
> being played. Nobody wants to play a second leg at home having
> lost the first game 5-1 but we gave it our best. A couple of scouts had
> seen me play in those games and it resulted in a move to Dutch club
> HFC Haarlem for me weeks later. I remember one game against
> Ajax out there when my manager told me to forget about scoring
> goals up front – my job was to come back and mark Frank Rijkaard
> instead!" –* **Paul Magee**

The rest of the decade held mid-table mediocrity and it was left to former
Bohemians and Dundalk midfielder Joey Malone to be responsible for the
next great chapter in the Tribesmen's history. This was achieved by defeating
Cobh Ramblers, Shelbourne, Limerick and St. James Gate on the way to the
1991 FAI Cup final. Standing in their way on May 12 – Shamrock Rovers.

For 85 minutes the game stayed deadlocked until possibly the finest moment in the club's history. Tommy Keane swung in a corner from the left-hand
side which a former Corrib Shamrocks man called Johnny Glynn got on the

end of to put the Tribesmen ahead with just five minutes remaining. The moment is the stuff of legend.

> *"I don't think many people gave us a chance as it was against Shamrock Rovers but we had a good side and people like Joey Malone and John Cleary who had won the cup before so their knowledge and experience helped. Of the goal I remember Tommy Keane's great cross but I actually scored with my right although I'm left footed. People still say to me these days, 'I'll always remember that header you scored in the final' – until I remind them I put it in with my foot!"* – **Johnny Glynn**

After a further few minutes, in which the ground was littered with about four stone worth of Galwegian fingernails, the full-time whistle finally blew and the Blue Riband of Irish football was travelling back across the road to Eyre Square and a place in the Terryland Park trophy cabinet.

The Galway faithful celebrate at the final whistle of the 1991 FAI Cup final
(photo credit: Paul O'Brien)

130

"I missed out on the final through injury. Obviously it was terrible not to be playing but in honesty I was more delighted for Joe Hanley, our Chairman at the time. He'd put his heart and soul into the club and this was a just reward." – **Eamon Deacy**

Once again the passports were out as United competed on the continent. The first qualifying round draw of the 1991/92 Cup Winners Cup pitted United against Danish club Odense. The Scandinavians had just won their nation's cup on a penalty shoot out and had Allan Nielsen (later of Spurs) and Lars Elstrup, a member of Denmark's Euro '92 winning side, in their ranks. The tie caught the local public imagination and 6,000 turned up to roar United on, but Odense won the first tie 3-0, and added four to that tally two weeks later at home.

Joey Malone resigned that summer, got re-instated straight away, then left again, and results took a turn for the worst. Tom Lally stepped in again as caretaker before Tony Mannion took the job on a full-time basis, but he couldn't save Galway from relegation despite having two home fixtures in the last two games against Derry City and Dundalk. Even one win would have been enough to keep them up, but in the end it meant the end of 15 years' unbroken service in the Premier Division.

Johnny Glynn scored the winning goal in the '91 FAI Cup final (photo credit: Paul O'Brien)

The club quickly regrouped (they were still lucky enough to have Gerry Mullan, a 300 plus appearance man and local legend) and returned to top flight football as First Division champions after just one season. It may have been at a lower level in a competition many seem to forget about, but Galway United did a double that season as a 3-0 win over Home Farm gave the Tribesmen the 1992/93 First Division League of Ireland Shield as well with basically an all local side.

On returning to the Premier Division, Mannion's squad surprised quite a few, finishing third in a season where they had to temporarily play at Crowley Park, the home of local rugby club Galwegians. There were also bright beaming lights into the Galway night air on October 22, 1994 when over 7,000 people turned up to see the first match under floodlights at a newly revamped

Terryland Park against Cork City. Everybody went home happy with a 2-1 win (well, bar the Cork supporters who had a long journey back home.)

However two seasons later the Maroon Army was travelling to St. Francis, Cobh Ramblers and Longford as the club recorded their worst points tally ever of 21 in the Premier Division to fall back out the trap door in 1996 under Denis Clarke. Again, United picked themselves up, won the First Division Shield and in the process shocked everyone by becoming the first club outside the Premier Division to win the League Cup.

Galway take on Cork City at a renovated Terryland Park in October 1994
(photo credit: Connaught Tribune)

The strange thing about 1996/97 was that a second success in the League Cup couldn't have been foreseen if United's patchy league form was anything to go by. Winning just four of their opening dozen games, along with losing their opening group fixture in the League Cup to Athlone, there was more chance of Rod Stewart appearing at Terryland and buying a round of drinks than Galway United having a successful season.

However a home win against collegiate side UCG and a battling 2-1 victory at Limerick, both in the League Cup, saw Clarke's men put some form together. That spilled over into the First Division Shield which was running at the same time (Galway eventually beat Limerick 2-0 in the final) and by the time December came around, the Tribesmen had dealt with Derry City and Athlone Town to reach the final of the 1996/97 League Cup.

The two-legged final saw Cork City come to Terryland Park a week before Christmas where goals from Donan Killeen, Mark Herrick and John "Jumbo" Brennan put United in the driving seat with a 3-1 scoreline. Despite a lot of pressure in the return leg, the Tribesmen had 11 heroes on the pitch and Fergal Coleman's goal at Turner's Cross that day made sure of the League Cup for the second time in the club's history.

There was yet another year slogging it out in the lower division before Don O'Riordan came along to take the Tribesmen by the scruff of the neck and drag them out of the First Division, courtesy of a 1998/99 runners-up spot to Drogheda – a mere six goals separated champions from bridesmaids.

The new millennium started with Galway in the Premier Division and dicing with death more times than is healthy. A ninth place finish in 2000 courtesy of an injury time Billy Clery goal condemned Waterford United to the relegation play-off, whilst a year later one win from their last eight games was just enough to finish above the relegation zone. Riordan left soon after and there was no Houdini act in 2002 as a poor season with just five wins from 33 games saw United relegated. By this stage Tony Mannion was back for his third stint in charge and immediately led Galway into a First Division play-off final the next season against Drogheda United. But despite Tony Folan and Barry Moran completing a 2-0 first leg win at Terryland Park, the lads agonisingly lost the second leg 3-0 after extra-time against Drogheda and failed to go up.

Again they regrouped and tried climbing the First Division mountain once more. Alan Murphy hit 21 goals in 2003, yet United still finished a distant seventh in the First Division, whilst 26 goals between Barry Moran and Damien Dupuy still wasn't enough to get Galway anywhere near the play-offs a year later in 2004.

Whichever way you look at the FAI's restructuring of the league in 2007, when clubs had to apply for a Premier or First Division licence, it certainly caused controversy. Galway United finished third in 2006 but gained a Premier Division licence ahead of Dundalk (who had finished second) due to the infrastructure and facilities at Terryland Park. The same season a new 1,500 seat stand was opened at Terryland which increased the seating capacity to almost 3,000. By this stage Nick Lesson, possibly the most surprising signing in Galway United history, was the club's CEO.

Stephen Lally had made way for Tony Cousins in the hot seat and the former Liverpool reserve guided the Tribesmen to a safe mid-table Premier position, before leaving in 2008. Derek Glynn chipped in with ten goals that year, the last United player to hit double figures in the Premier League (as of May 2011).

The following season went to the wire as a side now managed by Jeff Kenna needed a last day victory away to a relegated UCD to stay up. Over 700 Galway fans made it out of the City of the Tribes to the UCD Bowl and were rewarded when John Fitzgerald's goal kept United up and sent Finn Harps down.

The joys of being a manager! Sean Connor, current boss at Terryland
(photo credit: Andy McDonnell)

Kenna stepped down in January 2009, leaving Ian Foster to keep the club in the Premier Division. In 2010 under Foster the club entered their first relegation play-off of the decade. A highly entertaining game against second bottom Bray Wanderers at Terryland Park saw two sending-offs, a ton of goalmouth incidents and a star turn by Irish under-21 Seamus Conneely, as the Tribesmen kept their Premier Division status courtesy of a twelfth minute Karl Sheppard goal.

Sean Connor then took over and after the turmoil of February 2011, the five days of potential A Championship football, the last minute reprieve and the departure of Nick Lesson, the club started 2011 now under the control of GUST – a supporters' trust which has been working round the clock to make sure the Tribesmen have a football side for the foreseeable future.

Ground Info

Terryland Park is situated on Dyke Road just a couple of minutes from the City Centre. The ground is a huge improvement on the early years of the club's involvement in the league with the main 1,500 seated Corribside stand built in 2007 dominating the Waterworks Stand opposite, but both still seat almost 3,000 combined. For those who like a bit of thrill-seeking try sitting in front the club-house end which is as close to the action as you can get though a wayward striker might add a bit of hardship to your evening. Parking isn't a problem as there is room for 200 cars inside the ground.

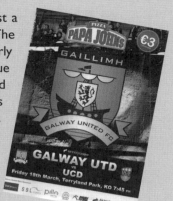

Record Attendance

7,260 v Cork City (October 22, 1994)

Cost

Adults: €12.00
Students/OAPs: €10.00
Secondary School Students: €5.00
Children: U-12 free with adult
Family Ticket: €20.00

Programme

I do love my stats, so thankfully the good quality home programme delivered a few whilst I was waiting for kick off. Refreshingly, a few articles weren't afraid to speak their mind on the perceived lack of support for the current club's situation. Galway United is now run by a Trust and has done well to bring in average crowds of 1,000-1,500, but interestingly, the "Maroon View" section pointed out it was only 1% of the population in Galway and made an impassioned plea for people to come out to support the team.

Rivals

Though fellow Galwegians Mervue United and Salthill Devon are within a five mile radius of Terryland Park, most fans opted for Shamrock Rovers as the more likely villains to fit the bill.

Mascot

Terry the Tiger.

Food and Drink

Hot food is available from a chipper with a wide selection (goujons anyone?) but what made the half-time nosh more delightful was a chat with former Galway United commercial manager/cum poet Sean Maguire. Not only did he fill out my fan's survey and give me some club information, but he regaled me with three poems from what I'm convinced is a vast repertoire.

If you're looking for a friendly pub with a great atmosphere then the Goalpost Bar in Woodquay is a firm favourite of Galway United supporters and is worth a visit before or after a game.

Club Shop

Located on the Waterworks Stand side on entry to the ground, and like most clubs Galway also has an online facility to cater for your needs.

Websites

www.galwayunitedfc.ie – official site
www.galwayunitedfc.net – fans' forum

Local Radio

Galway Bay FM 95.8

The Match – Galway United v UCD (Premier Division, March 18, 2011)

Two young sides served up ninety minutes of solid entertainment. Having visited UCD a week earlier and witnessed a tame display against Derry, I wasn't expecting anything other than a home banker, but the Students could easily have stolen the game at the death. The crowd of around 1,100 kept their vocal support going throughout the game, and the club will need them (as well as a few more through the turnstiles) to help with their current financial problems.

Limerick FC

Formed: 1937
Ground: Jackman Park
Capacity: 2,450
Nickname: The Super Blues

"Alec Ludzic said after the game, 'I don't know how you scored four goals, you only touched the ball four times!' To which I replied, 'It's lucky for you I didn't have a dozen touches then!'" – Eoin Hand

In whatever form they've taken over the years, Limerick is synonymous in League of Ireland circles as a proud club with a rich history in domestic football. They've seen hard times, years in the wilderness and it's been a while since they've knocked on the door of the Premier Division, but the fact that the club is still alive, kicking and functioning on a week-to-week basis is testament to groups of dedicated people throughout the years that have kept the provincial city playing at this level. Indeed, outside Dublin only Dundalk has had a longer unbroken run in senior football in Ireland. Even the likes of Cork, Waterford and Sligo have come and gone in one shape or another since the first league championship back in 1921.

137

Limerick was elected to the League of Ireland in 1937 as a direct replacement for Dublin club Dolphin (who ironically had just finished runners-up in the league), and played their first game in the highly popular Dublin City Cup against eventual league champions Shamrock Rovers on August 22, 1937. Johnny Curran entered Limerick football folklore by scoring the only goal of the game and gave the Shannonsiders a 1-0 win over the Hoops.

In that first season Limerick finished tenth from 12 teams with six wins and 17 points to their name, though they did win the Munster Cup and defeated Bohemians in their first Free-State Cup match as a league club 2-1 in Dalymount that year. They improved to fifth the next season, but then recorded their worst top flight season to date with just one win from 22 games in 1939/40.

Interestingly, a year later when Waterford resigned from the league, Limerick bought their blue shirts and changed from their club colours of Red and White stripes, hence the nickname of the club, "the Blues" (just when the "Super Blues" came in I really don't know!)

Limerick has been blessed with some great local talent throughout their history, and those early days were no exception – players like Tom "Bud" Ahearne, an Irish international who went on to play over 260 times for Luton Town, and winger Johnny Gavin who signed with Norwich and Spurs. Goalkeeper Willie Hayes was capped for his country whilst defender Rory Keane was a dual internationalist who went on to play for Swansea.

The '40s saw Limerick start challenging for honours and the Shannonsiders, who were now playing their football on the hallowed turf of Market's Field, finished runners-up in the league two years in a row. In 1943/44 Shelbourne pipped Limerick to the title by a single point, whilst Cork United, undoubtedly the best side of the decade, pushed the Blues into second place in 1944/45. In the cup the club could only point to a 1943 semi-final defeat to Drumcondra after a second replay and another last four appearance in '47 against Cork United as a frustrating decade came to an end.

The fifties started much the same. An awful beginning to the decade saw Limerick finish bottom of the pile in both 1950/51 and 1951/52. Despite their poor league position, crowds at Market's Field were healthy. Where Rovers had Glenmalure and Bohemians Dalymount, Limerick fans worshipped at the altar that was Market's Field. The spiritual home of Limerick football has just as iconic stature as any ground in the country with an atmosphere to match.

The club reached another cup semi-final in March of 1953, losing to Cork Athletic, but the Market's Field faithful finally rejoiced that November when Limerick Football Club won their first piece of national silverware in the shape of the League of Ireland Shield. A forerunner to the league championship, the

Shield was always fiercely competitive and laid down a marker for the upcoming title race, and indeed at one point carried a European spot. Needing to beat Dundalk in Oriel Park in the final game, and watched by probably the biggest sporting exodus ever to leave the city, Limerick quickly found themselves 2-0 down. However in a pulsating game they drew level with goals from George Lynam and Sean Cusack, before Paddy "Beaver" Cronin nicked a later winner to spark wild celebrations and a drink or two on the way back Shannonside.

Despite another see-saw existence in league terms, the Dublin City Cup was captured in 1958, defeating Drumcondra 4-3, with Gerry McCarthy hugely instrumental during that cup campaign. Poor Drumcondra. They created an unwanted record in the competition – losing eight finals in ten years between 1955-65.

The year 1960 started with JFK running for President, Elvis returning home from army duty in Germany (then make about 57 awful movies), and a four piece combo from Liverpool playing some low key gigs in Hamburg. John, Paul, George and Ringo managed to play a few bigger places in the following years. It was also the year Limerick Football Club finally won their first League of Ireland title after 23 years of trying. In truth, they didn't do things the easy way!

Astonishingly, Sonny Price's team lost seven of their 22 games, but still ended up winning the league, a feat never achieved before or since with that many defeats in so few games. A side with players like Joe Casey, Gerry McCarthy, Pat Skelly and Dessie McNamara, to name but a few, had battled it

Limerick's Fergus Crawford challenging Shay Gibbons (Longford) at a packed Market's Field in 1960 (photo credit: Brian O'Brien)

out with no less than five other teams for the title. Going into the penultimate game there were only two points separating Limerick from sixth place Cork Hibernians, with Cork Celtic, Shelbourne, Shamrock Rovers and Dundalk all waiting for the Shanonsiders to slip up. A final home win over Dundalk and results elsewhere left Limerick needing just a point required to lift the title as they travelled to St. Patrick's Athletic on the last day. An end-to-end five goal thriller saw Limerick score through Donie Wallace and Gerry O'Brien, however the Dubliners won the game 3-2.

I don't know if victory is sweeter when you've made a mess of things, only to find out you've been saved elsewhere, but the travelling Limerick support couldn't have given a hoot when the result came through that nearest challengers Shelbourne had lost to Cork Celtic, thus handing Limerick their first League of Ireland title.

> *"Coming off the field after losing felt horrible. We all thought we'd thrown it away. It wasn't until much later that we got the result from Cork. This was an age before the technology of today so you had no way of knowing seconds after the final whistle. I loved my time at Limerick. Harry McCue and Fergus Crawford were fantastic though I think Gerry McCarthy was the biggest influence in my time there. There used to be a bit of banter from fans as we only had a couple of local lads playing, most were from Dublin. When we played in the capital they used to say, 'Limerick will be travelling on a motorbike to today's game!'"* – **Donie Wallace**

Apart from winning the title, the result had huge significance as it put Limerick into European competition for the first time in their history. Drawing Swiss champions Young Boys of Berne in the preliminary round was always going to be an uphill task. Young Boys had just won four domestic league titles in a row, were managed by a former German international (Albert Sing) and just two years earlier had reached the semi-finals of the European Cup, missing out on tackling Real Madrid by losing over two legs to French side Stade Reims. Despite going down 5-0 in a match played in Thomond Park, Limerick put up a feisty return in the unfortunately titled Wankdorf Stadium in front of almost 25,000 people. Leo O'Reilly and George Lynam wrote themselves into Limerick football folklore by scoring the first goals for the club in European competition as the second leg finished 4-2.

By this stage, Sonny Price had been replaced by a Scotsman, playing in Wales and 29 years of age! However strange it may have seen (or a tad harsh on Price), Ewan Fenton introduced a whole array of local talent to Limerick FC as they reached their first FAI Cup final in 1965. Having seen off Drogheda, St. Patrick's and Drumcondra, the Shannonsiders were feeling confident of taking the cup, had it been any other side besides Shamrock Rovers! Put simply, the FAI Cup was the property of the Glenmalure club for almost the entire decade of the swinging sixties. Be it Sean Thomas or Liam Tuohy in charge it made little difference, as between them the Hoops won seven FAI Cups in the decade. Despite this, Fenton's Blues held Liam Tuohy's Rovers to a draw in the first game but lost out 1-0 in the replay at Dalymount Park. All of Limerick's hard work was not in vain though as it meant entry into the Cup Winners Cup and a second slice of European competition.

Limerick City take on C.S.K.A. Sofia in the 1965 Cup Winners Cup
Back (L-R): *Vinny. Quinn, Al Finucane, Kevin Fitzpatrick, Ewan Fenton, Dessie McNamara, Joe Casey.* Front (L-R): *Dick O'Connor, Tommy Hamilton, Eddie Mulvey, Joe O'Brien, Pascal Curtin (photo credit: Bernard Spain)*

Having previously drawn a side that had come off the back of four league titles in a row in Young Boys, Limerick decided they wanted a bigger challenge and promptly drew CSKA Sofia – a side who'd won nine championships in a row – a record still not beaten in Bulgarian football. This time however the Munster men had no intention of being roasted. The tie was switched to Dalymount Park and 13,000 showed up to see Dick O'Connor score in a 2-1 defeat to the Bulgarians, who finished off the tie 2-0 in Sofia.

"The away leg was amazing. CSKA were an army club yet there was about 60,000 at the game. It was an exciting time for me. I'd made my debut as a young boy in a friendly against Glasgow Celtic whilst sitting my leaving cert, and now here I was playing for Limerick in Europe in front of a huge crowd. We acquitted ourselves well over there. I'll always remember the flight back from Budapest to Sofia. Because they were an army club the plane was a DC3. Honestly, it was like something out of World War II. Though it took off and landed. I suppose that's what counted." – **Kevin Fitzpatrick**

A year later there was a terrible sense of déjà vu as having seen off Bohemians, Dundalk and Sligo Rovers in a semi-final replay, Tuohy's Shamrock Rovers yet again beat Limerick to win the 1966 FAI Cup final 2-0, making it back-to-back defeats in the Blue Riband.

Football was booming in Ireland. Crowds were healthy and competition fierce, though back in the Market's Field trouble was brewing. Despite having three Irish internationals in Al Finucane, Kevin Fitzpatrick and Andy McEvoy, the club ran into wage trouble as several players had refused to sign contracts due to their minimum wage of £7 – half the price of a cinema ticket and a bag of popcorn these days! It initially led to a stand-off but thankfully the dispute was eventually resolved. The last thing the club needed was high profile departures during such a successful period.

The league wasn't troubled for the rest of the decade, and in 1969 Limerick and Cork Celtic played out one of the longest running semi-final sagas in FAI Cup history. Four games were needed to separate the sides (they really went in for marathon cup ties in those days) with Cork's Donal Leahy finally settling the outcome with his solitary goal in the final game. It would be a different scenario in 1970/71.

Despite being bottom of the table in November and struggling desperately, club director Lord Petersham announced there would be a significant investment in the club which eventually led to Limerick winning the Blue Riband of Irish football. A 34 year wait to get their hands on the FAI Cup finally ended in Dalymount Park on April 21, 1971 when goals from Dave Barrett and a brace from Hughie Hamilton gave Limerick their first success in the competition.

The campaign had started with a solitary Tony Meaney goal against Shelbourne that February, before a 3-1 away win against Bohemians at Dalymount Park in a replay put Fenton's team into the semi-finals. Again, Meaney proved the hero when his semi-final goal against St. Patrick's at Tolka Park put Limerick into their first final in five years.

Joe O' Mahony and Tony Meaney drive on in the wind and rain for Limerick against Drogheda United in the 1971 FA Cup final (photo credit: Aidan Corr)

The final opposition was a Drogheda side only operating in the league for less than a decade, and under Mick Meagan playing in their first domestic cup final. The sides couldn't be separated in Dalymount that afternoon so a replay was called for three days later. However this time Hamilton and Brace helped to kill off the Boynesiders as Ewan Fenton's men brought the famous old cup back to Limerick for the first time in its 48-year history.

Having previously gone down to opposition from the lesser lights of Europe, Limerick drew a fashionable glamour tie with Italian side Torino FC in the 1971/72 Cup Winners Cup. Limerick entered at the first round stage of the last 32 (these days in the Europa League you need to play about 68 games over five months just to get to that point) against a side of internationals who had just beaten AC Milan in the Coppa Italia final and were managed by Gustavo Giagnoni, whose next managerial stop was actually AC Milan.

In Thomond Park on September 15, 1971, an eighth minute goal by the flamboyantly named Rosario Rampanti settled the tie in favour of the Italians. In the return leg, Limerick did manage to keep it scoreless at half-time but four second half goals, three in the last fifteen minutes as amateur legs tired, gave Torino an aggregate 5-0 victory. It provided great memories, however thoughts of players, staff and supporters at that time will also recall a period of financial dire straits as attendances fell.

A wage cut in 1972, the departure of Fenton and the need to apply for re-election knocked morale. A defeat to non-league Transport in the 1973/74 FAI Cup cost player-manager Kevin Fitzpatrick his job. Even the one success that the club did have in this time – the 1975 League Cup – was ruined by hooliganism.

Ewan Fenton returned and guided Limerick into that Bass League Cup final where on October 16, 1975 the Shannonsiders convincingly beat Sligo Rovers in the first leg 4-0 at Market's Field. However the game unfortunately was remembered for a group of around 100 Sligo fans causing mayhem, running riot around the greyhound track. Limerick won 4-1 on aggregate.

Under Frankie Johnson the Shannonsiders made an FAI Cup final appearance in 1977. It took six games to get to that stage including a mammoth three game semi-final tussle with Drogheda, but having got there Dundalk proved too strong in the final, winning 2-0 on the day.

There was a name change in 1979 to Limerick United. Still hovering in mid-table anonymity, Eoin Hand's appointment that year might not have raised any eyebrows, but within a year the former Portsmouth and Republic of Ireland international immediately made Limerick a different proposition altogether.

> *"In fairness to the Limerick board they had pitched the job well to me and I was happy to take the position on. Along with Dave Mahedy we worked a lot on the physical fitness side of things. We knew being that extra bit fitter was crucial going into the last ten minutes of a game and would give us an edge. Did I think we'd win the league? Maybe not at first but the lads responded so well to the training, we started winning, and it was the proverbial snowball down a hill after that. But we could play football as well, we had some wonderful players at the club."* – **Eoin Hand**

Hand's first league game in charge was also a milestone for UCD as the students were playing their first League of Ireland game, however three wins in their opening three games set the tone for the rest of the campaign. Aided by players like Joe O'Mahony, Johnny Walsh, Des Kennedy, Gerry Duggan and a Kevin Fitzpatrick now in his twentieth year in club colours, Hand didn't need to buy in half a team (though Gary Hulmes and John Delamare were welcome additions) and could always rely on himself to notch a few if needed. He scored all four goals in a 4-1 defeat of Cork United in one game.

> *"I met Cork's goalkeeper Alec Ludzic after the game. He said, 'How could you score four goals, you only touched the ball four times!' I just smiled and said, 'It's a good thing for you that I didn't touch it a dozen times then'."* – **Eoin Hand**

Current league champions Dundalk were Limerick's main rivals and the two teams soon broke clear of the chasing pack. In the end it came down to Hand's men needing a point away to Athlone at St. Mel's Park to clinch the championship. It was tight, nervy and sweatier than a g-string on a half ton man with a huge crowd paying £6,000 through the turnstiles, but a Tony Meaney penalty twenty minutes from time ultimately brought the title back to Market's Field for the first time in twenty years.

"We didn't really know what to expect at the start of the season, but we knew we'd be fit! Dave Mahedy was a PE teacher and along with Eoin they had us in great shape. Winning the league was so special for me as I grew up living just 400 feet from Market's Field - I could see it every day from my house. The crowds were unbelievable that year; we regularly drew well over 5,000 at games. It was a special time to be involved with the club." – **Des Kennedy**

Tony Meaney celebrating the goal against Athlone Town that clinched the 1979/1980 League of Ireland title for Limerick United (photo credit: Aidan Corr)

It got better. The first round draw for the 1980/81 European Cup paired Eoin Hand's men with some unknown Spanish side hailing from Madrid with Real as their first title. Payday!

Much debate had been made about where the game should be staged, but in the end the obvious choice of Thomond Park was overlooked for Lansdowne Road. Although Market's Field wasn't really an option, it was still a pity as the ground evoked such strong memories for Limerick football followers. Strangely enough, the pitch itself might have given Limerick a real edge.

"Market's Field was built on a bog! And because it was our home pitch we adapted to it better than anyone. Honestly, I've seen Garryowen play matches on a Saturday in the ground and Limerick play on the same pitch a day later! The game against Madrid would have been an interesting tie!" – **Brian O'Brien (Limerick Football historian)**

The switch to Lansdowne proved disastrous. Only 5,000 showed up in Dublin, however they were treated to the unbelievable sight of a part-time League of Ireland side taking the lead via Des Kennedy's effort (which he modestly says was a scrappy goal put in by his shin). Limerick should actually have been ahead earlier when ex-Waterford striker Johnny Matthews scored only to see a flag for a borderline offside decision which ensured one of the most talked about calls in Irish European football.

> *"I have run off and done a couple of cartwheels before I even noticed the flag was up. It's a good thing the ref didn't understand my Coventry English! But it was such a disappointment for us and personally as it would have completed a nice treble of having scored against Manchester United, Celtic and Real Madrid."* – **Johnny Matthews**

Facing the prospect of death by firing squad at worst (or a public stoning at best) on their return home, Madrid scored two goals in the last 20 minutes to win 2-1, a hotly disputed penalty and a Pineta goal five minutes from time doing the damage. The bite had been taken from the cherry and Real finished off the tie at home in front of 50,000 fans in the Bernabeu 5-1. However Des Kennedy wrote his own bit of history by scoring in each leg.

> *"There was a real sense of disappointment after the game as we had contained them so well until the last twenty minutes. Their equalizer had me fuming as Pineta had made the most of it. I came to smother the ball but he was clever enough to lean his body into me and go down. It was one of the first cases I'd seen of what seems to be standard practice in football these days."* – **Kevin Fitzpatrick**

> *"If you asked me before the game I'd have told you we were on a hammering to nothing. If you asked me at half-time I'd have told you we should win it."* – **Des Kennedy**

A third placed finish returned Limerick to Europe in the autumn of 1981, though the lads didn't have far to travel. The UEFA Cup placed the Shannonsiders against Lawrie McMenemy's Southampton. The Saints, with household names like Chris Nicholl, Mick Channon, Alan Ball and of course Kevin Keegan in their squad, comfortably won 3-0 at Market's Field but pride was restored with a battling 1-1 draw in The Den with Tony Morris scoring. Tony Ward, a man more familiar with kicking conversions from the turf of Thomond Park than scoring goals in Market's Field, also featured for Limerick in that tie.

On the second day of May 1982, the FAI Cup found its way out of Dublin and down the N7 to Limerick again when Eoin Hand's side won the FAI Cup, defeating Bohemians with a Brendan Storan goal in the final. Bluebell United, Shelbourne, Aer Lingus and Athlone were put to the sword before Tony Ward's corner was driven home by centre-half Storan. Again, it was a huge achievement for Hand, who had juggled the Limerick job with managing the Republic of Ireland, only missing out on World Cup qualification on goal difference due to a heart-breaking last-minute goal by Jean Ceulemans in Belgium (God will I ever forget) and a ref who, well – we won't comment.

It also marked the end of 22 year tenure between the sticks for Kevin Fitzpatrick, the Limerick legend keeping a clean sheet and the promise of several thousand free pints on his return home in his final 90 minutes.

A turbulent 1983/84 season threatened the existence of the club as a battle for ownership of Limerick United ensued. Football in the city was suspended for eight weeks before Kentucky Fried Chicken franchise owner Pat Grace finally won a high court action. The well known local businessman then changed the club name to Limerick City, and the club colours to Yellow and Green. They won the League of Ireland Shield (which had been revived that year) but lost Market's Field.

The last game at the spiritual home of Limerick football, on April 22, 1984, was a bitter experience. They won the Shield against UCD on a penalty shoot-out, but were distraught having to vacate a ground who if its walls could speak would tell some truly wonderful stories. A bittersweet experience. Though it could have been worse – by that stage the Premier Division had become known as the Pat Grace Kentucky Fried Chicken League!

Rathbane was the next port of call for Limerick where former Northern Ireland International Billy Hamilton brought some success to the club, leading them to a third place Premier Division spot in 1988/89 before moving on. The nineties heralded another name change – this time to Limerick FC – and a 1991 League Cup final appearance, however League Cup specialists Derry City won in the final 2-0.

Soon Limerick witnessed the managerial birth of one Sam Allardyce. Although the ex-Bolton, Newcastle and Blackburn Rovers manager (and personal friend of Arsene Wegner) has had success in the UK, and was once a candidate for the English national side's job, he arrived in Limerick untried as a manager courtesy of Father Joe Young. The priest's contribution to Limerick football will always be remembered (Allardyce talked of him fondly, even going round with him to local houses on a Friday night looking for money), and in his short spell at Limerick he led them to the 1992 First Division title by a clear five points.

Former Derry City manager Noel King soon took over the hot-seat vacated by "Big Sam" and proved an immediate success. The Dubliner brought Limerick through unscathed to the final of the 1992/93 League Cup where two goals from Howey King against St. Patrick's Athletic gave the Shannonsiders the cup for the second time in their history.

There was relegation from the Premier Division in the 1993/94 season and Finn Harps blocked them from a play-off spot in the First Division the season after, though they broke Cork City's stranglehold on the Munster Cup by beating them in the 1995 final. That demotion from the top flight was the last time a Limerick side has featured in the Premier Division to date. There was a play-off defeat to UCD in 1998, but that's as good as it's got for the folks on Shannonside.

The turn of the century however brought more pressing problems. In the 2000/01 season the club found itself in more financial trouble and without a ground at one point. Luckily for them, local club Pike Rovers became an unlikely knight in shining armour when they loaned their pitch to Limerick City.

If from playing in the Bernabeu to getting bailed out by a local junior league club seemed an unlikely story, then winning the 2002 League Cup was even more puzzling. That season the scriptwriters were working overtime as Limerick FC finished bottom of the First Division, applied for re-election yet still beat four Premier Division teams to win the League Cup!

It all started with a Derek Whyte extra-time winner against Galway United in the first round, which was followed by an eyebrow-raising victory away to Cork City. Noel O'Connor's men were on a roll (which is more than can be said for the league at that point) and progressed to the League Cup final by again shocking a Premier Division side when Brian Donnellan's late winner sent Shamrock Rovers crashing out.

Jackman Park, the club's ground at this point, hosted the first leg of the 2002 League Cup final that April, and despite the opposition coming in the shape of high-flying Derry City, the Shannonsiders came from behind to win the first leg 2-1 with goals from John Whyte and Ciaran Foley. Five days later Owen Coyle gave Derry a one goal victory to level it all up but a dramatic penalty shoot-out saw Limerick goalkeeper Jimmy Fyffe save twice to help the Munster men astonishingly win the cup 3-2 on penalties.

The club then spent a period of time in Hogan Park (reaching the First Division play-offs in 2003 but losing to Derry City) but then the failure to obtain a UEFA licence in 2006 meant a certain substance hit the fan for the club and it looked as if Limerick would sadly end their association with League of Ireland football after 69 years.

Limerick FC take on Cork City in the last league meeting between the two at Jackman Park. In 2012 the Shannonsiders return to Market's Field (photo credit: the author)

Several interested parties went after the franchise as FAI Chief Executive John Delaney had at this point dismissed Limerick FC's appeal to hold on to their league status, and on January 3, 2007, a consortium calling themselves Soccer Limerick confirmed that a new club – Limerick 37 – would compete in the League of Ireland First Division. No matter the packaging it had achieved its main goal – keeping football in Limerick City.

The club went back to Jackman Park and a 2-0 away win under manager Paul Magee saw Limerick 37 (the fourth name change in their history) start off on the right track and the much-travelled Sligo man guided them to a safe mid-table position that year before leaving in 2008.

There was a minor panic this year when licensing issues delayed their First Division licence, but Limerick kicked off the season on March 4 away to Finn Harps – as Limerick FC – and now with former Shamrock Rovers man Pat Scully in charge.

The club may just have the 75th anniversary the romantics among the Limerick faithful deserve when this year it was announced that Limerick native J.P. McManus put in a €1.5 million investment to finally bring Limerick back to their spiritual home of Market's Field. All going well, the Shannonsiders will step out for the first time in 27 years at their spiritual home in 2012. And the walls of the Market's Field will finally get to tell new stories to those old and new.

Ground Info

Snugly tucked in behind a row of houses on Carey Road in the city centre, Jackman Park has been home to the "Super Blues" of Limerick for the last four seasons now. The Main Stand on the Carey Road side houses 261 people, whilst the rest of the ground holds a standing capacity of 2,189. There is parking inside the ground for around 50 cars on the City End side, whilst away fans normally congregate on the Railway Station side. Of course, the future development of the club is all centred on their old stomping ground, and spiritual home of Limerick football, Market's Field. Ever since J.P. McManus made a generous donation to acquire the ground in March this year the club and city have been buzzing.

In June, Club Chairman Pat O'Sullivan hosted a press conference unveiling the plans, which include installing a new floodlit playing surface at Market's Field, renovating the existing stand and dressing rooms, upgrading the existing bar, opening a new club shop, offices and a club museum. Phase One of the project is expected to be finished in March 2012 with a capacity of 3,100, with the eventual aim of having an 8,100 all-seated stadium.

The deal which the Limerick Enterprise Development Partnership reached with Bord Na gGon is for a sum in excess of €1.5 million, which of course was made possible by a donation from the J.P. McManus Charitable Foundation.

Record Attendance

10,000 v Southampton (UEFA CUP, September 15, 1981, at Market's Field)

Cost

Adults: (stand) €12.00 / (ground) €10.00
Students: (stand) €10.00 / (ground) €7.00
OAPs, U-16s: (stand) €6.00 / (ground) €5.00
Under-12s: Free with adult

Programme

€3.00 – The *Super Blues Football Yearbook* is another labour of love with a nice layout and good contributors, including Gary Spain, probably Ireland's biggest memorabilia collector of everything League of Ireland, who writes a very witty column.

Rivals

Traditionally it's been Waterford through the years, though more recently teams like Shelbourne and Cobh Ramblers, when the Corkmen were in the league, took pride of place.

Mascot

Leo the Lion. Although he must have been hunting down wildebeest in the Serengeti on the night of my visit as he wasn't around. Leo can often be spotted on commercial photocalls online, and has produced some great stories from local and visiting fans over the years.

Food and Drink

There are two hot food vendors, one on the clubhouse side, the other directly opposite in the city end. It was here I found possibly the cheapest burger in Ireland. For a mere €2.50 I munched on a tasty bit of beef which went down well.

Outside the ground the Still House in Thomas Street has been a supporter of the club for a while now so local Limerick fans will often throw business their way, whilst Phil Flannerys in Denmark Street is also a haunt of many Super Blues Fans.

Club Shop

Located inside the ground next to the clubhouse. The club also has an online shop with some reasonable bargains and the fans do seem to back the club in terms of merchandise sales – on my visit the Limerick FC crest was more visible than the emblem of any English Premiership team.

Websites

www.limerickfc.ie – official site
www.limerickfcsc.com – fans' forum

Local Radio

Limerick's Live95 FM.

The Match – Limerick FC v Cork City (Airtricity First Division, May 30, 2011)

For several years Limerick hadn't bothered with the top half of the table (they've been down in the First Division since 1995), but under Pat Scully the Shannonsiders have become a genuinely tough nut to crack and were more than a match for league leaders Cork City in this scoreless draw. These are exciting times for the club off the field, whilst on it Scully has a team that can match anybody in the division as they challenge for promotion.

Longford Town

Formed: **1924**

Ground: **Flancare Park**

Capacity: **4,500**

Nickname: **"De Town"**

"Are you sure it's not Gary Gillespie?" – Longford supporter on hearing that the club had aquired the services of one Keith Gillespie

It's not often I'm speechless (ask my wife), but when former Newcastle, Blackburn and Northern Ireland international Keith Gillespie announced he was signing for League of Ireland First Division Longford Town in March 2011 you could have battered me with a baseball bat for a solid three days and it still wouldn't have registered with me. The 35-year-old's signature became headline news this spring and was seen as a major coup for the club from Flancare Park who've been kicking a ball about on these shores for a long time now.

Although founded in 1924, it was a full 60 years before the town built on the banks of the River Camlin finally took its place in our domestic football league. Since then they've managed to avoid some of the financial downfalls of many a league club and added a few honours along the way.

You have to hark back 87 years to 1924 and a Free State league that was still in its infancy for the formation of Longford Town Football Club. Whilst teams from yesteryear like Jacobs, Midland Athletic, Pioneers and Brooklyn

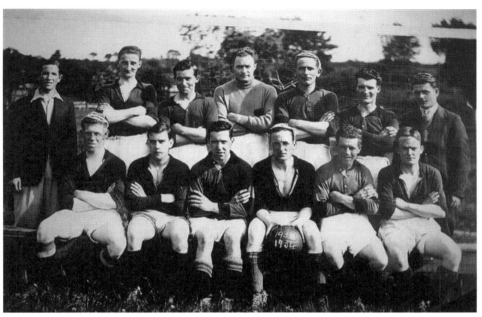

Winners of Athletic Union League Subsidiary Cup 1933–34. Back Row (L-R): *J. O'Reilly, P. Shine, Mel Gilleran, T. Beirne, M. Deane, Dennigan, C. Fallon* Front Row (L-R): *J. Malynn, P. Clarke, P. Barlow, J. Clarke, J. Breslin, W. Clarke (photo credit: Longford Town Supporters Club)*

contested the championship that season, Longford Town was plodding along at local junior league level.

The club achieved provincial success in the 1931 Lenister Junior Cup but more significantly captured the 1937 Intermediate Cup and progressed to the first round of the Free State Cup for the first time in their short history. There Longford faced similar non-league opposition in the shape of Evergreen United of Cork. On January 9, 1937, a 2-1 win over the Leesiders put the Leinster club into a quarter-final match against Drumcondra. The Drums had finished mid-table in the Free State League that year but had already won the FAI Cup in 1927 and contested the final again in 1928.

Overwhelming favourites on the day, the Dubliners were shocked by Longford with Peter Clarke scoring the winner in a 2-1 away win to reach the semi-finals of the Free State Cup. In doing so they became only the second non-league club outside Dublin to reach the last four of the cup, Alton United of Belfast being the other.

On March 10, 1937, Longford lined up for the biggest game of their short history against Waterford FC, a club that had already won the League of Ireland Shield that season and were pushing for their first Free State Cup. It proved a bridge too far for the non-leaguers as Waterford ran out 4-1 winners at Dalymount, though Town did have the consolation of Peter Clarke netting against the eventual Free State Cup champions. One of Longford's players from that cup run, Steve McManus, who played that day, sadly died in a Japanese prison camp a few short years later in World War II.

Despite not being a league club, Longford continued to pop up in and out of our nation's main domestic cup, whilst building a reputation for themselves at non-league level dipping into the FAI Cup twice in the forties against Waterford and Shelbourne. However the real golden era of Longford Town at non-league level came between 1954-62 with three FAI Intermediate Cups, with a fourth success in 1969.

Many League of Ireland clubs won the Intermediate Cup through the years before reaching the top flight in Ireland. Drumcondra was the first in 1927, a year before they entered the league, with clubs like Bray Wanderers, Cobh Ramblers and Home Farm also tasting victory in the competition.

Players like Lal Donlon, who went on to sign for Arsenal, the brilliantly named Mel "Garrincha" Mulligan, John "Hooky" O'Connor, Jimmy Clarke – a legend in the area – and Willie Browne, who went on to be capped three times for Ireland, starred throughout the decade for the club. With success at that level it was only a matter of time before they mixed it with the top flight in the FAI Cup again.

An attractive tie with Bohemians at Dalymount Park was the reward in the 1951 FAI Cup – going down to the Dubliners 3-1 – whilst the club put up a monumental battle with league side Limerick in early February '53 in a tie that took over a month and four games to separate the sides.

Longford had held Limerick at Market's Field with Donal Rochford scoring in a 1-1 draw, but failed to finish them off four days later at their home ground – the Longford Greyhound Stadium – where Paddy Gilbert scored in another 1-1 draw. The third game finished scoreless before the Shannonsiders finally saw off the challenge of the Leinster side 2-1 in the fourth game played in Dublin. Despite the defeat, Longford could take solace in the fact it was against a Limerick side that had won the League of Ireland Shield that year.

However, this was surpassed by reaching their second FAI Cup semi-final in 1955, beating Jacobs from Dublin in the first round before knocking out Transport away from home with goals from Ward and a brace from Gilbert.

On April 9, 1955, Longford lined up against Shamrock Rovers in the semi-final of the FAI Cup. It was the "Coad Colts" era at Glenmalure. Paddy

Coad's men were League of Ireland champions, had just won the Shield and were on the way to capturing this FAI Cup. It was a big ask of the non-leaguers on the day, and they accordingly went down 3-0. The decade ended with first round defeats again in the FAI Cup, to Bray Wanderers in 1956 and Drumcondra in '57.

By the start of the sixties Longford was still playing their football at the local Greyhound Stadium, but the success of the previous decade had given them a much bigger profile. On Valentine's Day 1960, Longford lined up against Limerick in the FAI Cup only to be shot down ninety minutes later and six goals worse off, whilst there was one more appearance in 1969 where after beating Sligo Rovers 2-0, "De Town" bowed out to Shelbourne in the next round by the same scoreline.

Having seen many triumphs within its cosy surroundings, the Longford Greyhound Stadium was vacated by the club in 1972 and Abbeycarton became the club's main residence for the next twenty years. The decade of free love had started with a 3-0 defeat at home to Dundalk on making the first round of the FAI Cup in 1972, and it proved to be "De Town's" last entry in any domestic cup for over a decade.

Whilst non-league clubs like Fanad United, Cobh Ramblers and Kilkenny City all gained entry to the FAI League Cup, Longford had to be content with Leinster Senior League football for the rest of the seventies. Still outside the top flight with no provincial or national title since 1969, any dreams harboured about one day finally playing League of Ireland football looked about as likely as Tottenham Hotspur ever winning the Premiership.

It looked even less likely at the start of the eighties. By 1983 the League of Ireland membership had fallen from 16 teams to 14. Clubs found it harder each year financially to stay afloat, and teams like Thurles Town went to the wall as did a bankrupt Cork United. Then out of nowhere a decision to pump the table up with two new teams for the 1984/85 season, along with the imminent arrival of a new First Division, was Longford's saviour.

Having applied that season, Longford's application was finally successful and along with the umpteenth version of a Cork club – Cork City – Longford Town Football Club was accepted into the League of Ireland – 60 years after they first kicked a ball in anger. Under manager Charlie Walker Longford's first game in top flight football took place in the mountains of Donegal. Ballybofey, home of Finn Harps, was the setting for the first game in Group 1 of the 1984/85 League Cup. Jim Mahon got the honour of scoring Town's first goal in top flight football. Unfortunately, Jim Finnerty also got the honour of picking the ball out of the net one more time than the Harps' goalkeeper, as Longford went down 2-1 on the day. The following week saw a 3-2 win against Sligo Rovers, but a defeat to Galway United in the last game killed off any chance of qualifying for the semi-finals.

> *"Longford was a great club to be part of at the time. I remember we gave Shamrock Rovers one hell of a game in one league game. We had to switch it to the local rugby ground as Abbeycarton was so small. They done us with a last minute goal but it was a fantastic game to be involved in. I knew I had to bring in a few players as the club was now playing League of Ireland football, and we done alright. The travelling from Dublin however took a toll on me in the end as I'd leave work at 5.00 and travel to Longford several times a week. That was the only downside in a time I really enjoyed managing the club."*
> – **Charlie Walker**

Longford Town 1990/91. Back row (L-R): *Heysham El Khersi, Zac Hackett, Alan Weldrick, Stephen Kelly, Jel Martin, Derek Chubb, Anthony Keenan, Gary McCormack, Donal Sweeney, Martin McCabe, Daniel Sweeney (young boy).*
Front row (L-R): *Mick Savage, Davy Flaherty, Leo Devlin, Peter Fagan, John Skeffington (photo credit: Longford Town Supporters Club)*

That first season was always going to be a steep learning curve. Thirty long hard games ensued with Town picking up just three wins and ten points. It meant a bottom placed finish but at least no re-election worries as Longford just dropped down to a newly created League of Ireland First Division, and they dragged Finn Harps, Drogheda United and Sligo Rovers down with them! Despite the 23 defeats that season, players like Zac Hackett, Liam Madden and Jim Mahon made their mark throughout the club's historic first year in the top flight and beyond.

Relegation to the new First Division wasn't be a bad thing at first. Despite falling into the league in its inaugural year, Longford had at least one year's league experience behind them and it was used to good effect against clubs like Cobh Ramblers, Monaghan United and Derry City as Longford, now managed by Billy Bagster, finished third, just missing out on promotion by two points. Longford also contested their first silverware at top flight level when they squared up to Derry City in the inaugural First Division Shield final. Played over two legs, the Candystripes got the better of Bagster's men, beating them 6-1 on aggregate, but it was still a highly promising start to their first year at this level. And that was about as good as it got!

"We were actually quite confident going into the Shield final as we'd beaten Derry twice in the league. The 2-1 win in the Brandywell would have been one of my highlights with the club. We switched the first leg to the Showgrounds in Sligo as Abbeycarton was too small and took something like a £14,000 gate – that was huge at the time. But I felt it wasn't invested back into the team, and subsequently we really struggled badly the next season." – **Billy Bagster**

In their second year at this level, Longford produced the worst season in their League of Ireland history, collecting just seven points from 18 games to finish rock bottom of the First Division. Things slightly improved in the next three seasons, and there was an FAI Cup semi-final defeat to Derry City in 1988, but by the start of the nineties, Abbeycarton was an all too familiar stopping point for League of Ireland First Division clubs. Managers came and went after Bagster (Ron Langford, Pat Hackett, Con Flanagan), even an experienced Dermot Keely tried his hand, but the club still remained entrenched in First Division anonymity.

"I really loved my time at Longford. When I arrived the club had about a -20 goal difference and getting pasted each week but we soon turned that around. The real problem I had at that point was the move to the new ground at Flancare Park. At Abbeycarton we had a tiny ground where we could push up on people and get in their faces. We'd become hard to beat there so when the proposed moved to Flancare came about I was pretty vocal. 'Fuck that, we're not going there', or words of that effect." – **Dermot Keely**

The move of course came about, and the lovingly titled "Flan-siro" on the Strokestown Road is now Longford Town's home ground.

Finally, in the 1999/2000 season after 14 years of depressing familiarity, Longford made their first serious attempt at getting out of the division. That

Abbeycarton – cosy little home ground for almost 30 years (photo credit: the author)

came under Stephen Kenny's watch. Despite being beaten in their opening game Longford convincingly won six of their next eight games to put themselves in the running. There they stayed on the coat-tails of Bray Wanderers all season, finally clinching promotion the last game of the season away to Cobh Ramblers with an own goal and a strike from Keith O'Connor. O'Connor's goals were vital to Longford that season – his 17 strikes along with another 13 from Richie Parsons accounted for almost half the goals Town scored that year. But the team had heroes all over the park. People like goalkeeper Stephen "Digger" O'Brien and the long serving Vinny Perth were as equally important to the side.

> *"When I came to Longford the club were struggling badly, expectations were low and there seemed to be empathy towards the club locally. I think we had a weekly budget of something like £1,000 for myself, the staff and the entire squad. Almost everyone was out of contract so I basically had a blank canvas to work with. Taking the club back into Premier football felt great so it was a wrench for me leaving the club three years later as I'd formed some good relationships."* – **Stephen Kenny**

Despite the pressure to completely overhaul the team, though players like Sean Prunty, Alan Kirby and Eric Lavine did come in, the men from Flancare Park defied the doom merchants to not only stay up in their first season back in the big time but to gradually build on it. A first FAI Cup final appeared that same 2001 season. Victories over Cork City, St. Patrick's Athletic, Portmarnock and a Stephen Kelly penalty in a replay against Waterford United sent them into their first FAI Cup final. Be it nerves, stage fright or the fact Bohemians were just better, a Tony O'Connor strike just after the hour was enough to give the Dubliners the Cup at Tolka Park for the sixth time in their history on May 13, 2001 and leave Longford still looking for their first.

However, because Bohemians had won the double it meant for the first time Longford Town would play on the continent. For a town of just over 10,000, with little top flight experience and still a novice in League of Ireland terms, it was a significant achievement. European football had come to Flancare Park.

The UEFA Cup first qualifying round draw had some notable names – Austria Vienna, Standard Liege, Dynamo Bucharest to name a few – but the likelihood of Longford drawing a team in the middle of nowhere was as predictable as the three months of rain we call summer. Sure enough, up popped Bulgarian top flight side Litex Lovech and on August 17, 2001, Longford hosted a European team in serious competition for the first time in their history.

Keith O'Connor had the privilege of scoring Town's first competitive European goal as the Leinster men acquitted themselves well, holding the Bulgarians 1-1. Two weeks later at Lovech Stadium in the small north-central town of Lovech, the hosts ended Longford's European odyssey, winning 2-0, but nevertheless it still marked a significant chapter in the club's career.

Stephen Kenny left that December, replaced by Derek O'Neill as a caretaker and then Martin Lawlor as manager (helping them just about survive a penalty shoot-out against Finn Harps in the promotion/relegation play-off of 2001/02), but it was Alan Matthews who presided over the most successful tenure in the club's history to date when he walked into the job in July 2002. The wait for silverware would be a short one.

The interim season of 2003 saw Longford come out all guns blazing in both League and FAI Cups. The Black and Red stripes started the FAI Cup campaign with a 4-1 win away to non-league Tolka Rovers, and quickly followed it up with a defeat of Limerick at Flancare Park. A 3-1 victory over Waterford (which put me in such a bad mood I produced a cataclysmic driving test that should have seen me banned from ever getting behind a wheel again) put Longford into the last four where a solitary Sean Francis goal was enough to see off Galway United and clinch another FAI Cup final spot.

By that stage Longford had also worked their way into the League Cup final as well, where they met St. Patrick's Athletic, but Eamonn Collins' Saints proved too strong in the final, though only by the smallest of margins, 1-0.

Attention had now turned to the big one. Again standing in their way – St. Patrick's Athletic.

What would normally have been a fresh spring afternoon in April became a cold, damp, Sunday in October because of the interim season dictating an end to proceedings in winter. It didn't bother Longford though. Alan Matthews' men were not to be denied and on October 26, 2003 goals from Sean Francis and Shane Barrett meant the 2003 FAI Cup would reside on the banks of the river Camlin for the first time in its history. Again, it meant a European date.

This time Matthews' men got what seemed a more favourable draw, at least on paper. The pretty alpine country of Liechtenstein and its national cup champions FC Vaduz were a handy stepping stone to bigger conquests . . . surely?

Despite losing the first leg 1-0 in the picturesque Rhienpark Stadium in late July, the Irishmen were still hot favourites back at Flancare, but it turned out to be a horrendous night as Longford humiliatingly found themselves 3-0 down after an hour to a team who annually adopted the word "minnows" on their travels in Europe. A late rally with two goals from Dean Fitzgerald and Barry Ferguson made the score more respectable, but a 4-2 aggregate defeat to the Liechtenstein outfit ranked as a very poor result.

The 2004 season saw the most productive year in the club's short League of Ireland history with a unique double and a growing reputation as cup specialists when both the FAI and League Cup were captured. Getting out of a group with Kildare County and Athlone Town, and then beating Dublin City in the quarter-finals, enabled Longford to reach the last four of the League Cup. A tough semi-final awaited them in Ballybofey against Finn Harps, but Sean Francis came up with a second half winner to see Matthews' men into the final. The "Flan-siro" faithful were being spoiled by this point.

Four full seasons of Premier Division football, cup finals on the horizon and the development of Flancare Park – even the notoriously football-outside-the-capital shy RTÉ began featuring the odd game involving the Red and Black stripes of Longford (mind you, I'm sure people tuned in and said, "Bohemians are playing well tonight, aren't they love?").

In fact, the 2004 League Cup final saw Longford face off against Bohemians. Despite the ground and obvious favourites' tag the Gypsies carried into the game, it was also a chance for their new manager, ex-Everton player Gareth Farrelly, to claim some early silverware. It was a challenge Matthews and his men relished. In the face of adversity an early strike from Sean Dillon combined with Sean Prunty's 81st minute goal won Longford the 2004 League Cup despite a late Bohemians penalty blotting their copybook. It was rather apt the local-born Prunty struck the winner. As one of the longest serving players in the club's history, he was also the only Longford player to play in all six of the club's senior cup finals.

The road to retaining the FAI Cup started in late July 2004 against non-league Leeds, and progressed with wins over Shamrock Rovers, Athlone Town and a semi-final replay strike from Sean Dillon away to Drogheda United which sent Matthews' men into their second consecutive final.

Back-to-back wins in the FAI Cup hadn't been achieved since Shelbourne, and for 86 minutes of the 2004 final on October 24 in Lansdowne Road Waterford United stood defiantly in the way of that achievement. Just as it looked as though Willie Bruton's goal for United was enough for the cup to head back over the River Suir for the first time in 24 years, a Waterfordian in Longford's ranks made sure that wouldn't be the case to start one of the most dramatic fightbacks in FAI Cup history.

Seizing on some hesitant United defending, Waterford-born Alan Kirby cut in from the left and drove home past United goalkeeper Dan Connor. Astonishingly, within two minutes the game was won. With Waterford visibly stunned, Eric Lavine set up Paul Keegan to slot home the winner, send the Town fans into rapture (and me contemplating suicide) for the first successful defence of an FAI Cup from a club outside the capital since Cork Hibernians in 1973.

> *"I hadn't planned on not celebrating as the truth was I hadn't planned on scoring but of course your natural reaction is to run and celebrate. Had circumstances being different I would have, I mean it's not every day you score in a cup final. However I had far too much respect for the Waterford manager, their players and supporters, and besides it was only the equalising goal, there was more drama to come! I remember our manager Alan Matthews giving me a hard time a few weeks after when he saw the team pictures of us celebrating on the pitch afterwards and me with a puss on me! I wouldn't change the goal or result – but I wish I could change the pictures."* – **Alan Kirby**

A third European road trip was then planned. No 27 hour bus trip or plane journey to the middle of nowhere, but instead Longford travelled to their Celtic neighbours Wales and a match against Carmarthen Town in the UEFA Cup. Like the Vaduz game, again the Irishmen had been favourites. It may have sat uneasy on Longford's shoulders after their previous European encounter but it certainly didn't show in the first leg with a well earned 2-0 home win with goals from Paisley and Ferguson.

However, the second leg.... If the second leg could be marked on a disaster scale of 1 to 10 – it would be 387. A blow up on par with the Hindenburg.

Put bluntly, Longford were torn apart in Wales. Beaten 5-1 on the night, 5-3 on aggregate and dumped out of the UEFA Cup.

Relegation after seven years of top flight football followed (they were deducted six points that season which would have kept them up), but Longford still managed to reach their fourth FAI Cup final in December 2007. However the fairytale ending of 2004 was this time replaced by the heartache of a single

Austin Skelly (no. 10) scores against rivals Athlone in a local derby at Flancare Park April 2011 (photo credit: Gary McGivney)

Denis Behan goal for Cork City on the hour in front of 10,000 on a rainy windswept (in other words normal) Irish day at the RDS as the Munster men clinched the 2007 FAI Cup.

And it's been the First Division ever since for "De Town". Now under the management of Tony Cousins, Longford kicked off the 2011 season rather anonymously until a certain Mr. Gillespie's arrival, press coverage and his subsequent debut in a 2-0 home win over their biggest rivals down the road – Athlone Town. From players in POW camps to former Premier League icons, we wait with bated breath to see what Longford gives us next.

Ground Info

Located about a mile outside of the main city centre on the Strokestown Road, Longford's Flancare Park is easy to find with parking space directly outside the ground.

Having undergone redevelopment in 2000 it's now a 4,500 all-seater stadium, though the capacity once stood at over 6,000. The impressive main stand dominates the skyline holding 1,500 and the further three enclosed seated sides give the ground a real football stadium look to it, although it's uncovered which leaves it open to the elements. Rain is a regular visitor up here and snow pops in on the odd occasion as well.

Filling those seats can be hard. When Longford reached the 2004 FAI Cup final the game was switched off in one local pub in favour of an Arsenal and Manchester United match, which summed up a certain attitude, although Keith Gillespie's signing brought renewed interest and a healthy crowd for his first game against local rivals Athlone Town.

Record Attendance

4,000 v Bohemians (League Cup final, August 30, 2004)

Cost

Adults: €10.00
OAPs/Students: €8.00
Children: €5.00

Programme

€3.00 – Under the late Noel "Butch" Treacy, Longford had produced a programme of great topical issues and statistical information over the years which suffered slightly after his passing, however with contributors like Marty Stapleton and Seamus Leavey still penning articles the programme is still worth a flick through, and you know they love the club in the way they write.

Rivals

Just as Barcelona have Real Madrid, Longford have Athlone Town. This "El Classico" might be on a different scale to their Spanish counterparts, but that doesn't mean Longford's rivalry with their neighbours down the road is any less passionate. You get space and time on the ball at the Nou Camp – that goes out the window at Flancare when Athlone comes to town!

Mascot

Leo the Lion lovingly sports the costume and loves his job, even though he got beaten up by a bunch of excitable kids at a Longford Town friendly against Liverpool in Flancare Park not too long ago! "Nobody came to help me – not one person!"

Food and Drink

There is a supporter's bar under the main stand that is free, friendly and open to home and away fans. A nice cup of tea is €1.00, though if there was a bar licence I have a feeling takings would be considerably higher. That said, it was all hands to the deck on my visit, which was a freezing Monday night in a League Cup game. In town the Markets Bar on Ballymahon Street or John Browns Pub are both favourites of home supporters.

Club Shop

Located just inside the ground and open on match days only.

Website

www.ltfc.ie

Local Radio

Shannonside FM 104.1

The Match – Longford Town v Athlone Town (EA Sports Cup, March 4, 2011)

Preliminary League Cup games never really attract huge crowds. Despite that, a decent crowd turned out but you just got the feeling the lads were so weather beaten up there that anything on the plus side of centigrade is like a balmy summer's night. Craig Walsh scored a quality free kick followed by stadium announcer Tony Gee coming over all American in his broadcast. Remember Vincent Hanley in Music Television USA on RTÉ? Well that's what he sounded like. The home side added a second on the hour before Athlone replied and with that the small contingent of Athlone fans started howling like a scene from the *Magnificent Seven* riding into town greeted by locals and warmed to the last twenty minutes shouting at Longford manager Tony Cousins every time he disputed something. It finished 2-1.

Mervue United

Formed:	1960
Ground:	Fahy's Field
Capacity:	2,500
Nickname:	The Claret & Blues

"I never have to complain about budgets at Mervue. We don't have one!"
– Johnny Glynn

There was a time not so long ago when no team from Galway had kicked a ball in anger at League of Ireland level. The country was in recession, unemployment was rife and we paid most our wages in taxes – so things haven't changed much. Now however there is a sibling rivalry in the province with three teams playing League of Ireland football for the first time. A ménage a trois of football teams made up of Galway United, Salthill Devon and a club from Fahy's Field who recently celebrated their fiftieth anniversary – Mervue United.

Declan McDonnell is their last original link to the past. The Galway councillor was just a 12-year-old tearaway when, along with his friend Jackie Keane, he joined a group of residents for a meeting in Hyacinth Darcy's House on McDonagh Avenue to set up a soccer club in Mervue for the youths. Their beginnings were humble. The first ground was a little patch on an area called the Redemptorist ground in the suburb of Mervue. At the time it seems two trees acted as goalposts and there were no nets!

It took divine intervention to improve things. Father Jack O'Connor managed to get the Galway Corporation to give the club a site on Monivea Road which they shared with Mervue Athletic Club. A local house garage owned by Mick Halpin doubled as the clubs' dressing rooms. The innocence of it all.

The Trojan work of people like Colie Smyth, Joe Flaherty and John Murphy helped in the early years, and the club made a breakthrough on the local scene in just their first season. In the area two clubs ruled the roost – Galway Bohemians and Galway Rovers – however Mervue sprung a surprise by getting to the local cup final, the Schweppes Cup, in 1961, although Bohemians didn't take too kindly to this and promptly hammered Mervue 7-2. Undeterred, the club continued to develop making a mark provincially at youth level by winning the 1975 Connaught Cup.

By this stage their neighbours up the road in Terryland Park were about to enter the League of Ireland. Galway Rovers had just finished playing in the 1976 League Cup and became the first club from the province to enter the league a year later. As gratifying as it was to finally have a club represent the province for the first time in top flight Irish football, it didn't mean Mervue were over the moon for their neighbours – they are rivals after all.

Brendan Concar for Mervue against UCD in the 1985 FAI Cup (photo credit: Mervue United FC)

In 1981, Mervue stepped up to the Connaught League and throughout the eighties became an established side around the province. Through fundraising and sponsorship the club developed facilities at their Fahy's Field ground, making the pitch one of the best in Connaught if not Ireland.

Their first breakthrough on a national scale threw the spotlight on United. It was one they wouldn't let the light die on for a few years. Having battled through several qualifying rounds, Mervue United, under Jimmy O'Sullivan, took on UCD on February 10, 1985 in the first round of the FAI Cup. To add even more to the occasion, UCD were the current cup holders. The game caught the imagination of the local public and a gate that produced £4,000 turned up to witness a potential David versus Goliath moment.

A field full of romantics and scriptwriters prayed for the happy ending and superlatives in the next day's sports pages, but were left heartbroken as despite Tony "Ginger" Collins scoring Mervue's first goal at this level, the Students went on to win 2-1. However, it did whet the appetite whilst temporarily stealing Galway United's limelight!

Mervue stepped back into it in January 1987, however this time the scriptwriters got it right. First Division Longford Town came visiting in the FAI Cup and a goal by Tony Collins on a bitterly cold winter's day was enough to shock the Longford team and send Mervue through to the last sixteen. Amazingly, it was another non-league club that stood between United and a place in the last eight of the FAI Cup. But of course Cork club Rockmount

The Mervue United side who defeated Longford Town in the 1987 FAI Cup
Back (L-R): *Jarlath Connolly, Eamon Ryan, Donnie Farragher, Michael Grealish, Tom Cahill, Tony Collins* Front (L-R): *Jimmy Nolan, Dermot McSweeney, Noel Gallagher, Aidan Fallon, Ollie Neary (photo credit: Mervue United FC)*

was thinking the exact same thing and both sides went for the jugular when they met. It resulted in a 2-2 draw but the game would always be remembered for two things. First, the ref allowed the game to be played in snow, and then he refused to play extra-time as expected!

"The weather was awful down in Cork, but we still played and actually went 2-0 up in the snow before being pegged back to 2-2. At the end of 90 minutes the referee suddenly decided no extra-time would be played. This of course meant the match hadn't been fully completed and the game would have to be played again down in Cork which robbed us of a home replay!" – **Declan McDonnell, Current Mervue United Chairman**

With this strange set of circumstances it obviously meant a replay where Rockmount prevailed, meaning the Galwegians missed out on a quarter-final tie at home to Dundalk. It proved a wasted opportunity, but they came back for one more stab at the FAI Cup the next season.

Managed this time by John Herrick, a win away to Letterkenny Rovers brought up Monaghan United in a last 32 meeting. With the tie at home against a struggling Monaghan side second from bottom in the First Division, a shock may have been on the cards but Mervue went down 2-1, despite Mike McDonnell's goal, meaning United missed out on a trip to Premier Division Cork City.

By the late eighties the club needed to upgrade their facilities. Although Mervue had first applied to the Galway Corporation in 1986 for planning permission to build a new clubhouse and develop two soccer pitches up to the required standard, there was some red tape until eventually on June 15, 1991 Minister Bobby Molloy turned the sod for the first phase of Mervue's new clubhouse.

Throughout the first few years of the nineties Mervue continued to perform consistently in the province (winning all four senior Connaught trophies in 1992/93) before the club got another chance to participate with the big boys. A first call up to the League of Ireland League Cup presented an eager Mervue with a chance to finally lock horns with Galway United. Before that meeting Athlone Town presented the opposition on August 15, 1997, however Mervue's big day was soured with a 3-0 defeat, and Limerick didn't make the introduction to top flight clubs any easier a week later, hammering Mervue 5-1. At least Gerry Mullan got the honour that day of scoring the club's first goal in a League of Ireland competition.

Three days later Mervue finally took on their peers in Fahys' Field in a fixture that at one stage both clubs could only have dreamt about fulfilling. Their League Cup meeting on August 27, 1997 however didn't go to plan, and Galway proved too strong over ninety minutes. Donnie Farragher scored but his goal was made irrelevant by the four that Galway notched that day.

There again was participation against League of Ireland opposition in 1998 when Mervue popped up the road to the Showgrounds to lock horns with Sligo Rovers in the FAI Cup. Despite being overwhelming underdogs, Alan Joyce put United ahead and a huge shock seemed on the cards until a late equalizer brought the game back to Terryland Park. The replay saw 3,500 supporters turn out to watch Mike Long and Eamon Ryan's men try to finish the job, but the class of their Premier Division counterparts eventually told and Sligo went on to win 2-0. It proved one of the last memories of Mike Long with the club as he sadly passed away at a young age a year later.

After the steep but essential learning curve in their previous League Cup outing, Mervue returned to the competition three years later in 2001, again in a group with Limerick FC and Galway United. Another step up in class and regrettably again the same result as both sides beat Mervue without conceding to the non-leaguers, however the CV was further enhanced when United reached the FAI Cup first round, losing to Derry City 2-0.

It proved to be a significant year as the club entered the Eircom U-21 league for the first time, making an impressive debut that saw them finish top of their section before going down to Athlone Town at the semi-final stage. This was regular football on a much higher level for United as many Premier Division clubs had teams situated in this league, indeed many who actually played for their first team every weekend.

In January 2003, Mervue United reached their first national final in the shape of the Enda McGill Eircom U-21 League Cup. It was an impressive route to the final, beating established reserve sides like Dublin City, Finn Harps, Shamrock Rovers and then Bohemians on penalties with goalkeeper Ryan Griffin the hero between the posts. However Longford Town proved a bridge too far in the final 90 minutes of that campaign, and despite goals from Jason Finn and Benny Lawless, Mervue was beaten 4-2. It could have been different had Seamie Rabbit's penalty been converted after 15 minutes, but I'm sure the man doesn't want to be reminded of it again. Even though I just have!

A year later a young kid born in Carnmore arrived to sign with the club from Cregmore FC as a 13-year-old. The precocious talent that is Greg Cunningham blossomed at Mervue, signed for Manchester City and made his Republic of Ireland debut against Algeria in 2010 on the club's fiftieth anniversary.

The Galwegians continued to improve, stepping up to the A Championship in its inaugural 2008 season. Now only one division separated them from League of Ireland football. Despite competing in an eight-team league, six of which were reserve teams of established League of Ireland clubs, Mervue wasn't fazed and went on to finish third behind Finn Harps A and eventual winners Bohemians A. This was good enough for a crack at First Division strugglers Kildare County in a promotion/relegation play-off in November 2008. The Newbridge-based club had struggled all year, with manager John Ryan ending a four-year association with the club by resigning with four games left in the season. Times had been hard for Kildare. Rooted to the bottom of the First Division and drained of confidence, your local bookie might just have favoured the 11 men from Galway. It was also the first tie of its kind, a winner-take-all match-up with the victor either gaining or retaining First Division status.

The first match took place in Fahy's Field on November 18, 2008. It certainly had drama. A two goal lead lost, floodlight failure and a cunning four-legged animal that could have altered the course of League of Ireland history. Mervue had started brightly and scored after just ten minutes through Ollie Keogh, and when David Goldbey added to that just before the half hour things had an air of inevitability for Kildare. Two goals up, controlling the game and an elated home support about to repopulate Galway later that night, the lights went out, literally, at the worst possible time.

> *"At the time it was an awful thing to happen. It was our first game under floodlights and what a time for them to fail! Thankfully, Mervue had an electrician on hand on the night to make sure everything ran smoothly so it was a blessing he was there!"* – **Johnny Glynn**

After a heart-in-mouth 15 minutes for the home supporters (and probably a "Paddy make sure that electrician doesn't get inside the gate" moment from the away fans), the game restarted, only to be stopped some time later by a stray dog who risked being kicked to death had it somehow got the game abandoned. The delay broke Mervue's concentration and Philip Hughes replied with a brace for Kildare to leave the game finely poised at 2-2.

Having come back from two goals down, County were obvious favourites for the return leg at Station Road four days later, but Johnny Glynn's men pulled off a massive shock, and quite easily as it turned out. Again Mervue went ahead in the tie through David O'Brien, but this time there was no stopping the Galwegians. David Goldbey made it 2-0 on 64 minutes, and with no floodlight failure or four-legged mongrel on the horizon Kildare looked doomed, a point rammed home by Goldbey with his second goal ten minutes from time. At 9.37 on November 21, 2008 Mervue United became a League of Ireland club.

Almost 50 years after they first started kicking a ball about between two trees, United's promotion to the First Division meant for the first time in history Galway had two League of Ireland teams.

> *"The realisation of what we were about to achieve set in with about five minutes left. Despite losing the two goal lead in the first game we were still confident that we could come out with a result at Kildare, so to be part of the club making history was special. On a personal*

level it meant a lot as when I was at Galway United, Tony Cousins had let me go. He was in the opposite dug out that night managing Kildare." – **David Goldbey**

Fahy's Field was not up to the required standard for their League of Ireland maiden voyage so the club popped up the road to Terryland Park to share with Galway United for their 2009 debut season.

Athlone Town wrote themselves into the club's history books by becoming the first side to kick-off against Mervue United in their League of Ireland First Division game on March 6, 2009. A large crowd was there to witness this historic occasion as eleven nervy hopefuls looked towards the tricolour as *Amhran na Fhiann* rang out on the Dyke Road.

Unfortunately for Glynn's men, the midlanders didn't care too much for the carnival atmosphere and excited local support and ninety minutes later walked away with a 1-0 win. Ironically, Athlone did exactly the same thing a year later to another Galway club making a league debut, Salthill Devon.

Eric Browne became the club's first top flight goal scorer in a 4-1 defeat to Limerick, and that all important first win came away against Monaghan Town in their fourth game with goals from Mike Tierney and David Goldbey.

A first appearance in the last 32 of the FAI Cup for over 21 years arrived in June, but United lost to Premier Division Dundalk, and the brave new world for Glynn's men also saw an EA Sports Cup game against local rivals Salthill. Mervue was familiar with their friends up the road from the A Championship, and United started favourites as the league club, however after a 2-2 draw in normal time, Devon progressed 4-3 on penalties.

That first season was obviously a struggle for the club. Many United players were home grown and not used to this higher level, but despite the step up in division Mervue did manage to avoid the wooden spoon, notch six wins and finish ahead of a doomed Kildare County.

Kildare County? Hang on! Am I missing something? Just in case you think I'm losing it, despite the play-off defeat Kildare was given a reprieve and granted a First Division licence ahead of Cobh Ramblers, though it still ended in tears as the club said goodbye to League of Ireland football the same year, folding at the end of the 2009 season.

A little bit older and a wee bit wiser, Mervue entered the 2010 First Division knowing it would still be a struggle, but the fact they were a solvent League of Ireland club in an era where pipe dreams and foolish expectations had threatened to ruin more established clubs at least made sure there was no tabloid headlines or sports pages devoted to them for the wrong reasons.

An eagerly anticipated local derby for the first time in the top flight against Salthill Devon finished 2-2, whilst other highlights included a 3-2 win away to

Mervue United team for their historic first League of Ireland game at Fahy's Field.
Back Row (L-R): *Jason Molloy, Michael Collins, Ger Hanley, Mike Tierney (capt) and*
Martin Conneely. Front Row (L-R): *Dan Cunningham, David O'Brien, Mark Ludden,*
Eric Browne, Noel Varley and Nicky Curran (photo credit: Eric Barry, blinkofaneye.ie)

Finn Harps, and home victories against Athlone, Longford and play-off final-ists Monaghan United. Despite losing 24 of their 33 games, Mervue managed for a second season not to finish last and in 2011 moved back to their spiritual home of Fahy's Field. That historic first League of Ireland home game took place there on March 11 this year, with Mike Tierney scoring an 88th minute equaliser against Cork City in a 1-1 draw to send a sizeable home crowd home happy.

> *"I didn't know what to expect from that game but thankfully we got*
> *a result. Although there might not be an expectation for Mervue to*
> *do anything in the league, in many ways that makes the challenge*
> *bigger. We are still an amateur club but have some fine young talent*
> *coming through and a real community spirit about the place. As for*
> *budgets? I never have to complain about them at Mervue . . . we*
> *never have one!"* – **Johnny Glynn**

And the club has surprised many this year and adapted extremely well. When Mervue beat Wexford Youths earlier this season six of the players that took the field came through their youth system, with nine on the full senior panel. The club is stable, solvent and actually do have a budget! In terms of the League of Ireland stairs it's still baby steps for Mervue, but they're climbing them confidently one at a time.

Ground Info

On entering the City of the Tribes, Mervue United will be the first of the three Galwegian clubs you'll run into. Located just right of Flannerys Hotel before the city centre, Fahy's Field had been used by the club since the seventies, but of course just recently hosted its first League of Ireland game on March 11, 2011 against Cork City after work had been carried out to bring the ground up to League of Ireland standard.

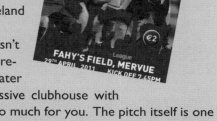

Although the ground currently doesn't have a stand or terracing, plans have recently been unveiled for a new 500 seater stand, and United do boast an impressive clubhouse with good views should the elements get too much for you. The pitch itself is one of the finest in Ireland.

Record Attendance

650 v Shelbourne (March 25, 2011 – so far!). Outside of Fahy's Field, United did have a paying gate of £4,000 at their FAI Cup first round game against UCD on February 10, 1985, though Terryland Park was used as the "home" venue.

Cost

Adults: €10.00
OAPs/Students: €7.00
Children: Under-14 free with adult

Programme

€2.00 – small and functional with a slightly cheaper price. Programmes tend to be a labour of love that editors put together with very little money and for small reward, but that doesn't stop them being churned out every home game by people who care, even if it's only a handful who buy them.

Rivals

Galway United has been a source of annoyment to a lot of the fans I spoke to, though that wasn't surprising given their proximity. Surprisingly, Salthill Devon, the other Galway club, escaped without as much as one sarky comment.

Mascot

None.

Food and Drink

There is a small shop inside the ground whilst the club has a healthy connection with local pub the Trappers Inn, which sits on the Tuam Road. Even on my afternoon visit there I found plenty of Mervue fans willing to talk to me about the club.

Club Shop

None.

Website

www.mervueunited.com

Local Radio

Galway Bay FM 95.8

The Match – Mervue United v Monaghan United (Airtricity League, First Division, April 29, 2011)

Take one form book. Place in hand. Quickly rip up. Mervue came into the game on the back of three straight defeats and Monaghan United on four straight wins. Even the local bookies would have quoted you odds of 5/1, but Mervue won 3-1 with Monaghan finishing the game with nine men! Jason Molloy gave Mervue an early lead (per usual, my late arrival = missed goal) and though the reliable Declan O'Brien levelled it up soon after, Mervue scored again through Eric Browne and another from Molloy. Paul Whelan and Declan O'Brien were sent off for Monaghan as Mervue recorded its first league win since returning to Fahy's Field. Having been cute enough to put €10.00 on Mervue, I retreated to the pub for the night to spend my winnings on my friend Jack Daniels and his cousin Jim Beam!

Monaghan United

Formed: 1979

Ground: Gortakeegan

Capacity: 3,500

Nickname: The Mons

"Joey was alright until they done away with the pass-back rule. Then he was on life-support!" – Billy Bagster on former defender Joey Malone

Apparently it's not the winning but competing that counts in football. That once you've given your best nothing else matters. That after all it's only a game. What a load of balls. Monaghan United and their supporters know exactly what I mean.

On Monday, November 8, 2010, the club experienced absolute heartbreak by losing out on Premier Division status having snatched defeat from the jaws of victory . . . twice! Having drawn at home to Bray Wanderers in the first leg of their promotion/relegation play-off tie, Mick Cooke's First Division side lost a last minute lead in extra time at the Carlisle Grounds and then a suicide-inducing sudden death shoot-out robbed them of a place among Ireland's elite. For any Monagahan fan that didn't opt for the river or a rope that night, here's a look back at your history!

Formed only 32 years ago, the club was a marriage of two local sides, Monaghan Town and Monaghan Hibernians. Gerry Reynolds had the honour of becoming the club's first Chairman when they came into formation in 1979. At that point the club were plying their trade in the AUL and playing their home games at Belgium Park.

The make-up of the League of Ireland had changed that decade. No longer predominantly clubs from the capital, new teams from the provinces had emerged. Finn Harps and Athlone Town had joined at the start of the seventies, whilst Thurles Town and Galway United made their league debuts in 1977. County Louth-based Dundalk won the league the year of Monaghan's foundation, with Limerick and Athlone dominating procedures in the early eighties. Between 1970-85, only two Dublin sides won the League of Ireland title so it made food for thought at Belgium Park.

A step up to the League of Ireland B Division got the "Mons" a little closer to the promised land. Under the watchful eye of Sean McCaffrey (the former Irish U-17 and U-19 manager), the club competed well against established reserve sides, but it was the announcement of a new League of Ireland First Division in 1985 that ultimately gave the Northerners a shot at the big time. Despite only existing a mere six years, Monaghan was granted a place in the inaugural First Division for the 1985/86 season, however they wouldn't be the shy boys at the back of the classroom on the first day of school.

A host of other clubs followed them into unfamiliar territory. Cobh Ramblers, EMFA, Newcastle United from Limerick, Bray Wanderers and fellow northerners Derry City also stepped into the unknown. Throw in a Longford Town side that had just been relegated in their first season and it left seven of the ten clubs as complete novices in the first year of the new league.

Monaghan United's first game in Irish top flight football took place on September 8, 1985 away to UCD at Belfield Park in the League Cup. Frank Treacy achieved the honour of scoring the club's first goal in a 2-0 win. As pleasurable a win as it was for John Murphy's side, their first home tie at senior level was even better. A week later Murphy led out Monaghan United for the first time in their own backyard against Derry City. Their fellow Ulstermen had kicked off their League of Ireland odyssey in front of 9,000 in the Brandywell the week before against Home Farm, and their fans and unfurled flags waving in the wind added more colour to Monaghan's historic first home tie. If the Mons were slight underdogs on the day it didn't show and goals from Willie Crawley and a late effort by Greg Turley gave Monaghan United a 2-0 win.

The League Cup wins offered an early relief from what was going to be a tough introduction to life at this level. Seamus Finnegan scored the club's

*The Monaghan United side that played Derry City at home in the League Cup
on September 15, 1985 (photo credit: J. McAviney)*

first league goal in a 2-1 defeat to Cobh Ramblers and the club won their first home game in the league against Finn Harps, but as the season progressed it got harder. Only three more victories were added and United eventually finished second-last with just EMFA padding their arse from the bottom.

> *"It felt great scoring Monaghan United's first league goal, and of course it went in the club's history books, but at the end of the day it didn't win the game, that's all I was worried about!"* – **Seamus Finnegan**

In 1987 the club moved to Gortakeegan, and handed back to the town council the long-term lease they had on Belgium Park. They have been positioned there ever since. The rest of the decade was spent occupying the lower regions of the First Division, finishing bottom in 1989/90 with Rockmount causing an upset in the 1987 FAI Cup by knocking Monaghan out at Gortakeegan 3-1. Things changed, however, with the arrival of Billy Bagster.

The charismatic Dubliner added a much needed boost to a faltering team in front of dwindling attendances. United had watched Bray, Cobh and Derry City, all fellow inductees into the league in 1985, win promotion whilst even perennial strugglers EMFA had won the First Division Shield. An awful defeat to non-league Elm Rovers in the 1991 FAI Cup just about summed up the problems before Billy's arrival.

Under Bagster, Monaghan United finally got their act together and a 1992/93 First Division campaign saw the club post their highest placing to date, finishing third behind Cobh Ramblers and eventual champions Galway United. That was enough to clinch a promotion/relegation play-off place

*The charismatic Billy Bagster
(photo credit: Northern Standard)*

against Premier Division strugglers Waterford United. The first leg at Kilcohan Park produced a highly entertaining 2-2 draw (I was at the game and somehow managed to miss every goal through a combination of visiting the toilet and searching for the half-eaten burger my friend threw away) with Mick Wilson and Noel Melvin scoring the Monaghan goals. The hard work had been done.

Now in the ascendancy under Billy there was no denying the men from Gortakeegan and Monaghan won the second leg in a canter with goals from Mick Byrne, Phillip Power and Noel Melvin again. Some clubs wait an absolute lifetime to play top flight Irish football. Monaghan had managed it in less than a decade.

> *"I've had some wonderful times at Monaghan; the highlight was obviously that promotion, though it was somewhat bittersweet as I broke my hand and missed out on all the excitement of the play-off. We had some fantastic players at the time – Mick Byrne, "Chippy" Devlin, Alan Kinsella and Noel Melvin to name a few, and you just couldn't go wrong with Billy in charge."* – **Seamus Finnegan**

Despite the pressure of competing with Ireland's elite for the first time in their history the next season, Bagster and his merry band of "ageing juveniles" not only finished seventh on a shoestring budget, but if the ridiculous "two tier" system, which split the Premier Division in two, had not been in operation United would actually have finished fourth.

> *"I only paid money for one player – £1,500 for Brian O'Shea from St. Pat's in a hire-purchase agreement. Paul Newe would be our top goal scorer and he couldn't even get into St. Pat's reserve squad when I signed him. The final piece of the jigsaw was Joey Malone and he was nearly on life-support – the pass back ruled killed him altogether!"* – **Billy Bagster**

The exception to a side with more golden oldies than Larry Gogan's record collection was a young Declan Geoghegan – signed from Bohemians after then manager Eamonn Gregg had phoned Bagster about him. It quickly led to the nickname the "Blue Rinse Brigade" being coined. Not that it bothered Billy and the lads. Though they lost their first Premier Division game against Cork in Bishopstown, only Shamrock Rovers beat them twice over that 1993/94 season and the club took some notable scalps whilst winning an impressive 13 games at the same time. When the two-tier split came at the half way point of the season Monaghan lay seventh, but in reality the 47 points they ended up with would have been enough to pop ahead of Derry City and finish fourth. However, things fell apart the season after.

United started the season badly and by Christmas the writing seemed to be on the wall. Only three wins had been taken from the first half of the season and by the time the 1994/95 season wrapped up in April, Monaghan had been long since relegated, finishing 13 points from safety.

"The trouble was the club relied on their discotheque for income, but soon after hotels around us started opening them and our income dropped. Honourable people were running Monaghan but they had to cut players' wages and the League of Ireland Chairman in his wisdom then decided all our players were free agents. We lost eight of them in two weeks. There was simply no surviving that. The FAI gave us £20,000 compensation but we didn't get our Premier status back. It was a sickening blow." – **Billy Bagster**

It set the club back big-time and Bagster departed soon after. The first season back in the First Division was an absolute disaster, winning just two of 27 games and scoring just ten goals, the lowest amount ever in the history of the First Division. The best the club could muster for the remainder of the decade was 10 wins and a seventh place in 1998/99.

Not to end the decade on a complete downer, there were some bright moments – mainly provided by the floodlights that were installed in Gortakeegan in 1995 and a new stand that had been paid for thanks to some amazing fundraising by the club, which was opened in 1996 by then Republic of Ireland manager Mick McCarthy.

As a new century dawned Monaghan entered it yet again in the role of perennial First Division underdogs. To date, no club has spent more time in the First Division than the "Mons", however the decade actually started with a bang and, under new manager Bobby Browne, Monaghan clinched only their second promotion in the 2000/01 season. Though top goal scorer Andy Myler had left for Athlone (having hit 17 for Monaghan the season before),

Browne had players like James O'Callaghan, Ken Lundy, Mick Scully, Paul Shiels and Gary Cummins among others to add silk and steel and United got off to a promising start, winning six of their first ten games and keeping pace at the top of the table. On the last day of the season Dundalk had clinched the First Division title whilst Monaghan lay in third. That would have been good enough for a play-off position, but if they could win away to Limerick and Athlone slip up at home to Waterford then Browne's men would gain automatic promotion.

Before you could say "please choke at St. Mel's", Athlone failed to net against Waterford in a scoreless draw and a Peter Rogers' penalty combined with a John Carroll goal just after the hour at Limerick sealed a win for Browne's men to complete a dramatic thieving of the second spot ahead of a disbelieving Athlone. Monaghan United was back among Ireland's finest again.

However the flirtation with Premier Division football was again brief as Bobby Browne's side was relegated in their first season back among the big boys. It was a hard, brutal campaign and by the end the players, staff and supporters were glad to see the back of it. Just three points were harvested in the opening ten games before their first win in the eleventh against Dundalk. Galway United inflicted a club record 8-0 hammering in October, and by December the writing was well and truly on the wall and they eventually finished bottom with just twelve points.

Back to familiar ground in the First Division, Monaghan parted company with Bobby Browne soon after as United endured several seasons of hardship, making the uncanny and unfortunate habit of finishing second last in the First Division for four seasons in a row!

In 2003, the club was docked three points for an illegible player and finished second bottom, something they did again in 2004. Trevor Vaughan became the club's top goal scorer in that time, but otherwise things didn't improve and for the next two seasons the Ulstermen just avoided the wooden spoon. The only good thing about that time was the fact that Kilkenny made a habit of finishing beneath them each year!

However manager Mick Cooke eventually made inroads and stopped the rot. Results began to improve and all of a sudden Gortakeegan wasn't the handy three points and few jars on the road for away fans that it had depressingly been for most of the decade. The steady improvement under Cooke led to a fifth place finish in 2009 with Karl Bermingham equalling Andy Myler's record of 17 goals in a season. And then to 2010 . . . the year of what might have been.

The league campaign saw them occupy the top four from the opening day, losing just once in their first 10 games. Along the way they used the EA Sports

Cup as a lovely distraction. United surprised many by taking out Shelbourne, Tullamore Town, Bohemians, Limerick and Dundalk along the way to contesting the 2010 final against Premier outfit Sligo Rovers at The Showgrounds in September. It was the club's first senior final in League of Ireland football though try as they might a Matthew Blinkhorn 14th minute strike for Rovers was enough to kill off Monaghan's fairytale ending.

Oh Brother! Stephen Geoghegan scores for Shamrock Rovers against brother Declan Geoghegan who had to fill in on the Monaghan goal after the goalkeeper was sent off! (photo credit: Northern Standard)

But there had already been huge momentum to United's season by that point. Monaghan finished third with Philip Hughes and Karl Bermingham hitting 24 goals between them, and then impressively beat Waterford in the play-offs away from home. This, of course, led to Bray Wanderers, extra time and those penalties.

After a scoreless first game in the 2010 promotion/relegation play-off in Gortakeegan, where the home side had several chances to win the match, the return leg remained deadlocked at Bray's Carlisle Grounds until Don Tierney's strike deflected off of Bray midfielder Gary Shields in the 118th minute of the pulsating away tie to put United within 120 seconds of Premier League football. Queue mass delirium, grown men crying and half the travelling support finding themselves on the pitch, not through the aid of their legs, more their arse as a wall around the ground collapsed.

Now God sometimes has a funny way of winding up people, so I'm pretty sure he enjoyed his fun at the expense of practically every Monaghan fan who was praying for him to end the torture within seconds of this goal. Surely he couldn't be so cruel for Wanderers to kick-off, go up the field and score? Surely, this is what fairytales are for? For those of a nervous disposition (or Monaghan goalkeeper Gabriel Sava) please stop reading now.

Monaghan goalkeeper Gabriel Sava complaining to the bench that someone is trying to take his job! Midfielder Eric Foley is about to break the poor lad's heart by telling him he can't go in goal (photo credit: Simon Crowe)

In the 122nd minute with literally seconds left, Gary Shields' cross was spilled by United's goalkeeper and Jake Kelly was on hand to slot home the most unlikely of equalizers. The home crowd rejoiced whilst a goalkeeper formally on the books of Lazio wondered just exactly where he had run over that black cat. It was harsh on United but incredibly cruel on the Italian who had produced a flawless display of bravery and shot-stopping the entire game.

Now at that point if I had been a Monaghan fan I would have calmly headed for the exits, taken the bus home and waited for the inevitable text from the suicidal friend who stayed at the ground to watch the penalty shoot-out. Despite this, the odds dramatically swung Monaghan's way again when at 3-2 in the shoot-out (Bermingham, Hughes and Gartland slotting home their penalties), Wanderers' substitute Gary Shaw missed for the home side. Barry Clancy struck his spot-kick home to put Monaghan 4-2 up and yet again United were on the verge of their first Premier League appearance in almost ten years. Lighting doesn't strike twice? Well, actually it does. Several times. In fact, there was a Park Ranger from Virginia who got hit seven times with it in his life, so he would have scoffed at what unfolded next had he been in the Carlisle Grounds that night.

Bray made it 4-3 but with a 12 yard penalty holding the makings of several hundred hangovers the next morning, Monaghan defender Alan Byrne smacked his effort against the Bray crossbar and the home side levelled with the very next kick to send the contest into sudden death. Those of you with an even more nervous disposition (or Paul Whelan) either pour yourself a large brandy or put the book down . . . again!

With the shoot-out on its 15th penalty, Monaghan defender Paul Whelan crucially missed his spot kick to ironically leave Gary Shields' to drive home the deciding penalty for Bray to give Pat Devlin's men an incredible win and ensure a nightmare return home for the visitors.

"We'd been building over a couple of seasons and I was quietly confident of doing well. Losing against Mervue in our penultimate game was a big blow as it would have meant a title decider against Derry on the last day otherwise. When it came to the play-off against Bray we really should have had it done and dusted at home. When we did score late in the second leg at the Carlisle Grounds there was a lapse in concentration after the wall had fallen down and I think the break of five minutes let our player's minds start thinking of places like Bohemians, Rovers and St. Pat's! It was one of those things, nobody was to blame – Bray's name was just on the overall tie. After the tears dried up in the dressing room I told them, 'If this is the worst thing that's going to happen to you in your life, then you're going to have a great life'." – **Mick Cooke**

Some light seemed to flicker at the end of the Premier Division tunnel in mid-February 2011, when it looked as if Monaghan would after all play Premier football following Galway United's apparent demotion to the A Championship. However reports of the Tribesmen's demise were off the mark, and following an appeal Galway was re-instated into the League of Ireland Premier Division at the expense of Monaghan. In the last week of February Mick Cooke left to manage Drogheda United and the Northerners kicked off the season managerless until the irrepressible, love-him-or-loathe-him Roddy Collins took over two games in, guiding the club to a win in his first game against Waterford.

"Its no secret I'd applied for jobs before Monaghan but didn't even get the courtesy of an interview so after nearly seven years I'm very grateful to the club and people of Monaghan to be given the privilege of managing the club. There's a wonderful spirit here." – **Roddy Collins**

Monaghan remain a force in the First Division and under the mercurial Collins the club once mocked for having more cows than people watching games may just bring Premier Division football back for their fans and those grateful livestock next year.

Ground Info

Gortakeegan is a mile from the city centre on the R189 not far from the Clones Road. It's been the happy home of Monaghan United for almost 25 years now having moved from Belgium Park in 1987.

Inside the ground the main stand holds just over 600 people which was lively enough for the visit of Dundalk. Opposite there is a grass verge running the length of the field with the old reliable weather beaten scoreboard which harks back to more innocent times. Behind the ground there are impressive training facilities along with an all-weather pitch.

Record Attendance

2,000 v Derry City (First Division, September 15, 1985)

Cost

Adults: €10.00
Students: €10.00
Children: €5.00
Concessions: €8.00

Programme

€3.00 – Some programmes seem to value style over substance with an eye for glossy visuals rather than what matters – content. Thankfully, United's programme focuses on giving solid information and plenty of articles without worrying that it's in black and white. It also has contributors ranging from Monaghan to Dundalk to Geneva, where United fan Adrian Harte works for UEFA. Simply one of the best in the entire league.

Rivals

Dundalk.

Mascot

Football-Head: It's that simple folks. A guy wandering around Gortakeegan with a giant football on his head!

Food and Drink

Gortakeegan is home of the "Mon Dog". Forget about eating a hot dog anywhere else. This was awesome!! A tad cheaper than a lot of grounds, but a bigger hot dog by far. So tasty I wolfed down two back to back with a cup of tea for possibly the best €8.00 spent at a football ground. Complemented with three lovely wee girls serving me, it set the tone for a great day out.

For drink look no further then "The Bagster" – the main supporters' bar in the ground named of course after the charismatic Billy Bagster, whilst the "Greg Turley Suite" is mainly for players and match officials. In town supporters normally frequent the wonderfully named Squealing Pig Pub which often sponsor games for United.

Club Shop

Located just next to the stand. Local *Northern Standard* Journo Ronan Killmurry keeps guard in a little barn building that did a brisk trade, particularly the programme. A walk-in megastore it's not, but if you want a hat, scarf or half-time ticket for the draw Ronan's your man!

Websites

www.monaghanunited.com
www.monaghanunited.tv

Local Radio

Northern sound 94-98 FM.

The Match – Monaghan United v Dundalk (EA Sports Cup, April 25, 2011)

An Easter Bank Holiday Monday, local rivals and a cup match in the middle of a heat wave made a tasty combination so I could have done worse. Under Roddy Collins United had started the league well and this win proved to be a fourth straight consecutive victory at Gortakeegan.

Dundalk took the lead through a sublime Keith Ward free-kick, but never quite imposed themselves afterwards. Monaghan equalised ten minutes from time at precisely the moment I was being chased by a bull down the main hill overlooking the ground as I tried to get a better picture of Gortakeegan, before Declan O'Brien won it in extra time for Monaghan.

Salthill Devon

Formed:	1977
Ground:	Drom
Capacity:	2,000
Nickname:	–

"We played Waterford away and got beat 8-0. After the game our
goalkeeper, Marty Mannion, said, 'I'm glad none of them were my fault!'"
– Emlyn Long, former Sathill Devon manager

There was a time when there was more chance of Fianna Fáil coming to power again in this country than having three League of Ireland teams from Galway. It had always been the domain of Dublin clubs to have featured heavily throughout the years so by the mid-seventies the nearest any League of Ireland team came to Galway was if they were passing through it on the way to play Sligo Rovers.

It changed with the election of Galway United and 30 odd years on the west is wide awake as along with the men from Terryland Park and Mervue United, Salthill Devon are fully paid up members of the fraternity that is the League of Ireland. It's been a long road for the Galwegians, where struggle and success have crossed paths, but the lads from Salthill are currently experiencing the highest point of their 34-year career as a football club.

Although the newest members of the league, Salthill has had, in one form or another, a team in the area for almost 70 years. The first version emerged in the 1940s when Salthill Athletic was formed and played their football in the local Galway District League. Shortly after, they gave way to Salthill Crusaders before a barren spell in the sixties where the area didn't have a team representing it. In 1970, Salthill Athletic emerged again with games being played in Salthill Park (which is right on the promenade) and the club also would be instrumental in setting up the Connaught Senior League in the early eighties. However it was the amalgamation of Salthill Athletic and another local club, Devon Celtic, that created the club you see today. A lot of credit must go to Tess Brennan (mother of the late Seamus Brennan TD) who was instrumental in pulling the two clubs together and went on to become the club president for a time.

Salthill Athletic 40 years ago in 1971 – they didn't become Salthill Devon until a few years later (photo credit: Salthill Devon FC)

The '80s were again spent playing their football in the Galway District League, but 1991 saw the club participate with top flight teams on a national scale for the first time in their history. This came about when, under former Galway United manager Tony Mannion, Salthill Devon gained entry into the 1991/92 League Cup. There the Westerners got drawn in a group with Longford, Limerick and Galway United.

The League Cup has been an outlet for some non-league clubs throughout the years with teams like Cobh Ramblers, Mervue United and Kilkenny City all playing in it before entering the league. Dubliners Bluebell United had also participated one year whilst Fanad United from Donegal became the biggest success by making the semi-finals in 1987. This was finally Salthill's chance, and on Thursday, August 15, 1991, they took on Galway United in Group Two of the League Cup.

The Tribesmen had been a league club for almost fifteen years to that point so it wasn't a surprise when they ran out 4-0 winners in a game played at Terryland Park, however their next group fixture was a tighter affair – losing 2-1 to Longford Town with Brian Long having the pleasure of scoring Salthill Devon's first goal at senior level.

> *"I had played for Salthill in the seventies so it was lovely to lead them into this competition. It didn't matter that it was the League Cup with a side who were non-league moreso than if it was with Galway United in Europe. You go about your job preparing properly and send them over the white line. We played United with a local inexperienced side so the result wasn't a huge surprise, but as a manager it doesn't stop you thinking that we might get a result here."* – Tony Mannion

The lads decided to double their goal scoring tally in the next game against Limerick FC. It was notable not only for their first draw (2-2) but the fact the opposing team was managed by one Sam Allardyce in only his third game in charge of the club, and Limerick went on to win the First Division title that season. By the start of a new century Salthill had another meeting with Galway United – this time to take them over!

> *"We were approached by then Galway Chairman Gerry Grey to look after the running of United as he had gone as far as he could with the club. So we took it on. One of the first things we done was to install Tony Mannion as our manager, not only for his experience but at the time Tony was the project manager of our ground – Drom. We handled every aspect of the club though after a few years it began to clash with trying to take Salthill Devon forward, but we handed back a debt-free Galway United."* – Pete Kelly (Club PRO)

However it became a case of two steps forward, one step back before they could get near the League of Ireland. Having progressed nicely in local circles, the Connaught League suddenly folded, leaving Salthill Devon back playing in the Galway District League. At one point they had even managed to play in the inaugural League of Ireland U-21 League in 2001, but dropped out after a year. However a lifeline was thrown when the competition was completely restructured and expanded to include several non-league clubs in 2005.

Seizing on the opportunity, the club took the Under-21 championship by storm. Under Emlyn Long and Mick Quirke, Devon became the surprise package of the two-sectioned league and despite playing against the Under-21 teams of established League of Ireland clubs, Salthill went on to stun everyone and beat Cork City in the 2005/06 final on a damp blustery evening in Terryland Park in December, with goals from Michael Gilmore and Cian McBrien in a 2-1 victory to win the league at their very first attempt. It was an even bigger achievement knowing that a good sprinkling of Cork's players had been part of their Premier League squad and sampled football at that level. Having raised a few eyebrows the Connaught men continued to impress – making the final again in 2007. It also was the year that Devon finally made the first round proper of the FAI Cup.

Having beaten Munster Senior League side Avondale of Cork, Salthill squared up against Premier Division UCD in the last 32 of the competition. The game was played on June 16, 2007 at home in Drom, against a UCD side struggling desperately to hold on to their Premier Division status. Despite the potential of a cup upset, the Students struck early and never looked back, comfortably winning 4-0 and booking a place with Dundalk in the next round before going out in the semi-finals. However it still proved a great experience for the club. Having won that 2005/06 Under-21 league, the next logical step was to apply for the A Championship. The runaway snowball kept gathering momentum and Salthill was accepted into that division in 2008. However things didn't exactly go to plan when then they got there!

> *"We got approved alright and then got absolutely slaughtered in each game! All of our players were young and home grown and it was a huge step up and we ended up finishing bottom. It was a steep learning curve but we knew that."* – **Pete Kelly**

Having been spanked more times than a three hour session with a dominatrix sometimes you've just got to roll with the punches, and though it may have felt a little like pissing against the wind when your goalkeeper has arthritis from picking the ball out of the net, it was a learning experience the club knew they'd have to go through.

A year later and twelve months wiser, Salthill Devon again reached the first round of the FAI Cup (losing to Tralee Dynamos) but more importantly topped the nine team Group A section of the A Championship, losing just two of their 16 games. Shamrock Rovers A side came through Group B and set up a winner-takes-all in a final with €20,000 on offer to the victor.

The final, played in Drom on October 31, 2009, proved to be anything but a horror show with Salthill more than holding their own . . . that is, until the 97th minute when Rovers cruelly won it through a Don Cowan goal to give them the A Championship title and twenty grand to boot. However the real reward was a promotion/relegation play-off against First Division Kildare County that November.

Kildare had been here before. Just twelve months previously they had lost to Mervue United and faced A Championship football, but got a reprieve through a First Division licence at the expense of Cobh Ramblers – however 2009 proved even harder. Hit with massive financial difficulties and needing a huge effort just to fulfil their remaining league fixtures, Kildare County was wound up in November 2009, meaning they could not field a team to play their promotion/relegation play-off against Salthill Devon, thus leaving the A Championship runners-up duly elected to the First Division.

Though they would have liked to have won it on the field of play, Salthill wasn't complaining – League of Ireland football had come to a third Galwegian club.

> *"It was a real anti-climax for us. We were confident having topped our group in the A Championship and even though the lads were devastated after losing so late to Rovers, we had had a fantastic season. We knew Kildare were having trouble at the end of the season and that they might not be able to fulfil the fixture but we obviously still prepared professionally, but I still think we would have won the tie on the field."* – **Emlyn Long**

Though the facilities at Drom boasted all-weather playing surfaces, two beautiful manicured pitches and a clubhouse with possibly the best vantage point to watch a League of Ireland match, the players and staff knew exactly what was about to confront them and had just four short months to get themselves ready for their League of Ireland debut.

Salthill Devon's historic first game in League of Ireland football took place in Drom on Saturday, March 6, 2010 against Athlone Town in the Airtricity First Division. Sean Boyle could have put the home side ahead as early as the fifth minute but missed a glorious chance before Town's striker Austin Skelly proved he hadn't a single romantic bone in his body by scoring the only goal of the game to spoil the party.

Their first FAI Cup tie as a league club yielded better success when a brace from Charlie Burke and one from Mike Kennedy ensured a 3-1 win away to A

Championship side Tullamore Town. This set up a local derby against Galway United at Drom. It was the first time both sides met in the top flight since their League Cup meeting back in 1991. The last 16 meeting took place on the last weekend of August and Devon proved more than a capable match for the Tribesmen, drawing 1-1 with the goal coming from Ciprian Straut before Emlyn Long's men went down 3-1 in the reply at Terryland Park.

> *"We went into the season with our eyes open. It was a case of get through it and learn as much as you can. What made myself, Mike Quirke and everyone at the club proud was the fact seven of our players that took to the field in our opening game against Athlone had come through the club."* – **Emlyn Long**

Taking on Cork City in the First Division - April 2011
(photo credit: Tony Tobin)

Yes, it was a long hard season. Yes, it was the proverbial boulder up a mountain. And yes, the lads probably got a bit teed off losing 24 of their games. But Salthill managed to win their biggest battle in 2010 with the very last kick of the season. Having finished bottom of the table, the Connaught club was forced into a promotion/relegation play-off with A Championship winners Cobh Ramblers. The Cork men had a League of Ireland pedigree having spent almost 25 years in the top flight, winning a First Division title, reaching an FAI Cup semi-final and starting the career of one Roy ... Roy ... I can't remember his name right now but he played for Manchester United and had an argument with Mick McCarthy in Saipan.

The first leg took take place at St. Coleman's Park on November 2, 2010. With so much at stake it was Devon who settled better and took the lead courtesy of Mikey Gilmore's first half strike. It proved to be the only goal of

2011 Squad: Back (L-R): *Victor Collins, Cian Fadden, Ronan Forde, James Whelan, Luke McConnell, Eugene Greaney.* Front (L-R): *Ciprian Straut, Cian McBrien, Gearoid Leidhinn, Etanda Nkololo, Daniel Rupa (photo credit: Ian McDonald)*

the game and when Robbie Porter doubled that advantage in the second leg at Drom four days later things looked rosy. However the men from the Rebel County weren't about to give in without a fight, and Ramblers' player Jamie Murphy made the tie interesting (if you're a Salthill fan, replace the word "interesting" with "terrifying") by pulling a goal back and the tie remained nervy until the game was finally put to bed with Ciprian Straut's 93rd minute winner to end the Corkmen's hopes, thus making sure Salthill Devon survived to play League of Ireland football in 2011.

The club has a great infrastructure, producing dozens of players who have represented the Republic from U-15 to U-19 level, both boys and girls, in the last few seasons and have been stationed at Drom since the middle of the last decade. It's a top-notch facility which, aside from some small outside funding, the club has built through pulling most of the money together themselves. There is a self-sufficient streak running through the club (they bought and sold their previous ground, Miller's Lane, to the City Council for a profit) and a determination to do well, with old-stager Paul "Ski" Magee now in charge.

Ground Info

Not the easiest of grounds to find (I'm pretty sure Lennon and McCartney wrote *The Long and Winding Road* with Salthill Devon's ground in mind), Drom is situated about a mile north of the Cybaun Hotel in Knocknacarra. As a facility for players Drom is excellent. Eight all-weather pitches, four full-size ones, in immaculate condition I may add, and a club house with four changing rooms, office space and a lounge upstairs should you find the wind chill factor a bit much.

It may seem a bit fan unfriendly for the lack of a stand or terrace, but Salthill's main concern is growing local talent, paying the bills and getting a foothold in a city that already has two other League of Ireland clubs. It also hosts the Umbro Cup, one of the best youth tournaments in Europe each year, which has attracted academy teams from Celtic, Newcastle, Leeds United and Ipswich Town in the past.

Record Attendance

600 v Mervue United (July 17, 2010 – First Division)

Cost

Adults: €10.00
Students/OAPs: €3.00 (the cheapest in Ireland)
Children: Free

Programme

€2.00 – fairly basic and could do with some more contributors to it. The sponsors take pride of place in between the pages, which is understandable for the revenue it brings in to the club. Any turnover from sales would be small in any case as Salthill doesn't have a big support base.

Rivals

With three Galway clubs within such a short distance of each other fans can take their pick from either Mervue or Galway United – though most picked the latter!

Mascot

None.

Food and Drink

Though the upstairs lounge in Drom just does coffee you won't find a better place to watch a game of football in the league as it looks directly down on Devon's pitch and is a safe refuge from the harsh Atlantic winds that often come in from Galway Bay.

The nearest "local" is Tom Sheridan's Bar & Restaurant, just about a mile away. They are sponsors of the club and host the team and supporters after each home game.

Club Shop

The shop is open every Saturday morning from 10.00 am to 12.00 noon in the cabin beside the five-a-side cages.

Website

www.salthilldevon.ie

Local Radio

Galway Bay FM 97.4

The Match – Salthill Devon v Waterford United (Airtricity League First Division, April 2, 2011)

The proximity between the surrounding fences meant you could have a bit of banter with the linesman and players. Waterford controlled the match and scored through Paul Murphy and Conor Sinnott, though Devon's winger Nkololo proved tricky throughout.

During the match I mislaid one of my programmes and asked a steward for one after the game, which he handed me no problem. Coupled with the relaxed atmosphere, this more than made up for the fact we made a wrong turn on the way up.

Shamrock Rovers

Formed: 1901

Ground: Tallaght Stadium

Capacity: 5,947

Nickname: The Hoops

"A small crowd would be 10,000. You'd get up to 30,000 into Milltown. The PA system would be asking people to take care. The perimeter wall fell down a few times the crowd was so big."
– Shamrock Rovers supporter Ned Armstrong

The most successful club in League of Ireland history. A team that conjures up stirring memories, household names and unforgettable moments. Domestic days of wonder. European nights of pride.

No team seems to evoke nostalgia like Shamrock Rovers. A club embedded into the history of Irish football and the psyche of the clubs around them. Locking horns with the Hoops was always something special in days gone by. Practically every club has had a rivalry with them, such was their dominance throughout the ages.

The Glenmalure club has seen a litany of Irish football greats wear the jersey and mentioning but a handful evoke memories for the thousands who

195

stood in Milltown to watch them ply their trade. Love them or hate them, you cannot deny their rich heritage which is woven into the fabric of Irish football.

In 1901 the population of the Emerald Isle was a shade over 4 million. Ireland was under British rule and Queen Victoria had just popped her clogs. At Harland & Wolff, the world's biggest steam ship, Celtic, was launched whilst Thomas O'Donnell was thrown out of the British Parliament for speaking in Irish (what a revolutionary, it's astonishing he wasn't shot!). It was the year that saw the formation of a club from the Southside suburb of Ringsend who, after a meeting in Number 4 Irishtown Road, called themselves Shamrock Rovers, which was derived from Shamrock Avenue in Ringsend, and applied for membership of the Leinster Football Association. Initially the club started in the Dublin County League but progressed to the Leinster Senior League playing their matches at Ringsend Park.

The Free State League appeared in 1921 and the same year the inaugural Free State Cup saw a non-league Shamrock Rovers side reach the final and fight it out against league champions St. James Gate. The first game ended in deadlock with Rovers losing out 1-0 in a replay to a goal by Jack Kelly in front of 10,000 spectators at Dalymount Park. However the supporters didn't take it too well and invaded the St. James' Gate dressing room after the game, where the mother of all punch ups occurred. It was only halted when the brother of one of the St. James' Gate players took out a gun and shot into the roof! Bet the referees back then felt safe! "Hey Paddy, don't book the centre-half today, his brother's got a rifle on the north terrace."

Rovers gained entry to the Free State League the following season, however, winning it in their first attempt. For a club just out of the Leinster League it was an impressive debut, winning 18 of their 22 games and amassing 77 goals along the way. It was the start of a great opening decade to league life for the club and Rovers won the title twice more in the twenties (1924/25, 1926/27), as well as the Free State Cup in 1925 and 1929. Throughout that time Rovers had the quality of players like John Joe Flood, Dinny Doyle, William "Sacky" Glen, Alec Kirkland and Joseph Golding. Throw in the League of Ireland Shield that was captured in 1925 and '27 (a year that saw them first wear their famed Green & White hooped jerseys), Shamrock Rovers had amassed an astonishing six league or cups in eight seasons.

There may have been a great depression in the thirties but that extended to any side who played Shamrock Rovers that decade. Yet again, the Free State Cup was captured in 1930 through a last minute goal scored by David Byrne against fellow Dubliners Brideville. Byrne became the first League of Ireland player to score 100 goals and the first to be transferred to Manchester United.

The league title was drunk to three times in the thirties (good thing there wasn't prohibition) whilst the Free State Cup was toasted no less than five times that decade.

Glenmalure Park, a ground that first featured the likes of Fullam, Fagan, Farrell and Flood (the famous "four Fs") in 1926, was the altar on which the Shamrock faithful came to worship. Opened on Sunday, September 19, 1926, 18,000 watched Bob Fullam score the only goal of the game against Belfast Celtic. It was when the Cunningham family took over the club the next decade that the ground was re-named Glenmalure Park in honour of their family ancestral home in the Wicklow Mountains.

Even by 1940, Shamrock Rovers had already chalked up seven FAI Cups, so it wasn't a surprise that the forties started with an eighth. Having beaten Limerick, Drumcondra and then Bray Unknowns at Shelbourne Park, Rovers recorded an eighth FAI Cup beating Sligo Rovers with goals from Joe Ward, Willie Fallon and Jimmy Dunne in front of a massive crowd of 38,059, all crammed into Dalymount Park. Healthy and safety just wasn't an issue back in the day!

It was fitting that a man born within earshot of the ground masterminded the victory. Jimmy Dunne had taken over at Rovers in 1937, coming back to his native Dublin after significant spells with Sheffield United, Southampton and Arsenal. On his return to the Emerald Isle he immediately led the Hoops

Shamrock Rovers in action during the 1938/39 season (photo courtesy of Robert Goggins)

to back to back League of Ireland titles in 1938 and '39, plus that FAI Cup against Sligo as well as two Shield victories before joining Bohemians.

Now I have to point out something before I go on. I've hopefully managed to record most of the defining moments in clubs' histories in this book, be it a Dundalk double or Salthill Devon's first steps in the league. But because sodding Rovers have won so much it's impossible to go into every defining moment in a league championship or FAI Cup! If I did that there would be only one book in the world bigger than this one and that's a scripture written thousands of years ago and read by Catholics the world over. Explanation over, let's continue!

Bob Fullam led the club to further FAI Cup success in 1944 (beating league champions Shelbourne 3-2), and then in 1945 with a 1-0 win over Bohemians in front of a crowd of 41,238. Jimmy Dunne then returned to master a 2-1 victory over Drumcondra in the 1948 final, but his untimely passing due to heart failure in 1949 meant a young 29-year-old Waterfordian took over at Glenmalure Park. Paddy Coad had played inside-right for his native Waterford FC side, making his debut as a tender 17-year-old in 1937, before he moved to Rovers in 1942. Having then been part of three FAI Cup winning teams with the Hoops, he enjoyed the playing side so rather reluctantly took up the player manager's job at Glenmalure Park. His tenure as boss would go down in club folklore. Introducing a radical youth policy and bringing in players like Liam Tuohy, Paddy Ambrose, Ronnie Nolan, "Maxie" McCann and Shay Keogh, Paddy moulded a vibrant young exciting side and the 1950s belonged to "Coad's Colts".

> *"That was a special side with so many great players, but Paddy was by far the best I'd ever played with. He was a magnificent player and of course when we were on the field together he played inside left with me outside left so I was the recipient of everything good he done!"* – **Liam Tuohy**

It started with a League of Ireland Shield win over Transport in 1950, and four years later the club captured their first League of Ireland title since 1939 when the Hoops pipped Cork side Evergreen United by two points to win the 1953/54 title with Paddy Ambrose as the league's top goal scorer. Two back-to-back FAI Cups followed, beating Drumcondra in the 1955 final and Cork Athletic 3-2 a year later in an amazing game where Athletic had been 2-0 up with ten minutes left, but Rovers still won 3-2 courtesy of a last minute Ronnie Nolan winner. Talk of the town, best in the land. It was truly a golden era.

"It was a great time to play for Rovers. Mind you, I'd been a Drums' fan all my life and loved watching Drumcondra when they played at Tolka Park, but there was no divided loyalty when I had a Rovers shirt on! Tolka was a great place to play, unless my friend 'Bunny' Fullam was lining out for Drums. 'Bunny' played right back for Drumcondra and always used to man mark me – and I mean man mark me, every time we played there, but it was always fair. I think along with John Herrick of Cork Hibs they were the two most difficult players I ever encountered in Ireland." – Liam Tuohy

The Shamrock Rovers team that won the 1956/1957 League of Ireland title
Back row (L-R): *Gerry Mackey, Liam Hennessy, Christy O'Callaghan, Paddy Coad, Shay Keogh, Ronnie Nolan.* Front row (L-R): *Jimmy "Maxie" McCann, Noel Peyton, Tommy Hamilton, Paddy Ambrose, Liam Tuohy (photo courtesy of Dublin Evening Mail)*

Another league title followed in 1957 and a first trip to European football where the Hoops drew Manchester United in the European Cup. On September 25, 1957, 45,000 people popped along to Dalymount Park (Milltown was deemed too small to cope with the crowds) to see United win 6-0 with goals from John Berry, David Pegg and a brace each for Liam Whelan and Tommy Taylor. There was no disgrace in losing to Matt Busby's side, and a week later at Old Trafford James McCann's 55th minute strike created history as the club's first European goal. They only had to wait another ten minutes for another when Tommy Hamilton also notched in a 3-2 defeat. Just four months later, on February 6, 1958, David Pegg, Liam Whelan and Tommy Taylor, who had all scored in the first leg at Dalymount, were three of eight United players who perished on a snow-covered runway in Munich.

A ninth league title arrived in 1959 and twelve months later Paddy Coad departed having fulfilled his legacy at the club in a year that Rovers narrowly lost out to Nice 4-3 in the European Cup. The Waterfordian was replaced by "Albie" Murphy who had rejoined the club after several years with Clyde in Scotland, but it was under Sean Thomas that Shamrock Rovers again began a period of dominance. Two goals each from Paddy Ambrose and Tommy Hamilton helped the Hoops to a 4-1 victory over Shelbourne in the 1962 FAI Cup and an appearance in the Cup Winners Cup against Botev Plovdiv (if it was a dish you'd chew your own leg off first), and a Fairs Cup defeat to Valencia twelve months later at least kept the momentum going.

Sean Thomas guided Rovers to the League title in the 1963/64 season, losing just one game in 22, and with a comfortable five point gap over nearest rivals Dundalk with Eddie Bailham the league's top goal scorer with 18 goals. Not content with that league championship, Thomas's side won Shamrock Rovers their first double since 1932 with victory over Cork Celtic in the FAI Cup final.

1965 FAI Cup Champions Back row (L-R): *Jackie Mooney, Paddy Mulligan, Tommy Farrell, Mick Smyth, Ronnie Nolan, Johnny Fullam.* Front row (L-R): *Pat Courtney, Frank O'Neill, Liam Tuohy, John Keogh and Noel Dunne.* *(photo credit: Connolly Collection/Sportsfile)*

Just to hammer home their dominance even more, the League of Ireland Shield was also captured giving the Ringsend club the treble.

Rapid Vienna came calling (and left happy) in the 1964/65 European Cup, but after winning the FAI Cup the same season with a Johnny Fullam goal against Limerick, Shamrock Rovers, now being managed by former "Coad Colt" Liam Tuohy, gave Spanish giants Real Zaragoza a real fright in the 1965/66 Fairs Cup. Tuohy's side, boasting players like Bobby Gilbert, Mick Smyth, Paddy Mulligan, Pat Courtney and Ronnie Nolan, drew the first leg 1-1 with a goal from Johnny Fullam but went down 2-1 in Spain where Liam Tuohy scored. Having come close to going out at the hands of the Irishmen, Zaragoza went all the way to the final where fellow Spaniards Barcelona beat them.

Limerick got a feeling of Déjà Vu in the 1966 FAI Cup final when Rovers beat the Shannonsiders 2-0 for the second year in a row (the only time in Irish history the same teams have met in consecutive finals) with goals from Tony O'Connell and Frank O'Neill in front of almost 27,000 people in Dalymount. This led to one of the greatest European adventures in the club's history.

Defeating Spora Luxembourg in the first round of the 1966/67 Cup Winners Cup, the Hoops landed German giants Bayern Munich in the last 16. Dalymount was rocking on November 9, 1966 when a team with the likes of Franz Beckenbauer, Gerd Muller and Sepp Maier on its books was held 1-1 on Irish soil. The Germans took an early lead but Billy Dixon's second half equalizer meant the tie wasn't done and dusted.

If you were a German arriving at the Grunwalder Stadium for the second leg two weeks later you would have expected the Germans to comfortably win and things were going according to plan when Munich went 2-0 ahead after just 13 minutes, however goals from Bobby Gilbert and player-manager Tuohy stunned the Germans in their own backyard. Rovers were now in control of their own destiny with just 30 minutes left to play. Going through on away goals. Bayern going out. Lynch mob for Franz and the boys at the ready. What a lovely dream it was.

Alas, with just seven minutes remaining it took the class of Gerd Muller to rescue the tie as "Der Bomber" drove a winner past Mick Smyth. Bayern then went on to beat Glasgow Rangers to win the Cup Winners Cup.

> *"I literally heard a whistle going over my head and it was in. I reacted to the whistle all right but by this stage the ball had already come back out of the net! It was one of the hardest shots I'd ever seen in my life; from the moment it left his boot I didn't see it. His thighs were like tree trunks"* – **Mick Smyth, from** *We Are Rovers* **by Eoghan Rice**

Rovers had many rivals in the sixties. Obviously in the capital there was Bohemians, St. Patrick's (who they beat in the 1967 FAI Cup final) and Shelbourne, but one club with whom they shared a combative history yet mutual respect was Waterford. The Blues had given the Glenmalure club Paddy Coad in the forties and Rovers returned the favour with Coad coming back to the banks of the River Suir to win Waterford's first league title in 1966.

Both sides contested games that have become the stuff of legend throughout the years (the 6-5 game in Kilcohan Park in 1959 when Waterford came back from 4-1 down still holds fond memories . . . in the South East anyway!), so by the time the sides met in the 1968 FAI Cup final, their first time ever, the excitement was fever pitch.

Rovers under Liam Tuohy had won four cups in a row; Waterford had won two of the last three titles. A game for the purists from the best two sides in the land. The Hoops took the lead through Mick Leech and never looked back. Try as Vinny Maguire's team might, the Milltown club was just invincible in this tournament and won 3-0 with futher goals by Leech again and Mick Lawlor.

> *"Back then everybody wanted to win the cup and I loved the fact there was always an extra buzz around the training ground whenever there was a cup weekend. Waterford had invested in a lot of good players and played such attractive football in winning the league so beating them in the final made it that bit more special."*
> – **Damien Richardson**

There would be Cup Winners Cup defeats to Cardiff and Randers Freja of Norway before Liam Tuohy's men won the last of their bewildering six in a row on April 23, 1969. Victims in the final were Cork Celtic. The Leesiders came very close to causing a shock before John Keogh's equalizer got Rovers the draw, but the replay three days later was far more one-sided as the Hoops ran out 4-1 winners.

At this point, with packed houses, the healthy revolving turnstiles and football in its halcyon era in the country, Hoops fans were quite rightly thinking the good days would never end, but Shamrock Rovers' second leg defeat in the Cup Winners Cup to German side FC Schalke in the autumn of 1969 represented the club's last foray into Europe for a decade.

The magnificent 32 game unbeaten run in the FAI Cup came to an end against Shelbourne, and three consecutive League of Ireland runner-up spots in 1969, 1970 and in a play-off with Cork Hibs in 1971 gave way to midtable mediocrity. Managers came and went like the seasons. Arthur Fitzsimons, Frank O'Neill, Billy Young and Paddy Ambrose all tried between 1969 and 1972. Even Liam Tuohy returned for a season in 1972/73. The 1975/76 season was a new low with the humiliation of their first bottom placed finish under former Republic of Ireland manager Mick Meagan. Something had to be done.

Sean Thomas, whose pedigree was undeniable, having led Rovers to league and cup success before working his magic down the road at Bohemians, again took charge of the hot seat. The following season Shamrock Rovers battled their way through a group of Dundalk, Shelbourne and Home Farm and then a semi-final against Cobh Ramblers to reach their first final since 1969 in the shape of a newly revamped League Cup.

Although not as popular as the Blue Riband, there wouldn't be any Arsene Wegner throw-the-kids-out-there mentality and a goal from Mick Leech in the final on October 6 against Sligo Rovers gave the Hoops the 1976 League Cup and a collective sigh of relief was breathed around Milltown.

> *"The League Cup win proved significant as we had young players like Robbie Gaffney, Larry Wyse and Harry McCue in the side, but signing for Rovers second time round was different for me. The game just seemed more physical. I remember we won the first couple of games of the next season before we met Dundalk around the time Jim McLaughlin was making his mark with them. And those boys were big. Players like Tommy McConville, Paddy Dunning and Hilary Carlyle, I don't think there was one guy under six foot in the team."*
> – Mick Leech

A true legend of Irish football arrived in 1977 to begin a six-year stint with the club. Johnny Giles needs no introduction, but I'm going to give him one anyway. The midfielder started his career under Matt Busby at Manchester United before moving on to Leeds (Busby still admits it was one of his biggest mistakes letting him go) and by that point had already been player-manager of the Republic since 1973, combining the job with club management at West Brom. Resigning from the Hawthorns in 1977, Giles came back to Dublin (bringing the lovable Eamon Dunphy with him) the same year and took over the reins at Milltown.

In his first full season Rovers finished fourth but beat Sligo Rovers to win the 1978 FAI Cup (Rovers' 21st) with a goal courtesy of Ray Treacy. Passports were at the ready again as the Hoops took their first trip into Europe for ten years to play Cypriot side Apoel FC in the 1978/79 Cup Winners Cup. There they recorded victory over two legs for the first time since 1966 with a 3-0 aggregate win, but came up against a different proposition in Czech side Banik

Ostrava in the next leg, going down 6-1 to a side who eventually went out at the semi-finals stage.

A new breed of players emerged at the club, among them striker Alan Campbell who won the Golden Boot for his 22 goals that season, and then bettered it by two in 1984. A runners-up spot in the 1981/82 championship led to Shamrock Rovers competing on the continent again where they recorded their biggest victory in Europe against Icelandic outfit Fram Reykjavik (or Knattspyrnufelagio Fram as they like to be known – that language must be a doddle!), before going out to Romanian side FC Universitatea Craiova (trust me, I'm not making these names up).

Another manager of pedigree arrived in 1983 in the shape of Jim McLaughlin. Brought in by the Kilcoyne Family who owned the club at the time, the Derry native had already made a name in management under Dundalk and just picked up where he left off having arrived on the longest day of the year in 1983, June 21st.

With a side including players like Pat Byrne, Liam Buckley, Peter Eccles, Mick Neville, Dermot Keely, Kevin Brady and the ever reliable Jody Byrne, Shamrock Rovers won their first league title in twenty years on April 1, 1984, making fools of Shelbourne in a 3-1 defeat to finish six points clear of their most hated rivals Bohemians in a season where they'd won an impressive 19 of 26 games.

Hitting a purple patch that Prince would have been proud of, Rovers began another period of domination not seen since, well, the last time they had a period of domination! Between 1983-87 the club recreated both dominant eras of the fifties and sixties. With more or less the same core of players, the Hoops won four League of Ireland titles in a row (three under the wily Derryman) and two FAI Cups (the 1987 League and Cup double came under Dermot Keely's watch).

> *"I had my own ideas for running the club but to be honest I was blessed I had so many good players at Shamrock Rovers. Getting Pat Byrne was very important to us and I was delighted he signed on his return from England. At the time we had some outstanding individuals, take for instance young strikers like Alan Campbell and Liam Buckley, but it was always about how the team performed as a whole – that was always the most important thing to me."* – Jim McLaughlin

A year later the title was retained, again with the Gypsies playing bridesmaids much to the delight of the Glenmalure faithful. Surprisingly, the threat came from outside the capital in McLaughlin's last year in charge as Tony

Mannion's Galway United put together a 16 game unbeaten run to lead the league coming to the closing stages of the 1985/86 season, until a 3-1 win at Terryland Park turned the tide in the Hoops' favour and they clinched the title with a last day defeat of Cork City. UCD beat them in the 1984 FAI Cup final but both Uniteds – Galway and Waterford – then felt the wrath of those defeats as they were put to the sword in the 1985 and 1986 FAI Cup finals.

McLaughlin passed the keys of the Porsche on to Dermot Keely soon after, and the Home Farm man with a passion for algebra drove the finely-tuned Glenmalure machine to more victory, clinching a League and Cup double in his first season in charge. The championship was a canter with nine points to spare from Dundalk, and the Lilywhites also suffered in the 1987 FAI Cup final where goals from Harry Kenny, Noel Larkin and Mick Byrne completed the double. Seriously, I'd wish they'd stop winning stuff as it's taking up too much space!

> *"I always knew I would go into management and being in charge of that Rovers side was the best job in Irish football at the time. Although I'd been at UCD and Home Farm this seemed a natural progression to take over at Milltown, having played and won titles under Jim. I had such quality to work with. You could say it made my job a little bit easier!"* – **Dermot Keely**

Between February 3, 1984 and February 12, 1988, Rovers had won 15 of their 16 FAI Cup ties, taken home the trophy three times, with only that 1984 Cup final defeat against the Students of UCD to blot their copybook. Amazingly, it was UCD again that stopped that run on that day in February 1988!

During that dominant period Shamrock Rovers also competed in four consecutive European Cup campaigns for the first time ever. The first of the four started in 1984/85 with a disappointing exit to IFA club Linfield. The Northerners won through a David Jeffrey away goal in Milltown, and though Peter Eccles equalized it wasn't enough and the Belfast club walked away with bragging rights. Defeats to Budapest Honved (5-1) followed a year later, whilst a slightly more famed Hoops arrived at Milltown in 1986 when David Hay's Glasgow Celtic nicked a 1-0 win before finishing off the job at Parkhead.

> *"The atmosphere in Milltown at the time was probably the best in the country. It certainly had the best pitch! It was immaculate. To play a team like Celtic there, a club who had so much similarity to Rovers, and the return leg in Parkhead was simply one of my best experiences I ever had as a player."* – **Paul Doolin**

Defeat to the Glaswegians may have been expected. Defeat to Cypriot side Omonia a year later wasn't.

Not that the Rovers faithful were too worried at that point as one of the most tragic events of Irish football was unfolding before the watching public in 1987. There had been whispers among sportwriters of the Kilcoyne Family selling Glenmalure Park with the aim of relocating the club to Tolka Park to share with Home Farm. However when journalist Charlie Stewart broke the story in the *Irish Press* full-scale war broke out between Louie Kilcoyne and the Milltown faithful. Fans vented their anger, matches at Tolka Park were boycotted, and the KRAM (Keep Rovers at Milltown) group took up several column inches during the standoff. Brought to its knees with no revenue, no crowd and no compromise, Milltown closed its doors forever after an FAI Cup semi-final against Sligo Rovers on April 12, 1987, with Mick Byrne scoring the final goal at the famous old venue. As one fan remarked, "It was our altar. Our religion. And we worshipped there."

> *"To be honest, I wasn't sure how long Milltown would have lasted even if it wasn't closed. At the time it was on a main road out of the city, with no parking. Look at how facilities changed from the nineties to what they are now. Going to Tallaght Stadium is a great experience."* – Mick Leech

The Kilcoyne family sold their interest in Shamrock Rovers a year later to a consortium led by John McNamara, but efforts to buy back the lush green grass at Glenmalure proved fruitless. The ground was demolished in 1990. What a waste and shameful end to a ground embedded into the memory of League of Ireland fans everywhere.

A move into an area more common with horse droppings, oval balls and unfortunately Jon Bon Jovi concerts saw the Hoops share the RDS with showjumping fanatics and Leinster rugby from 1990, however their first game there on September 16, 1990 against St. Patrick's Athletic was attended by 22,000.

Noel King spent four years at the helm in a period where Vinnie Arkins came to prominence, before Ray Treacy took a break from itineraries, arrivals and plane tickets to lead the Hoops to the 1993/94 League of Ireland title. Treacy's side had a full seven point winning margin and an unstoppable striker in Stephen Geoghegan, who came to within four goals of equalling Bobby Fullam's 27 goal haul in the 1928/29 season.

Ray might have wished he was back at the travel agency that autumn as Rovers endured the worst ninety minutes in their European football history when Polish side Gornik Zabrze annihilated them 7-0 in Poland. Irish sides

Mick Byrne contesting the ball as Rovers play their first game in the RDS against St. Pat's, September 16, 1990 (photo credit: Ray McManus/Sportsfile)

aren't generally expected to last longer than November in European Competition each year, but this was an awful result, one that Ray Treacy admitted the club was ill prepared for.

The nineties ended with John McNamara selling his interest in the club, a League Cup final, an Intertoto Cup thriller with Turkish side Altay (losing 5-4) and some talk about a new pitch. Ah yes. Tallaght.

Tallaght Stadium was first brought to public attention in 1996, shortly after John McNamara had sold his stake to a new consortium. The idea was to have a 10,000 all-seater stadium, however local residents had a thing or two to say about that. More red tape followed and when planning permission was finally granted in 2000 Rovers ran out of money! Yet more legal issues followed and when the South Dublin City Council refused planning permission for a further extension in 2004 the whole idea had the ring of Cork's Bishopstown ground, or a certain politician who wanted to name a national stadium after himself.

By the new millennium former Rovers legend Damien Richardson was now at the helm after the club had been struggling to make an impact for some time. He brought them to a runners-up spot behind 2002 league champions Shelbourne and qualified for the UEFA Cup where Swedish outfit Djurgarden proved too strong. Sean Francis and Noel Hunt had hit double figures in consecutive seasons, and the Hoops still had the raw young talent of Trevor Molloy, Tony Grant, Glen Fitzpatrick and Shane Robinson in their arsenal.

"It was a difficult time at the club. At one stage we had about 18 different training grounds and two of them were public parks! Perhaps the most difficult thing however was running out at Santry Stadium – quite possibly the worst venue ever to play a game of football. It's fair to say I'd seen both sides of the coin having been a supporter of the club since I was seven then joining them as a young man and been grateful of the good times. But you learn more about yourself during times like this and you persevere because I believe romance is an integral part of the game of football." – **Damien Richardson**

A year later they qualified for the Intertoto Cup and beat Polish opposition home and away in Orda Wodzislaw (making up for the debacle of Gornik Zabrze), before going out to Czech side FC Slovan Liberec 4-0 over two legs. Although adored by their huge loyal fanbase there was always spitting venom from several directions from those envious of the Ringsend club's success. What goes up most come down didn't seem to apply a club not familiar with the rules of physics. However, that all changed in 2005.

For the first time in the club's illustrious history, Shamrock Rovers was relegated from the top flight of Irish football. Under Roddy Collins the Hoops had made a poor start to the season and a further blow came in the shape of an eight point deduction for alleged financial irregularities. It led to a promotion/relegation play-off in November 2005. The opposition – Dublin City Football Club. The Dublin City that Roddy Collins used to manage. The Dublin City Roddy had left to join Rovers. If you were a Hoops fan, this had bad news written all over it.

Despite being overwhelming underdogs, Dublin City had pulled off a 2-1 victory at Dalymount Park in the first leg to put them in the driving seat. Rovers' fate was sealed in the second leg on November 25, 2005. There might have been a touch of irony about the surname of Dublin City's next goalscorer as Robbie Collins put City 3-1 ahead, and though Derek Treacy pulled the game level two minutes later it wouldn't be enough. For the first time since their introduction to the Free State League in 1922, Shamrock Rovers, the most successful club in Ireland, was relegated. Depressed, humiliated and with the sniggering of several Dublin clubs echoing in their ears, Rovers picked themselves up, dusted themselves down and under former legend Pat Scully started life in the First Division. Their stay there was brief.

Playing their first game outside the top flight in 84 years against Dundalk on March 10, 2006, a 2-1 victory that day proved crucial as Rovers, with the loss of just three games and a goal difference of +40 (of which Tadgh Purcell helped with a dozen) won the 2006 First Division championship, pipping their opponents that day, Dundalk, by a point, and returning the Hoops to the Premier Division for the first time of asking.

In 2007 there was a comfortable fifth place finish, and then the rather surprising departure of Pat Scully, replaced by Michael O'Neill, who left Scottish club Brechin City to manage the Dubliners. He brought in several players including Ollie Cahill, Steven Bradley and some unknown Glaswegian called Gary Twigg, who had been on the books at the Scottish Second Division club. Again, Rovers comfortably held their Premier Division status in 2008.

Finally, on Friday the 13th of March (of all days) Tallaght Stadium opened its doors to the public when Shamrock Rovers hosted Sligo Rovers in their first home game of the 2009 Premier Division season. Ironically, Sligo had played in the last game at Rovers' beloved Milltown in April 1987. A crowd of 3,000 saw Gary Twigg become the first man to score in Tallaght Stadium in a 2-1 win over the Bit O'Red.

The prolific Gary Twigg celebrates yet another goal (photo credit: Fergus McNally)

The feel-good factor had reached proportions that only an illegal drug (or seeing Wayne Rooney lose his hair) could possibly equal. With the wind in their sails, Shamrock Rovers ended up finishing runners-up behind Bohemians in the Premier Division that season, earning themselves a Europa League spot. With so many great European nights and historic moments behind them on the continent, Tallaght Stadium sooner or later needed to sample a slice of that nostalgia. That time came when Juventus was added to the names of

Manchester United, Bayern Munich, Valencia and Glasgow Celtic as the Italian giants came to Dublin on July 29, 2010 in the Europa League.

Having produced a magnificent away performance against Israeli club Bnei Yehunda to get there in the first place, Rovers knew this was the plum tie of the third qualifying round. A capacity crowd piled into Tallaght Stadium hoping for a glimpse of Alexandro Del Piero – oh, and for a home win of course.

The Hoops didn't secure that victory (going down to two Amauri goals) but the former darling of the Azzurri did oblige with a cameo appearance in the last eight minutes. Del Piero notched the only goal of the game a week later in the Stadio Alberto Braglia to secure a 3-0 aggregate win with a sizeable Rovers contingent making the trip, though they did get to see Del Piero walk off with his Woodies DIY Rovers shirt at the end!

The real magic, however, was left for a cold October night in Bray last year when Shamrock Rovers won their first league championship in 16 years. Having played catch up to Pat Fenlon's Bohemians for most of the Premier Division championship, an unexpected slip by the Gypsies away to Galway United in the penultimate week left O'Neill's men in the driving seat for the last week of the season, and on Friday, October 29 last year a sea of Green and White hooped shirts from every age and size made the short 12-mile trip south to the Carlisle Grounds in Bray to see goals from Tommy Stewart and 20-goal man Gary Twigg seal the title in a 2-2 draw, despite Bohemians winning against Dundalk.

The year 2011 marked the 110th anniversary of the Ringsend club that started out as a side under British rule in a corner of Dublin embedded into football folklore, and has continued as a footballing dynasty that draws admiration and jealousy in one breath. Loved and hated over the course of 90 minutes, but through it all, undeniably our nation's most successful club.

Ground Info

An impressive ground which seats almost 6,000 people, Tallaght Stadium was a modern day soap opera with a plotline of twists and turns that ran for over a decade before Rovers could finally move into the ground in 2009.

The main West Stand houses just over 3,000 people, whilst the facing East Stand is 100 seats shy of the same number. The lay-out of the stadium also means there's plenty of room to expand. There's a members' car park which holds close to 200 cars at the back of the ground, but unless you're a member you'll be parking across the street.

Record Attendance

10,600 v Real Madrid (Friendly, July 20, 2009)
Shamrock Rovers record attendance at Milltown was 24,000 v Waterford in 1968

Cost

Adults, unreserved seating: €15.00
Students and Senior Citizens: €10.00
Children (under 14): €7.00

Programme

€4.00 – Bigger size + smaller font = a winning formula. Plenty in the 52 page *Hoops Scene* to keep me entertained. Good balance of retro articles and current news. There didn't seem to be a lack of sponsors between the pages either, so the club seems to be in demand. Some good contributors as well, including Robert Goggins whose wrote the definite history of the club.

Rivals

Though the Hoops would be rivals to a lot of clubs in the capital and around the country, for Shamrock Rovers' fans there can be only one – Bohemians Football Club.

Mascot

Is it a bird, is it a plane? No, it's a Celtic version of the "Man of Steel" running around Tallaght Stadium in his spare time. Hooperman – the Shamrock Rovers' mascot – has endeared himself to all ages at the ground. He got a soaking on my visit but that didn't deter him from hopping around like a lunatic.

Food and Drink

Burger, chips and a drink for €5.00? I'll have some of that! There are six different outlets for fans to quench their thirst or stuff themselves silly around the ground.

The Trophy Room is a coffee shop to the front of the main entrance where you can sip on a latte and curse the memorabilia around you if you're not a Hoops fan! The Glenmalure Suite in the main stand is open to club members only on match days.

Club Shop

The club Megastore is located at the front of the building where practically everything you'd want in Rovers' merchandise is on sale, and that now includes your very own Shamrock Rovers prepaid MasterCard!

Websites

www.shamrockrovers.ie – club website
www.srfc-ultras.com – fans' website

Local Radio

98 FM is a sponsor of the club so look no further.

The Match – Shamrock Rovers v Dundalk (Airtricity League, Premier Division, June 21, 2011)

Six yellow cards, four goals, good crowd, great game. Just how Rovers came away with a point I'll never know. Well, I do actually. They got two goals in the last ten minutes and for the first time on my travels I got a soaking.

Dundalk had taken the lead on 23 minutes courtesy of Mark Griffin, and the Lilywhites extended the lead on the hour, again through Griffin from a Ross Gaynor free-kick. Despite the fact I had no coat and only a pink bib above my clothes as an article of warmth, I learned from previous experience that leaving a ground early almost certainly results in goals. So I hung on, Rovers got two in the last ten minutes (Turner, Dennehy) and drove home having actually seen all the action.

Shelbourne FC

Formed: **1895**

Ground: **Tolka Park**

Capacity: **4,750**

Nickname: **Shels**

"It was the best and worst night of my managerial career."
– Dermot Keely, on seeing Shelbourne go 3-0 up against Rangers in the
UEFA Cup only to lose 5-3

I will always remember a particular half-time cup of tea in late August 2004. Jeff Stelling was presenting his *Gillette Soccer Special* with his usual dry wit, and Phil Thompson was still harping on about Liverpool, but it was the flash on the screen of two football teams, Deportivo La Coruna and Shelbourne, along with the numbers 0-0 that raised my eyebrows to the rafters.

The Dubliners were holding the Spanish giants scoreless at half-time in the second leg of their final third qualifying round match in the Champions League. Shelbourne was a possible 45 minutes from becoming the first Irish side to play in the group stages of the greatest club competition in the world. Alas, the fairytale would not materialise but it was a moment in time for a League of Ireland club, almost making the impossible dream come true.

Shelbourne has been knocking about for 116 years now. Founder members of the league, winners of both national cups north and south of the border, a club who has won almost every major honour in the land, yet like many came close to closure. Founded in 1895 by a group of men led by James Rowan, and taking their name from nearby Shelbourne Road, the club had a whip-round, bought a set of kit and played their first games at Havelock Square, just behind the north terrace of Lansdowne Road (or the Aviva Stadium if you like).

The Shelbourne side that won the 1906 IFA Cup and Leinster Senior Cup
Standing (L-R): *Kelly, Heslin, Rowe, McGrath, Ledwidge, Monks (trainer)*
Seated (L-R): *John Owens, Byrne, Harris (capt.), James Owen and Clery.*
Sitting: *Abbott, Wall (photo credit: Peter Byrne,* Football Association of Ireland: 75 years*)*

In 1904, Shelbourne joined the only game in town – the Irish League north of the border – and competed along with Bohemians as the only other southern side in the competition. In March 1905 they made the Irish Cup final but lost out to Distillery in front of 13,000 at Solitude, home of Cliftonville FC. Despite that defeat there was only a delay of twelve months as a year later the Dubliners, captained by Ringsend-born and bred Val Harris, beat Belfast Celtic 2-0 in the IFA Cup and became the first southern club to win the trophy in a game played at Dalymount Park. Shelbourne lost successive cup finals in 1907 and 1908, though clinched the competition again against Bohemians in 1911. The 1908 final, also against Bohemians, became the first to feature two clubs south of the border and showcased the talents of Bill Lacey, who later played for Everton and then won two league titles with Liverpool. Soon

*Just another Dublin Derby – St. Patrick's Athletic v Shamrock Rovers
(photo credit: Andy McDonnell)*

*St. Patrick's captain Damien Lynch sides in on Ger O'Brien of Sporting Fingal
– a club sadly now defunct (photo credit: Andy McDonnell)*

Waterford and Sligo Rovers line up for a minute's silence in memory of the Munich Air Disaster, 1958

St. James Gate – 1921/22 Free State League and Cup Champions (photo courtesy of St. James Gate)

Cork away fans watch the action at Salthill Devon
(photo credit: Tony Tobin)

Shamrock Rovers and Cork Hibernians get acquainted during a 1962 league game
(photo courtesy of Plunkett Carter)

Andy McEvoy, centre, with the FAI Cup and some happy Limerick AFC fans after winning the 1971 FAI Cup (photo credit: Aidan Corr)

UCD's Samir Belhout in slightly dramatic pose (photo credit: Fergus McNally)

Memories are made of this – the famous Shed End at Turner's Cross (photo credit: stadionweld.de)

Limerick FC v Waterford FC, 1960
(photo courtesy of Brian O'Brien)

Cork City in action against Wexford Youths
(photo credit: Tony Tobin and Alan Mooney)

Galway United run out at a newly revamped Terryland Park, 1994
(photo credit: Paul O'Brien)

Terry Harkin scores for Finn Harps against Aberdeen – UEFA Cup, 1973
(photo credit: Derry Journal)

An excitable bunch of Galway United ball-boys before the Lynby game in 1985

Pat Devlin is all smiles as he collects the FAI Cup in 1999
(photo credit: Michael Tierney)

Benny the Bull, the Sligo mascot, helps the author celebrate completion of his visits to all 21 grounds in the League of Ireland

after, in 1913, the club moved to Shelbourne Park, which became their home for the next 37 years.

The formation of a new Free State League in 1921 saw Shelbourne enter its inaugural season finishing third behind Bohemians and champions St. James Gate. Shels quickly got into their stride finishing runners-up the following two seasons, before taking their first League of Ireland championship in 1925/26 with the loss of just one game, with Jock Simpson's 18 goals one of the main factors in the two points that separated them and Shamrock Rovers. The club did not finish outside the top two for the next five seasons, taking the title again in 1928/29 and 1930/31 when Scotsman Alex Hair hit 29 goals in just 22 matches! Sammy McIlvenny also managed 22 in the 1927/28 season in 29 games. Astonishing tallies from both strikers. Either that or the defending was atrocious.

An almighty row with the Free State FA over the national side arranging a game the same day as the Dubliners, astonishingly, ended in Shelbourne's resignation from the league in 1934, though they rejoined two seasons later.

The good times returned and with it the club's first Free State Cup victory in 1939 when they defeated Sligo Rovers with a William "Sacky" Glen free kick after just two minutes in a replay after the first game ended 1-1. John Feenan became one of the club's first managers (before that it was committees picking the team) in 1942, having been at the club two years playing with players like Paddy Bradshaw and Willie Fallon, and kept the momentum going. Another League of Ireland title arrived in 1943/44 and the club was denied a treble (they had won the Shield) by Shamrock Rovers in the FAI Cup final that season, going down 3-2 despite goals from Willie Fanning and Mick McCluskey.

But it was an age of greatness for the club that had challenged the dominance of Shamrock Rovers and Bohemians. Between all three clubs they won 16 of the first 25 league titles. Drumcondra was pipped for the title (Shelbourne's fifth) in 1947 and a move away from the Greyhound Stadium materialised in 1949 with a 2-2 draw against Waterford being the last competitive game played at Shelbourne Park. Shelbourne Stadium in Irishtown was supposed to be the club's permanent new ground, but it was another three decades before the Reds owned their own pad. Despite a combined total of 12 league and shield triumphs to that point, it was proving a real pain in the arse to bring the FAI Cup back to the club's trophy cabinet.

Hopes were high in 1951 after seeing off Waterford, Shamrock Rovers and Drumcondra, with Tommy Carberry scoring in every round, but Shelbourne fell at the final hurdle to a Johnny Vaughan goal for Cork Athletic, losing 1-0 in a replay. Bob Thomas was responsible for Shelbourne's first league title of the fifties, pipping Drumcondra to the 1952/53 championship. Central to the club's success at the time were players like Martin Colfer and forward Rory Dwyer, who hit over 60 goals for the club in three seasons.

David Jack then took over the manager's reins from Thomas. The Lancastrian-born inside forward played almost 300 games with his native Bolton, and notched 113 goals in 180 appearances for Arsenal, before ending up on our shores, and it was seen as a coup to have him managing at the time, although he stayed for just two seasons.

Despite great work being carried out by volunteers, the club only played one season in their Shelbourne Stadium as it offered no shelter from the primary import into Ireland – rain – so the club had to hop into bed with Drumcondra at Tolka Park.

Gerry Doyle then broke a 21-year hoodoo and finally landed Shelbourne their second FAI Cup with a 2-0 victory over Cork Hibernians on April 24, 1960. Having got there via Bohemians, Shamrock Rovers and Dundalk, goals from Eric Barber and Joey Wilson took the trophy from Cork Hibernians. That team included players like Finbarr Flood, Theo Dunne, Brendan O'Brien

1960 FAI Cup winners Back Row (L-R): *Eric Barber, Christy Doyle, Tony Dunne, Jack Kelly, Finbarr Flood, Brendan O'Brien* Front Row (L-R): *Jack Hennessy, Ollie Conroy, Joey Wilson, Theo Dunne, Freddie Strahan (mascots and name of black cat not known!) (photo courtesy of Shelbourne Football Club)*

and Jack Kelly. The unlucky Andy Fitzpatrick, Shelbourne's wing-half and captain, would miss out that day through injury.

"Although it was a huge occasion playing in an FAI Cup final and most of us were still only 19 or 20, we really had no fear. We were just excited and took it all in our stride. I remember my goal well as I lobbed it from about 40 yards! The ball came to me just past the half way line and I'd seen Sean O'Brien off his line so I took it down off my chest and drove it high in the air towards him. I was delighted when it flew over him and ended up in the net!" – **Eric Barber**

"I was delighted with the victory as I had to play the game with three fingers strapped together. I'd injured them in our semi-final victory over Dundalk and I knew I'd have to look after myself in the final. Back in those days goalkeepers didn't get any protection. If you ever see old photographs of goalkeepers catching a ball from the sixties you can be sure their knees are up in it!" – **Finbarr Flood**

Doyle was a visionary. Having seen the youth team win the FAI Youth Cup in 1959, he promoted six of that side into the senior team, one of which was an 18-year-old left-back called Tony Dunne. Less than ten years later, the Dubliner won the most prestigious medal in world club football, winning the European Cup with Manchester United, and went on to make over 400 appearances at Old Trafford. Gerry was still in charge when the club added their seventh League of Ireland championship in 1961/62, this time in the first play-off game in league history against Cork Celtic.

"I remember playing Cork Celtic in probably the last game of the season that year down in Turner's Cross with both of us level on points. We should have got absolutely hammered that day but John Heavey in goal was absolutely brilliant. To say he kept us in the game was an understatement. Coming off the field at the end we knew we held the psychological advantage going into the play-off." – **Freddie Strahan**

Both sides finished on 35 points – unable to be separated after 22 games. The play-off game took place at Dalymount Park, and a Ben Hannigan goal was the deciding factor as Doyle's men clinched the title. The elusive double however had to be put on hold as Shamrock Rovers defeated Shelbourne in the 1962 FAI Cup final. The sixties produced players like Jackie Hennessy, Eric Barber, Christy Doyle, Freddie Strahan and Tommy Carroll, who were all capped for the Republic.

A first trip into Europe came about in September 1962 when the Dubliners drew Sporting Lisbon in the European Cup. The game was played at Dalymount Park but Sporting, a side who had won 11 national titles in their homeland, came away with victory in Dublin. The first goalscorer in that 2-0 win was Joao Morais, a tough-nut international who produced one of the worst tackles (one of many) on Pele during the 1966 World Cup, when the Brazilian was literally kicked off the field. The second leg ended in a 5-1 defeat with Jackie Hennessy becoming the first Shelbourne player to score in Europe.

A third FAI Cup came the way of Doyle's men again in 1963 when Shelbourne beat Cork Hibs in a carbon copy of the 1960 final, with the same result – 2-0. This put the Reds into the 1963/64 Cup Winners Cup and a tie with Barcelona. The Catalan giants arrived in the Emerald Isle firmly in the shadow of the great Real Madrid side of Di Stefano and Puskas in one of the leaner periods of their history, but won 2-0 in Dublin and 3-1 at home (though Shelbourne frightened the life out of them by taking the lead in that game through a Paddy Bonham penalty). The Catalans went out to Hamburg in the next round.

A significant success was achieved in the 1964/65 Inter-Cities Fairs Cup when Shelbourne progressed past the first round in European competition for the first time with an impressive play-off victory against Portuguese side Belenenses. Both legs finished 1-1 and 0-0 (away goals didn't count), but goals from Mick Conroy and Eric Barber in a play-off match sent the Reds through to meet Athletico Madrid. Again, the Irishmen acquitted themselves well, only going down 2-0 on aggregate to a Spanish side that went all the way to the semi-finals.

Shelbourne's Jimmy O'Connor in action against Shamrock Rovers. Jimmy's 2 minute 13 second hat-trick against Bohemians on November 19, 1967 still holds the world record for the fastest hat-trick in domestic football (photo credit: Connolly Collection/Sportsfile)

Gerry Doyle left the club in 1965, but came back two years later, though Shels had to wait until 1971 to taste success again when Noel Quinn scored the winner in a second replay against Athlone Town in the final of the 1971 League of Ireland Shield. The club entered Europe that season, acquitting themselves well before going down to Hungarian side Vasas.

That League of Ireland Shield success had to be savoured as, amazingly, it was the last taste of silverware for the club for 20 years. Though Shelbourne reached the 1973 FAI Cup final (with Cork Hibs finally getting revenge for losing to Shels in 1960 and '63), the club went through a lean period and attendances weren't the only thing falling. In 1974, Shelbourne propped up the league table, winning just four games and collecting 13 points all season. With *Match of the Day* coming to prominence and English football more accessible through television, Shelbourne wasn't the only team suffering a big drop in revenue since the fifties and sixties.

Doyle departed soon after as one of his protégées, Tommy Carroll, stepped in the hot-seat, but Shelbourne continued to struggle. Despite not finishing once in the top half of the table for the rest of the decade, there was a 1975 FAI Cup final, however Shelbourne became part of Home Farm's history for all the wrong reasons that April as the former Leinster Senior League side won the cup 1-0 in only their third full season in the league, thus becoming the first all-amateur side to lift the famous old trophy since Bohemians in 1935. Things got decidedly worse before they got better.

The eighties brought a bottom-placed finish, financial woes and eventually the dreaded "R" word in the 1985/86 season. A dismal year in which Shelbourne won a paltry three games from 22 and managed to hit just 15 goals saw the club relegated after 65 years of top flight football. Former Rovers' legend Paddy Mulligan left in a season that also saw the club temporarily set up at Harold's Cross.

In life you find prosperity is a great teacher, but adversity a better one. Under John Byrne, Shelbourne made an immediate return at their first attempt, finishing runners-up in the First Division championship to Derry City. One Byrne made way for another in 1988. Former Shamrock Rovers' man Pat Byrne had won every accolade in the game and moved to Tolka Park after five successful years at Glenmalure. Under Pat Byrne, Shelbourne avoided any drop back down, slowly building on to a comfortable seventh place in 1989/90. It was here that Byrne dipped from the pool of Glenmalure greatness. In 1990 Mick Neville and Jody Byrne came across town to Tolka Park, and with some more astute signings in Athlone striker Padraig Dully and Huddersfield hitman Gary Haylock, whilst nurturing the talent of players like midfielder Brian

Flood, the Reds went on to win the 1991/92 League of Ireland championship – their first in 30 years.

> *"I remember when I was at Bohemians seeing this guy pop into the home dressing room at Dalymount on occasion not having a clue who he was but he was always chatting to Billy Young. Somebody had said he was playing for Hearts at the time. Little did I know it was Pat Byrne and he'd be my boss a few years later at Shelbourne and help me win an FAI Cup medal."* – **Paul Doolin**

The title race had seen Derry and Cork City push Byrne's men all season long, but despite all the signings Byrne made it was the right foot of 21-year-old Flood that secured the title from 35 yards, when Shelbourne saw off Dundalk 3-1 in Oriel Park on the last day of the season in 1992. This meant a trip abroad and European competition for the first time in 20 years – unheard of in the club's history. But Byrne's men were grateful and tested Ukrainian champions (Christ, here we go again with another dyslexic spelling) SC Tavriya Simferpol, holding them scoreless in Tolka Park before losing 2-1 away. However, going into Europe as Irish champions was a proud return to form.

Central to the revival in fortunes was Tony Donnelly. The club chairman helped the club move from Harold's Cross in 1989 and transformed Drumcondra's former ground of Tolka Park into the finest stadium in the land. A heavy investment by the Donnelly family saw Shelbourne begin to dominate

Manager Pat Byrne (left) Fred Davis (middle) and Jim McLaughlin get ready to party after Shelbourne's '93 FAI Cup final victory over Dundalk (photo credit: David Maher/Sportsfile)

League of Ireland football in the '90s. Though Derry beat them in the 1993/94 League Cup final, Shelbourne took the FAI Cup in 1993. It wasn't just any old cup though as it ended a 30 year wait, way back to Cork Hibernians in April 1963. Greg Costello was the hero against Dundalk at Lansdowne Road as it was his effort that took the famous old trophy back to a cabinet it had last seen when a four-piece combo called the Beatles were just starting off.

The good times kept coming. That summer Shelbourne claimed their first victory in Europe since 1965 by extracting revenge on Ukrainian football by knocking out FC Karpaty Lviv 3-2 on aggregate in the Cup Winners Cup, before going out to Greek giants Panathinaikos. There was a rather disappointing UEFA Cup exit to Icelandic opposition in Akranes in 1995, and then to Norwegians Brann a year later, but 1995/96 was really all about a magnificent cup double under Damien Richardson. The League Cup was sitting pretty in the boardroom after a November win over Sligo Rovers in an epic final that saw the Dubliners come from behind with two late goals and then beat Sligo on penalties.

Five months later it was joined by the big one as Shelbourne beat St. Patrick's Athletic in the 1996 FAI Cup final in even more dramatic circumstances. As early as the 18th minute Shelbourne goalkeeper Alan Gough was sent off for a professional foul, and with no sub goalkeeper the Dubliners were forced to play an outfield player in goal for the remaining seventy minutes. Brian Flood, the man who had won Shelbourne's first title in 30 years back in 1992, stood in between the posts and held Athletic out until 15 minutes from time when Dave Campbell scored for the Saints. Astonishingly, Tony Sheridan equalised with two minutes left to force a replay for the ten men and you just knew St. Patrick's wouldn't recover. Gough would be back in goal for the replay which even saw him save a penalty before Stephen Geoghegan thought it needed even more drama and hit a late winner to capture the cup after Sheridan had levelled an early St. Patrick's goal.

> *"After Alan was sent off in the first game I remember I tried to delay the resulting free-kick a little, knowing it might help break up the play, and give Brian Flood time to adjust to the situation. Tony Sheridan's equalizer was typical of his talent, undoubtedly one of the best players I've ever worked with. I learned from my time at Shamrock Rovers there was such a thing as 'cup luck', that sometimes you're name is just on a trophy. When St. Patrick's missed the penalty in the second game you just knew what the outcome would be." – Damien Richardson*

The true dominance of the Tolka Park outfit was forced home yet again a year later. By beating Derry City in the 1997 FAI Cup at Dalymount Park, with goals from Dave Campbell (who the Reds had signed from St. Pat's) and Stephen Geoghegan in a 2-0 win, Damien Richardson's Shelbourne became the first League of Ireland side to retain the Blue Riband since 1986 when a Shamrock Rovers side of the mid-eighties dominated this competition. Only Rovers and Cork Hibernians had managed to retain it since the war so Pat Scully knew he was a privileged man lifting the cup that afternoon.

It again saw the Dubliners enter Europe and they may have been sneaky favourites going into their 1997/98 Cup Winners Cup tie against Scottish Premier club Kilmarnock. It seemed that way after Mark Rutherford gave the Dubliners the lead in the first leg at Rugby Park, but the home side soon levelled, and a winner with seconds left on the clock gave "Killie" the advantage going into the second leg at Tolka Park. Again, Shelbourne took the lead at Tolka Park in the return leg, only for Kilmarnock to reply and ultimately the 1-1 draw that night put Shelbourne out.

Sligo Rovers popped up for sweet revenge in the 1998 League Cup final, but the year will be remembered for possibly the strangest European tie in the club's history. Drawing Scottish giants Rangers in the first round of the UEFA Cup, new manager Dermot Keely saw his first game in charge of the Reds played on a neutral ground. Because of security fears, potential clashes and Rangers' fans history of going slightly mad when they'd come to Dublin in the past, the game took place at Tranmere's Prenton Park. On July 22, 1998 Pat Scully led the Dubliners out as the sides faced each other in the first round of the UEFA Cup.

By the hour mark Shelbourne was 3-0 up. As incomprehensible as it seemed to those in the ground (and for us watching at home with soggy biscuits floating in tea again), goals from Mark Rutherford, Pat Morley and an earlier own goal from Porrini had Keely's men destroying the Scottish giants and there seemed no way back. Surely this was too good to be true? Well, in the end, yes it was.

Rangers got one back within 60 seconds of the third goal after Albertz scored and within 15 minutes the Scottish giants were level with further goals from Amato and Van Bronckhorst. Dick Advocaat's men completed the turnaround in the last ten minutes with two more goals to win 5-3 in one of the weirdest matches in Shelbourne's history. Oh, and the Rangers fans still went mad! (They were fined £10,000 for their behaviour at Prenton Park that night.)

"It was the best and worst night of my managerial career. Here was this scoreboard saying Shelbourne 3-0 Rangers after an hour. I

should have changed the formation straight away and shut up shop but before we knew it they'd got one back. I was like a rabbit in the headlights from there on. The best hour in management yes, and the worst half hour – certainly." – **Dermot Keely**

To finish off the most successful decade in the club's history, the League of Ireland title was clinched again in the 1999/2000 season under Dermot Keely. But it wasn't just the end to a stylish league campaign, finishing a full 11 points clear of nearest challengers Cork City; it was one half of the first league and cup double in the club's history. Having lost out in their first Intertoto Cup match (to Swiss side Neuchatel Xamax), Keely's men went unbeaten in their first 20 league games (finally losing to a Liam Coyle goal for Derry in January) and steamed clear of the opposition, wrapping up the title long before the final game of the season which they lost to Shamrock Rovers – the only two defeats in the league that season.

They then won the FAI Cup, having been drawn away in every round. St. Francis was first to fall (1-0) then a 3-2 win against feisty fellow Dubliners Bangor Celtic. Another non-league side, Bluebell United, forced Keely's men to a replay before James Keedy and Tony McCarthy goals saw them off in Tolka Park four days later. Keedy was on the mark again (along with Dessie Baker) in the semi-final at Terryland Park against Galway, before Pat Fenlon's goal on May 5, 2000 against Bohemians in an FAI Cup final replay clinched the double – something the club had been waiting over a century for.

A first trip into Europe in the new millennium that autumn saw Richie Baker score a vital away goal to give Shelbourne a win on the road against Macedonians Sloga Jugomagnat (I think in future I'll just say, "an eastern European team"), and the first away win for any League of Ireland club in 18 years to that point.

"That meant a lot. Europe used to mean a nice trip, some duty free and maybe a suntan. It was all about the holiday but times were rapidly changing, and the 'moral victory' was going out the window. It was great to get the monkey off the back and I think that win changed things for us and Irish clubs in Europe." – **Dermot Keely**

Tolka Park was rocking in late July when 10,000 crammed in to watch Shels take on regular Champions League group qualifiers Rosenborg. Had this tie taken place twenty years previously you'd have probably put your mortgage on the Irish club, as Norwegian football was about as effective as a chocolate fireguard. Rosenborg had made a habit of upsetting the odds at that point, however, and were making a name for themselves in Europe, so it wasn't that much of a surprise that despite a spirited fight and a Richie Foran goal, the

Dermot Keely celebrates with Pat Scully after Shelbourne knock Sloga Jogomagnat out of the Champions League (photo credit: David Maher/Sportsfile)

Norwegians won 3-1 at Tolka Park, though Foran would score again to at least secure a 1-1 draw in the away leg.

The juggernaut rolled on. Despite a defeat to Brondby in the UEFA Cup the summer of 2001, Keely's last season in charge saw the 2001/02 title won back, this time at the expense of St. Patrick's Athletic in the most controversial season in league history. St. Patrick's had already sewn up the league title, but were subsequently docked 15 points over the improper registration of midfielder Charles Mbabazi Livingstone. This put Shelbourne clear at the top and the Reds collected the title and trophy instead. There could actually be another book written on the entire circumstances and arguments that raged on that season over the controversy and feuding, but we'll leave that for the sequel!

The prolific Jason Byrne arrived soon after, hitting 21 goals in his first season with the club. Players like Steve Williams, Owen Heary, Ollie Cahill, Jason Byrne, Tony McCarthy, Stephen Geoghegan and Wes Hoolahan were pivotal in the club's success around this time. Chief Executive Ollie Byrne and Chairman Finbarr Flood were putting huge resources behind the team, and the odd bit of banter about an Irish team finally making it to a Champions League group stage was thrown about on the factory floors of Ireland. Improbable – maybe? Impossible – no.

"I believed with a bit of luck it was possible. I remember before the Deportivo match chatting to Ollie about the prize money involved for getting into the Champions League group stages. According to him it was around the ten million mark and the money would actually arrive pretty quickly. Of course, in the same breath he said, 'Well, we would then need to buy three players just to be able to compete'. I asked him how much would that cost to which he replied, 'About twent-five million'. 'That's great,' I said. 'We qualify for ten million and then spend twenty-five!'" – **Finbarr Flood**

When Hibernians of Malta arrived in the autumn of 2002 it should have been the ideal opposition to launch an attack on those group stages, but Shelbourne produced an absolutely disastrous result in the second leg at Tolka Park. Even though the hard work seemed to have been accounted for in a 2-2 draw in Malta, Pat Fenlon's men looked nervy at home, but still would have progressed had it not been for a late Hibernians goal to put the Maltese through. There was no need for sugar-coating or trying to sell the impossible dream to an Irish public on that night. Shelbourne had let themselves and the believers down. A year later Champions League wouldn't even be on the menu as the Reds made do with the UEFA Cup and another disappointing exit – this time to Slovenians NK Olimpija.

An eleventh League of Ireland championship was clinched in 2003 under Pat Fenlon on the penultimate day of the season with a 2-0 win at home to Cork City to see off champions Bohemians in the interim season which saw the conversion to summer soccer.

The club aimed big again, recruiting Alan Moore who came in from Burnley. Having spent a decade with Middlesbrough before that (he was capped eight times for Ireland), it again showed the club's lofty ambitions and normal service was resumed domestically in 2004 as Shelbourne made it consecutive League of Ireland titles for the first time in their history. Cork City had pushed the Dubliners hard all season but two crucial away wins at Turner's Cross that year, along with two home draws against the Munstermen, saw Fenlon's side undefeated in their four tussles with Cork that season and a tame scoreless draw on the last day of the 2004 season away to St. Patrick's Athletic was enough to clinch a little piece of history for the club from Irishtown.

The Reds European exploits made even bigger waves that season. Mind you, Europe might not have been too worried when Shelbourne scraped past

KR Reykjavik in their first qualifying round. They were 2-0 down with ten minutes left when an Alan Moore strike and a lucky own goal grabbed precious away goals in Iceland, which saw Fenlon's side through after a scoreless stalemate at Tolka a week later.

> *"The hardest team we actually played in that Champions League run was Reykjavik. There was obvious pressure as we were expected to beat them but they were a good side and in truth we just ended up sneaking through."* – **Pat Fenlon**

However a few eyebrows were raised in the next round as Shels came up against Croatian champions Hadjuk Split. Not only had the Croats produced players like Slaven Bilic, Alen Boksic and Robert Jarni, they also played in one of the most intimidating atmospheres in European football. The Poljud Stadium holds over 35,000 and is home to the *Torcida*, a slightly passionate supporters' group. I'm not saying they're mad, but when Spurs visited for a UEFA Cup match in 1984 they slaughtered a cockerel in the centre circle before the game. Good thing Shelbourne's crest doesn't have a puppy on it.

Despite the hostility, Shels got out of Dodge with a 3-2 defeat. Having taken the lead through Glen Fitzpatrick, only to then concede three goals, Alan Moore's late goal gave the Dubliners real hope for the second leg.

> *"Hadjuk were a great side but at the end they were rattled. You could see that. There was an incident in the tunnel afterwards, and I knew we'd upset them and it became obvious they wouldn't fancy the second leg over here. The return leg at Tolka would be one of those games when absolutely 100% of our game plan went exactly according to plan."* – **Pat Fenlon**

A week later a Dave Rogers' goal on 78 minutes levelled the tie before Alan Moore's injury-time winner took the roof off of Tolka and sent 11,000 Shelbourne fans delirious. Through to the third round. The impossible dream back on.

Shelbourne was now one tie away from a place in the 2004/05 Champions' League group stage. The opponents standing in the way – Spanish club Deportivo La Coruna. Because of the interest the first leg was switched to Lansdowne Road where a tentative Shelbourne ground out a nervy 0-0 draw in front of a crowd of 24,000 against a Spanish side seemingly convinced that they could finish off the job at home.

I wonder whether there were many visits to the home dressing room toilet a fortnight later on August 24 when the score remained 0-0 after the first 45 minutes at the Riazor Stadium in La Coruna. After all, this was a Deportivo side with Spanish internationals like Manuel Pablo, Juan Valeron and Albert Luque who had reached the semi-finals of the Champions League just three months earlier! Alas, we dared to dream and got punished for that, as despite their best efforts, Shelbourne eventually went down 3-0 and the dream was over.

Despite losing it gained Shels entry into the UEFA Cup. Again, the lunatics staged a dramatic comeback a la Reykjavik with two goals in the last ten minutes against French side Lille to grab another 2-2 draw, but the French aristocrats crushed Pat Fenlon's four leaf clover in the second leg in a 2-0 defeat.

> *"I was lucky at Shelbourne to be surrounded by some great players and staff - the run in Europe was proof of that. It's easy to forget that during that eight game stretch in Europe we actually managed to retain the League of Ireland championship the same year which I thought was a big achievement. Deportivo was obviously the most crucial game. They had reached the semi-finals the year before so on paper it was daunting, though by this stage nearly all the squad had some European experience. The emphasis was to keep it tight so by half-time in La Coruna and the tie still scoreless we were delighted, but we always knew the game would open up in the last half hour. It was just a little lack in concentration that killed us, though Jason Byrne had a good chance that night for us just after 20 minutes which might have made things different. As good as Deportivo were and as tough a game we had in Reykjavik, Lille were certainly the best team we played. They had such flair and talent."* – **Pat Fenlon**

Something strange happened in 2005 – Shelbourne didn't win anything. Glentoran accounted for them in the Champions League. They then reached the first Setanta Cup final, but lost to Linfield 2-0 with the phenomenal Jason Byrne becoming the first League of Ireland player to win the Golden Boot four years in a row, having hit over 100 goals in four domestic seasons.

The 2006 season was a year of contrast for the Tolka Park outfit – a league championship, financial problems and the temporary demise of one of the nation's most honoured and respected clubs. Amid the backdrop of ongoing financial difficulty, with a wage bill considerably higher than the gates at Tolka were bringing in, Pat Fenlon led Shelbourne to the 2006 Premier Division championship beating off Derry City in one of the closest Premier Division races ever. A mere seven goals separated the sides at the end of the season with Shelbourne holding their nerve with a last day home win against Bohemians to clinch the league championship as Derry was beating Cork City.

The thirteenth title in the club's history proved to be the unluckiest. Shelbourne was forced to pull out of both the Premier Division and Setanta Cup, having not being granted a licence for the upcoming 2007 season. Derry City took their place in Europe, a mass exodus of players left Tolka Park and Pat Fenlon resigned. To make matters worse, Ollie Byrne – for so long the driving force behind Shelbourne – passed away. It looked like 101 years of history would be consigned to the record books and one of the nation's most decorated clubs would fold, ironically like another giant of yesteryear who had plied their trade at Tolka – Drumcondra. But, again, there is no education like adversity. Once again, a League of Ireland club had to gather itself from a dark well and pull themselves out.

Demoted to the First Division and with Derry City playing in Europe instead of them, it may have been a source of amusement for some to see Shelbourne slugging it out at a lower level, but the club was surviving having at least been granted that all important licence. Dermot Keely was drafted back in as manager and only a last minute slip up at home to Limerick 37 in 2008 denied Shelbourne an automatic return to Premier Division, something that the now defunct Sporting Fingal enforced in their semi-final promotion relegation play-off in 2009.

Fast approaching their 120th anniversary, Shelbourne is an institution, a cornerstone of Irish football that have produced amazing talent throughout the decades and as many memories that resonate among not only their fans but supporters of League of Ireland football. Long may it stay that way.

> *"One of my fondest memories at the time was representing the League of Ireland as a Shels' player in a game against an English First Division side in 1964. This was an English team with people like Roger Hunt, Martin Peters and Ian Callaghan who all went on to win the 1966 World Cup. It was such an honour to captain the side and a bonus to win it 2-1. I'll always remember Tony O'Connell absolutely roasting Jimmy Armfield for the entire ninety minutes!"*
> – Freddie Strahan

Did You Know?

Shels won the league in 1952/53 managed by Bob Thomas, who had won a league winners medal with Shels earlier. Bob Thomas was the uncle of future Shels club captain Theo Dunne, who in turn is the father of present Cork City manager, Thomas Dunne, and the uncle of Irish international Richard Dunne.

Ground Info

Tolka Park was the first ground in Ireland to become all-seated. The former home of Drumcondra Football Club, Tolka was transformed in the early nineties by Shelbourne at a time an all-seated stadium was unheard of in this country. For most of the eighties the club had been playing at Harold's Cross, however a major investment by Tony Donnelly led to the purchase of Tolka Park in 1989, and with it a complete overhaul of a stadium that today stands as testimony to all the hard work, time and money that's been put into it.

    Located in Dublin's Northside, the ground is easily accessible and lies on Richmond Road just off the Upper Drumcondra Road. The impressive Riverside Stand, which is partially covered, has a massive 4,000 seats with the Richmond Road stand accommodating a further 1,600. In 1999, the Drumcondra Stand was added to facilitate another 800, however safety restrictions have cut Tolka Park to a safe holding capacity of just under 5,000 (the Ballybough end, for instance, is no longer used).

    For car parking, as you approach the ground from Drumcondra, there is a small car park on your left, but there is ample roadside parking on Grace Park Road almost opposite the ground.

Record Attendance

12,000 v Manchester United (friendly, August 11, 1995). Crowds of 20,000 were a regular occurrence at Tolka in bygone days when playing local derbies against clubs like Drumcondra, Bohemians and Shamrock Rovers.

Cost

Adults: €15.00
Students: €10.00
OAPs/Children: €5.00

Programme

€3.00 – and a solid read. The SSDG (Shelbourne Supporters Development Group), who have produced and funded the programme for the past five years, took a decision that with attendances growing smaller – and consequently fewer programmes being sold – to produce one programme to cover two games, rather than printing in black and white or reducing the size, thus saving on production costs while maintaining a professional publication. It's worked well. The programme is well laid out and packed with views from some quality contributors.

Rivals

Because both clubs where founded in the Ringsend area of Dublin, Shamrock Rovers have historically been Shelbourne's biggest rivals, and though the club has built up rivalries with the like of Bohemians and St. Patrick's, The Hoops are always first in most fans' eyes.

Mascot

Alas, Shels don't have one.

Food and Drink

Bar@Tolka, the main bar under the Richmond Stand, is very popular with home supporters and does a brisk trade, whilst hot food is available on both sides of the ground. Outside of Tolka Park fan favourites include Kennedy's in Drumcondra and Smyth's in Fairview, owned by Vincent Smyth, a former director of the club.

Club Shop

Located inside the ground beside the Drumcondra Stand. Money generated here is so important to the overall finances of a League of Ireland side and Shels supporters aren't afraid to dip into their pockets if the home jerseys on display on my visit are anything to go by.

Websites

www.shelbournefc.ie – official site
www.shelschat.com – fans' forum

Local Radio

NEAR FM 90.3 (north east access radio).

The Match – Shelbourne v Limerick (First Division, April 1, 2011)

Limerick controlled most of the opening half of this First Division clash, which quickly led to one or two of the home faithful muttering ,"It's coming, its coming, I know it!" But it didn't. In fact, with just five minutes left Shelbourne took the lead through Philip Hughes which should have sent the Tolka Park faithful home happy. However, the Shannonsiders levelled things in injury time with a goal from Paudie Quinn, and I left the ground with the words, "It was coming, it was coming, I knew it!" ringing in my ears.

Sligo Rovers

Formed:	1928
Ground:	The Showgrounds
Capacity:	4,500
Nickname:	The Bit O'Red

"I was carrying an injury going into the '83 final and had to mark of all people Jackie Jameson. It was bad enough trying to mark him with two legs never mind one!" – Chris Rutherford

Many League of Ireland clubs' foundations can be attributed to local Junior League football. The "Bit O'Red" from the west of Ireland is no different. It would be the amalgamation of two local sides over 83 years ago that formed the basis of the Sligo Rovers you see today. Sligo Town and Sligo Blues played their football locally, but joined forces under a new banner, Sligo Rovers, and entered the Connaught league in 1928. Ballyshannon FC had the privilege of being Rovers' first opponents, and thoughtfully they didn't spoil the day – letting in nine goals in their Connaught Cup match!

Success was immediate, winning the national Junior Cup in their first season, beating Dubliners Grangegorman on their home turf, the Showgrounds, in front of almost 3,000 supporters. A move to the Leinster League followed and their first appearance as a non-league club in the Free State Cup popped up in 1933, beating former league side Brideville 3-1 before losing out to Shelbourne 5-2 in the quarter-finals – a Shelbourne side that had already won the League of Ireland three times to that point and possessed several Irish internationals. Not bad for a side around a mere five years.

The Bit O'Red got a taste for mixing it with the best and a year later popped up again in the first round but league side Dundalk emerged victorious 4-0. The club won a unique treble of Leinster Senior League, Intermediate Cup and Metropolitan Cup in 1934, then set their eyes on top flight football. Though many current League of Ireland clubs formed around this era, not all of them entered the league as quickly as Rovers. Longford (formed 1924) took 60 years to gain League of Ireland status, Derry City (1928) didn't kick a ball in the South for 57 years, whilst St. Patrick's Athletic (1929) didn't join the elite until 1951. Rovers, however, sat at the top table a hell of a lot sooner.

With Cork Bohemians resigning from the league at the end of the 1933/34 season, Sligo Rovers was elected for the following season, playing their first game as a League of Ireland club on August 26, 1934 against St. James Gate in the Shield, losing 5-1 with Tommy Callaghan scoring at the Iveagh Grounds that day.

Sporting players like Gerry McDaid, Paddy Monaghan and Johnny McManus, Rovers went on to an impressive first Free State League season and reached the semi-final of the Free State Cup, going down to Dundalk 2-0.

The whirlwind start in League of Ireland football continued 24 months later when Rovers became the first club outside Leinster to capture the Free State League championship in 1937. And boy did they do it in style. Now under coach Jimmy Surgeoner, Rovers took the league by storm, winning in an absolute canter finishing ten points clear with striker Harry Litherland notching 19 goals that season – still a club record. Ah, those were the days!

Without doubt the biggest name of the era to play on these shores arrived in January 1939. Birkenhead-born William Ralph Dean started his career with Tranmere Rangers, scoring 27 goals in his 30 appearances and even losing a testicle in a reserve game! The football world knew him as "Dixie". For the next 12 years Dixie Dean made 433 appearances for Everton, scoring an absolutely astonishing 383 goals. Not bad for a man who was given a £30 signing-on fee for Everton. His arrival in Sligo stunned Irish football. Such was the interest in Dixie that thousands converged on the local railway station in anticipation of his arrival. His debut was against Shelbourne (naturally scoring in a 3-2 win) but his five goals in a 7-1 tonking of Waterford was the highlight of his ten games with the club. That season ended with an FAI Cup final in front of over 36,000 at Dalymount Park against Shelbourne. Dean scored, but

The legendary Dixie Dean who joined Sligo Rovers in January 1939

the game ended level 1-1. The replay went the way of the Dubliners.

Lighting struck twice a year later when, having battled their way past Cobh Ramblers, Brideville and St. James Gate, the Bit O'Red was foiled again by another Dublin club at the final stage as Jimmy Dunne's Shamrock Rovers won the 1940 FAI Cup 3-0 in front of a crowd of just over 38,500 at Dalymount Park. Citing World War II and finances as deterrents, the Bit O'Red withdrew from the league that season eventually returning in 1948.

The club's best league showing since 1939 arrived in 1950/51, finishing runners-up to Cork Athletic under Glaswegian Bob Mooney. With five games to go Rovers had been top of the league, but a last day draw against lowly Transport handed the title to Cork Athletic. And that's as good as it got for a while.

In 1958 the club finished in the bottom two for the first time in their history and a succession of managers were used throughout the fifties, including ex-Manchester City player Tommy Wright, Englishmen Dick Groves, Scotsman Jock Shearer and fellow native John Black. The fifties however did give Rovers one of their all-time heroes in Johnny Armstrong – a man who scored 138 goals in 12 seasons with the club. Not bad considering he was a winger!

The start of the sixties was anything but swinging for the Bit O'Red. After an absolutely disastrous 1960/61 season under former Celtic defender Alex Rollo (finishing bottom with one win and six points), the club appointed former Shamrock Rovers double cup winner Peter Farrell in the hope of turning the tide, however again the club finished stone last. Ironically, a man called Sean Thomas had been at the club coaching in 1959. The Dubliner would of course go on to have huge success with Shamrock Rovers, win the FAI Cup with Bohemians and become Republic of Ireland manager (albeit for one game) in 1973. That bottom-placed 1962 finish proved disastrous. The club

An aerial view of the Showgrounds in 1959
(photo credit: Sligo Rovers Football Club)

wasn't re-elected and along with Transport dropped out of senior football for a second time in the club's history. Thankfully for the club, the break only lasted a season.

With the league being extended to 12 clubs, Rovers returned to top flight football and managed to avoid any re-election issues by finishing ninth that year. Bar an FAI Cup semi-final in 1966, their first in 14 years, it was a quiet decade. By this stage former "Coad Colt" Shay Keogh was in charge and the club had notable names like Jackie Quinn, Finbarr Flood and David Pugh. The arrival of Johnny Brookes in 1966/67 saw him become the league's top goal scorer – the only time in history a Sligo player has done it at the top level.

Soon after Keogh left and was replaced by former York City and Shrewsbury Town player Ken Turner, and in 1970 the Englishman led Sligo Rovers to two cup finals but came away empty-handed from both. The cross-border Blaxnit Cup featured Rovers in the final that year, but saw them lose to Coleraine 4-2. However Turner led Sligo Rovers to their first FAI Cup final since 1940. It started with a 3-0 away win against St. Patrick's Athletic with two David Pugh goals and a Joey Wilson strike, and continued with a 4-0 hammering of non-league Dubliners Rialto.

This brought Turner's men into a semi-final pairing with Cork Hibernians. The clubs drew 0-0 on March 29, but the replay two days later saw a memorable Johnny Brooks' goal along with a Gerry Mitchell strike to contribute to a 2-1 win as the Connaught men marched on to their first final since the 3-0 defeat to Shamrock Rovers in 1940. Standing in their way was Bohemians, a side that had an equally average '60s but were now under a resurgence with one of Sligo's former coaches – Sean Thomas. It was a monumental struggle.

The first game at Dalymount on April 19, 1970 ended scoreless, as did the replay three days later. Finally, Rovers struck the onion bag in the second replay through John Cooke but still went down 2-1 to Bohemians. It was bitter disappointment for Turner's men.

In 1975 the club reached the League Cup final under Billy Sinclair. Despite a 4-1 defeat, Rovers wouldn't be denied silverware for long. The Scotsman's time in charge produced the club's most successful period since before the war. Sinclair had players like Glasgow-born Mick Leonard, a big frontman and the perfect foil for strikers Paul Magee and Gary Hulmes, the strong and fearless Tony Fagan, plus captain Graham Fox, and behind them all Alan Paterson, often touted as the best goalkeeper ever to defend a Rovers' goal.

In the 1976/77 season the Connaught men served notice early on that they were serious contenders for the league championship with just one defeat in the first ten games. Bohemians and Drogheda were their nearest rivals but after a topsy-turvy season of different leaders, Rovers' fate was in their own hands on Sunday, April 10, 1977. The equation was simple: beat Shamrock Rovers and the title was theirs.

The Ringsend club had beaten Sligo earlier that season in the League Cup final and had proved a bogey side down through the years so the Hoops were certainly the last side Sligo needed to be playing on the final day of the season. A paying gate of £3,278 watched Sligo Rovers take an early lead when Charlie Ferry's cross was put away by Gary Hulmes, but like true pantomime villains, the Hoops equalised shortly after. Ironically, that goal could have handed the title to their Dublin rivals Bohemians, who were winning at St. Pat's, but in the 69th minute Chris Rutherford won the Freedom of Sligo when he headed in Paul McGee's corner to tear the roof off both the net and the stand in the Showgrounds. Sligo Rovers – League of Ireland champions 1976/77.

"I was only 22 at the time and probably didn't see what all the fuss was about. I was a professional being paid to do my job. After the game I just walked into the dressing room. There was nobody there as they were all still celebrating out on the pitch. I think that celebration went on for at least three months in the town!" – **Chris Rutherford**

"Without doubt it was the highlight of my League of Ireland career and it meant so much as a local boy. I had remembered my father bringing me to the Showgrounds as a young boy and then signing for the club at 15. There was a massive build up to the game itself and of course you had all these emotions running through your head of fear, dread, excitement, and confidence when we finally stepped out on the field but thankfully it worked out." – **Paul Magee**

With a first league title secured since 1937, the Bit O'Red went to represent Ireland in Europe as league champions for the first time in their history. It saw Rovers take on Red Star Belgrade, a side with an undoubted European Cup pedigree, but a sunny and less hostile environment would have been more acceptable. After all, Juventus, Benfica and Athletico Madrid were also on offer – instead Sligo got Yugoslavia and a long bus ride.

The first leg took place away on September 14, 1977. Rovers did well to keep the game scoreless at half time, but the true class of winger Dragan Dzajic, a true great of the game in the former republic of Yugoslavia, soon came to the fore and his brace inspired a 3-0 win for the home side, with Red Star winning by the same margin in Sligo two weeks later. The title was relinquished a year later, but the seventies wouldn't end without another crack at the elusive FAI Cup. It yielded a fourth final and, unfortunately, a fourth box of Kleenex.

Sligo won two tricky away games to St. Patrick's and Cork Alberts before defeating Drogheda with a John Gilligan goal at Oriel Park in April to reach their second FAI Cup final of the decade and their fourth overall. Standing in their way, their nemesis Shamrock Rovers. The Hoops had beaten Sligo Rovers in the 1940 final and were now under the management of Johnny Giles. The final on the last day of April 1978 saw a controversial penalty awarded by referee John Carpenter, after Paul Fielding was judged to have fouled Stephen Lynex inside the box, which was put away by Ray Treacy to deny Sligo yet again in the Blue Riband event of Irish football.

The eighties saw former Finn Harps manager Patsy McGowan take the reins, and lead the Bit O'Red to another FAI Cup final, this time in 1981. McGowan had already guided the Donegal club to success in the competition in 1974, and the campaign saw victories over UCD and Home Farm before a Harry McLaughlin goal in a semi-final replay against Waterford got Rovers to the final. Their opponents this time were Dundalk. The County Louth club had won league and cup twice each in the five years previous, and were in the middle of a real purple patch under Jim McLaughlin.

It didn't end ninety minutes later that afternoon either. The Lilywhites proved too strong for McGowan's men, and won 2-0 to take the 1981 FAI

Cup, leaving another set of Sligo Rovers fans wondering whether they would ever get their hands on the Blue Riband.

> *"It felt different when I came to Sligo Rovers from Finn Harps. I wasn't a local and I felt I was treated with a bit more respect because of that. Getting to the final proved a highlight, and though it was Dundalk we were up against I still thought we had every chance. I've never gone into a match feeling inferior as to be honest you can't. However the one thing I had told the lads was to not give away set-pieces in dangerous areas as Dundalk were so good at them. Of course we lost 2-0 – both from set-pieces."* – **Patsy McGowan**

Finally, the FAI Cup hoodoo was broken in 1983 under Paul Fielding with victory over Bohemians in that year's final, clinching the famous old trophy at the sixth attempt. On their way Rovers defeated Home Farm, Shamrock Rovers and then Cobh Ramblers over a marathon four game semi-final, which when ended reading something like a tennis match from Wimbledon. It was eventually game set and match for Fielding's men winning 1-1, 2-2, 0-0 then crucially 3-2, the winner coming from Gus Gilligan in that final game.

Sixth time lucky! Tony Fagan finally lifts the FAI Cup for Sligo Rovers in 1983
(photo credit: Sligo Champion)

There just might have been some Sligo Rovers fans contemplating suicide on the way to Dalymount Park on the morning of April 24, 1983. Surely to Christ they would not be beaten for a record sixth time in the final? Surely God would throw a bit of luck their way this time? The final would be an all-time classic.

The homecoming – thousands turn out to welcome home the '83 champions
(photo credit: Sligo Champion)

Played in an absolute monsoon, Rovers fell behind just before half-time to the Dubliners but drew level on the hour when Tony Stenson hammered in a Martin McDonnell free-kick. The moment a generation of fans (their fathers and maybe the odd grandfather) had been waiting 55 years for came 15 minutes from time when Harry McLoughlin's magnificent chip over a despairing Dermot O'Neill sent the North West fans absolutely delirious in the pouring rain at Dalymount. Sligo hung on to finally win the FAI Cup for the first time in their history.

Another fantastic voyage across Europe beckoned, their first since 1977. The Bit O'Red waited with bated breath for the draw to see who it would throw up. It could have been Barcelona, Porto, a trip to Old Trafford or a stroll around Turin before playing Juventus. Instead they got FC Haka.

The Finns might live in the most expensive country in Europe and have 24 hours daylight for months, but at least there wouldn't be any trouble for Sligo adjusting to the climate. It pisses rain in Finland too. The Showgrounds hosted the first leg. Try as they might, Fielding's men couldn't penetrate the Finns' net and the visitors ended up pinching a 1-0 win. They finished the job off at home, beating Rovers 3-0.

Soon after league form dipped significantly and having already flirted with relegation, Sligo Rovers dropped through the Premier Division trap-door in 1985. The creation of a new First Division meant for the first time four sides got demoted. In the penultimate game Sligo crucially lost to fellow strugglers Shelbourne and fell short by just seven goals having finished level on points with the Dubliners. Their stay in the First Division was brief as there was an immediate return to the top flight under Gerry Mitchell. Just two defeats in 18 games and Harry McLoughlin reaching double figures seemed a decent eight months work outside the big guns in the Premier Division.

Rovers lasted two seasons back in the big time before being relegated again, however former Shamrock Rovers' boss Dermot Keely took charge of proceedings in 1989 and immediately restored the club's fortunes, gaining them promotion that season. Though they lost in a First Division league title play-off to Waterford, it wouldn't dampen the promotion party too much.

"Sligo Rovers was a great club to manage at and I always look back at my time there with fondness. There just seems to be more meaning to a provincial club when success came their way and it was great to be part of that. Managing in Dublin was fine but it seemed more calculated. Like success was expected. But it was different at Sligo. It was a hotbed of football and had a history behind it. I always remember driving up from Dublin on Tuesday nights, training the team, crashing in a bed, then getting up at 5.00 in the morning the next day to drive back to Dublin and teach. But I wouldn't have changed a thing." – **Dermot Keely**

In 1991/92 it got a bit hairy, staying clear of the drop by a mere two points in their first season back up, before the insane two-tier league of 1992/93 (which I'm hoping was put down to a few too many brandies after an end of season bash) claimed Rovers for the First Division again. Whilst former Hoops hero Keely laid a foundation for success, it took another man in Green and White from across the sea to build a house on it.

Former Glasgow Celtic player Willie McStay's arrival soon after propelled Rovers to their greatest season ever. By the end of May 1994, the Bit O'Red had won a first treble at this level, cementing the Scotsman's name in the annuals of Sligo Rovers' history. The league started brightly with Sligo, Athlone and Finn Harps setting the pace, but Rovers always seemed a step ahead. A major boost to the campaign came in the First Division Shield, where having worked their way to the final, McStay's men took home silverware by beating Waterford United 2-1 over two legs. By the time the FAI Cup came around, Rovers looked primed for promotion.

They got a fright in the first round as non-league Glenmore Celtic held McStay's men at the Showgrounds before being dispatched in a replay, and with both Cork clubs (City and Cobh Ramblers) then being taken out it led Sligo to a semi-final tie against Limerick which the ever reliable Eddie Annand settled, sending the Bit O'Red into their first final since 1983.

Derry City provided the opposition in the final. The Ulstermen had finished a comfortable fourth in the Premier Division and beaten Shelbourne to capture the League Cup that season. Rovers had by that point also captured the First Division title, beating Athlone by four points, and with the Shield also in the bag and the pressure off the overwhelming underdogs clinched their second FAI Cup courtesy of a goal from Coventry-born Ger Carr and created a unique piece of history – a treble of trophies in one season.

> *"I was fortunate enough to have scored in the Shield final against Waterford as well so it was a nice double. I'd played most of my career in England as a centre back, but Willie had decided to push me into a defensive midfield role to give a bit of bite along with Declan Boyle and Gavin Dykes. I was there mainly to break things up. It just wasn't part of my game to be creative! The goal was slightly fortunate as it came off the side of my head, but it was a well rehearsed set-piece that we'd obviously worked on in training."* – **Ger Carr**

> *"We didn't have the resources to win a league at Sligo Rovers so the cup was always special in this town. It was an amazing day for the club and supporters, but also personally and for my family as my father was Chairman. To captain the side and lift the cup having seen Tony Fagan do it as a boy in 1983 was unreal."* – **Gavin Dykes**

A semi-final defeat to Shelbourne a year later saw Rovers reluctantly take the FAI Cup out of the Showgrounds' cabinet, but Premier Division status was maintained under new manager Lawrie Sanchez. The former Wimbledon match winner at Wembley in '88 would cut his managerial teeth at the Showgrounds before going on to manage Northern Ireland and Fulham.

Although a one season wonder at Sligo, Sanchez had the honour of being only the third manager in the club's history to lead them into Europe. A Cup Winners Cup tie against Floriana FC of Malta in September '94 was the re-

Sligo Rovers captain Gavin Dykes (left) and Willie McStay celebrate victory over Derry City in the 1994 FAI Cup final (photo credit: David Maher/Sportsfile)

ward for their cup final heroics of May and the Bit O'Red duly dispatched the Maltese outfit 3-2 on aggregate. That led them to a second round tie with Belgian side Club Brugge, and despite scoring in both ties through Johnny Kenny (home) and Adrian Rooney (away), Sligo bowed out 5-2 on aggregate.

Steve Cotterill took over a year later, leading Rovers to a League Cup final in which they led 2-0 against Shelbourne, before a heartbreaking loss on penalties in which Cotterill admitted the tears flowed freely. But the Englishman still brought Rovers into Europe via the 1996 Intertoto Cup.

Having only played three times in Europe before this, Sligo got to beat that record in the space of a month – playing four teams from the continent in the shape of Nantes, Lillestrom, Kaunas and Heerenveen. A scoreless draw with Dutch club Heerenveen and an impressive 3-3 draw with French club Nantes was a healthy return for Cotterill before he went off to manage sides like Burnley and Portsmouth.

> *"I remember the Heerenveen coach telling me he wished he had more Irish players in his team. Everybody knows about our spirit but we could also play football, and it seemed to him that Europe was the only place we expressed ourselves as he had coached over here and seen how the emphasis was on a more direct style of football."* – **Nick Broujos**

The Bit O'Red never settled on a manager long term. If you stayed in the Showgrounds longer than five years, chances are you were an advertising hoarding. Jimmy Mullen, Nicky Reid, Jim McInally and Tommy Cassidy all came and went before the end of the decade, but it was ex-Manchester City defender Reid who proved most successful, winning the club its first League Cup on February 23, 1998 with Neil Ogden's solitary goal over both legs clinching the cup against Shelbourne.

A new century started with Sligo back in the First Division. Don O'Riordan came in from Galway United but failed to get the club promoted. That honour went to Sean Connor in 2005, gaining promotion after six long seasons in the doldrums. The title was effectively secured with a 0-0 draw at home to Athlone Town in the penultimate week of the season. They could even afford a last day defeat to Kilkenny City. And in the Premier Division they have stayed ever since.

Despite those two well-worn words – "financial difficulty" – lurking about in 2008, the club has managed to survive and in 2009 went back into Europe under Paul Cook, drawing Albanian side KS Vllaznia Shkoder in the Europa League, but losing out 3-2 over two legs. There was heartbreak the same season losing out to Sporting Fingal in their first FAI Cup final since 1994. Getting beaten by those cheeky upstarts was one thing – losing it to two goals in the last eight minutes when you're up 1-0 is another. Rovers had led through Eoin Doyle's 52nd minute goal but a Colm James penalty and Gary O'Neill's 90th minute winner for Fingal proved to be a kick in the nuts Cook's men didn't deserve, having knocked out three of the five Premier Division sides that finished above them that year.

And so to last season. The Bit O'Red captured only their third FAI Cup in November 2010 in a memorable penalty shoot-out at the Aviva Stadium. The journey started with a John Dillion goal at home to Athlone, and gathered momentum with wins over Finn Harps in the local derby and Monaghan with 4,000 watching at the Showgrounds. The semi-finals saw Cook's men travel to Dalymount, where former Blackburn trainee Gavin Peers notched the winner to send Rovers into yet another final.

A crowd of 36,000 turned up at the plush new Lansdowne Road (OK, the Aviva Stadium) to watch the Bit O'Red and Shamrock Rovers drift to a penalty shoot-out. Sligo had dominated periods of the game and Michael O'Neill's side was hanging on for dear life after Stephen Bradley's dismissal, but Ciaran Kelly earned the Freedom of Sligo with an astonishing goalkeeping display in the penalty shoot-out, saving from Twigg, Flynn, Turner and Kavanagh and, combined with Eoin Doyle and Gary McCabe's successful spot-kicks, gave the Bit O'Red the Blue Riband of Irish football for the first time in 16 years.

Sligo Rovers – 2010 FAI Cup Champions Back Row (L-R): *Joseph N'Do, John Russell, Ciaran Kelly, Iarfhlaith Davoren, Eoin Doyle, Romauld Boco* Front Row (L-R): *Gavin Peers, Jim Laughlin, Gary McCabe, Danny Ventre, Alan Keane*

Rovers started 2011 taming Derry City at the Brandywell in front of 4,000 passionate home fans and drew over 4,200 in their first home game of the season against their old nemesis Shamrock Rovers which ended in defeat. They like to be known as just "Rovers" in the North West, and though their Dublin counterparts would dispute which is more famous, the men from Sligo have earned enough respect to be addressed as Rovers as well – especially when I'm writing about them and their fans are reading this!

> *"I remember meeting a busload of Brugge fans after the Cup Winners Cup home tie in 1994. They'd been out on the town (like us) and wanted something to eat. They hadn't any Irish money on them so I bought them all takeaways. When I walked outside the stadium in Brugge after the return leg the same fans amazingly were there, and they brought me out for a free night. I thought it was a lovely gesture that they hadn't forgotten."* – Gavin Dykes

Ground Info

For almost 84 years now this patch of green off Church Hill in the heart of the city has been the home of Sligo Rovers Football Club. The Showgrounds is not only part of the club and the city of Sligo, its woven into the fabric of League of Ireland football. Taking its name from the annual show held at the grounds by the County Sligo Agricultural Society, the ground was leased to the club until 1968 when they bought it for the princely sum of £6,500.

Inside the current ground the Treacy Stand holds 1,800 whilst the opposite Jink's Avenue Stand can accommodate another 900 people. On the far side of the ground the Railway End Terrace is landscaped by the majestic Benbulben Mountain which makes the Showgrounds one of the most picturesque grounds to visit in the league. Alas, in 2006 the club lost its famous "Shed" (which I included for you nostalgic Rovers fans in the main picture) and the area has since been redeveloped for new turnstiles, an office, a hospitality suite and car park.

Record Attendance

Unofficially, its 13,000 on April 17, 1983 v Cobh Ramblers for an FAI Cup semi-final, but there was a Eucharistic Prayer meeting in 1932 that brought 60,000 to the Showgrounds!

Cost

Adults: €15.00
Students/OAPs: €10.00
Children Under-12: €5.00

Programme

€4.00 – and easily one of the best programmes in the league. The substance of a programme is always more important than the style, but the club has got both in perfect measure here. Great attention to detail without cramming the publication with obligatory player snaps plus genuine contributors whose love for the club is obvious in their words.

Rivals

To the Bit O'Red faithful there is really only one Rovers in the league, and that's them! So you will always hear their Dublin counterparts referred to as "Shams" in this neck of the woods. Despite Galway slightly to the south and Finn Harps a wee bit north, Shamrock Rovers have always been the Bit O'Red's greatest adversaries.

Mascot

Benny the Bull – possibly the friendliest mascot in the League. When I finished my 2,856 mile trek around the 21 League of Ireland grounds in Sligo, Benny was the first one over to shake my hand, offer a free hug and even knew my name!

Food and Drink

A local burger van will greet you on entry as well as a shop located in the same area. For drink not only is Mooney's Bar the choice of almost every Rovers' supporter, it helps that it's located directly across the street on Church Hill. It's a friendly, inviting pub with wall to wall nostalgia from the Bit O'Red's history and a great place to celebrate or hold a post-mortem after a game at the Showgrounds.

Club Shop

The club doesn't have a merchandise shop in the ground, rather an online tie-in with local clothing company Jako Sports (for whom former Rovers goalkeeper Nicky Broujos looks after sales) where you can buy practically anything with the club's emblem.

Websites

www.sligorovers.com – club website
www.sligoroversforum.com – chat forum

Local Radio

Ocean FM 102.5.

The Match – Sligo Rovers v Drogheda United (Airtricity League, Premier Division, July 9, 2011)

The Showgrounds was actually the last ground on my travels and I finished on a high, as did Rovers, who went top of the Premier Division with a win over Drogheda United. Crowds are healthy in this part of the world at present, and manager Paul Cook has moulded a team capable of beating anyone in the league. It was a struggle at times against a Drogs side fighting for their life, but goals from Matthew Blinkhorn on the hour and a solid header from Eoin Doyle with ten minutes left sent the Bit O'Red home happy. Interestingly, the last time they'd beaten Drogheda United to go top of the league was in 1976/77. Hmmmm, I wonder?

(photo credit: Brendan Moran, Sportsfile)

St. Patrick's Athletic

Formed: **1929**

Ground: **Richmond Park**

Capacity: **5,340**

Nickname: **The Saints**

"At the time we didn't have a phone let alone a mobile! There was no club car so I got myself a bike!" – Pat Dolan on taking over the commerical manager's job at Richmond Park in 1992

When you share the same name as a patron saint and the guy who drove snakes out of Ireland, you have a lot to live up to. Fortunately, there's no need in the case of one club from Inchicore as they've spread joy throughout the land over the years, and even if they can't remove a boa constrictor from the Naas roundabout they've achieved great success in the Emerald Isle without the need for a staff and big hat.

St. Patrick's Athletic Football Club was founded in May 1929 by a group of men from the Inchicore area of Dublin. Calling themselves St. Patrick's FC, they approached Institute, a club playing in the local GSR (Great Southern

246

Railway) league, to take them under their wing, however Institute officials felt they had sufficient work on their hands at the time and were unable to accommodate the young aspirants from St. Patrick's.

St Patrick's Athletic at the GSR Ground in Inchicore, June 1929 – one of the very first photographs taken of the club (photo courtesy of Pat O' Callaghan)

Determined, the lads had a whip-round, paid a registration fee and instead gained entry into the Dublin Intermediate Novice League on the basis they extended their club name (half of Dublin had clubs called St. Patrick's), so Athletic was added.

The club played their first games in the Pond Field before moving to "The Acres" in Phoenix Park, then eventually negotiating a deal to rent Richmond Park from League of Ireland club Brideville and, having been accepted into Leinster Senior League, the club played their home games there during the 1939/40 season.

Although still a decade away from joining their Dublin peers, Bohemians, Shelbourne and Shamrock Rovers in the League of Ireland, the club did announce itself on a national scale by beating Galway Bohemians to win the 1941 FAI Junior Cup, and captured the Intermediate Cup twice in succession in 1948 and 1949, as well as winning the Leinster Senior League on four occasions. It was in 1948 they got the chance to mix it with the best the top flight could offer when St. Patrick's qualified for the FAI Cup for the first time.

A St. Valentine's Day massacre of Cobh Ramblers, with goals from Mc-Donald, McCormack and two from Cassidy, and then a bye set them up for what must have been a surreal semi-final tie on March 21 against an all-conquering Shamrock Rovers side that included Paddy Coad, Frank Glennon and Paddy Ambrose, and was managed by former Arsenal player Jimmy Dunne. The occasion and Rovers got the better of them as the Ringsend club ran out 8-2 winners with Shields and McCormack scoring.

A year later, however, there would be sweet revenge as Athletic caused one of the biggest shocks in League of Ireland history by knocking Shamrock Rovers out of the 1949 FAI Cup after a replay. The fact the Hoops had dominated Irish football, had dozens of internationals plus 24 domestic titles to their name at that point was one thing, but that they were the current cup holders made it even more amazing.

There had been a warning when Rovers just squeezed past the Saints in the semi-finals of the Leinster Cup a year previously, however not many expected this cup tie in Milltown would end level 1-1. The replay on February 23, 1949 was truly one of the first early highlights in the club's history when goals from Gregg and Bobby Rogers gave St. Pat's a 2-1 win over a disbelieving Shamrock Rovers. Shelbourne unfortunately killed the dream in the last eight.

With their profile significantly raised through their cup exploits and Leinster Senior League status, an application for League of Ireland football was finally accepted in 1951 – 22 years after they first kicked a ball at the Pond Field. St. Patrick's Athletic was admitted into the senior ranks and, along with Cork club Evergreen United, joined the League of Ireland. It would be an astonishing first season.

Not since Shamrock Rovers made their Free State League debut in 1922 did a club make such an impact in their inaugural year in the League of Ireland. Lining up with players now embedded into the club's very fabric, like Shay Gibbons and Jimmy "Timber" Cummins, the Inchicore club astonished the league by losing just four of their 22 games and taking the 1951/52 Championship with three points to spare over second placed Shelbourne, with Gibbons becoming the Golden Boot winner with 26 goals. St. Patrick's had arrived and with their foot in the door they would jam it there throughout a glorious decade which saw more success with a conveyor belt of new young talent.

Shay Gibbons was the first to earn an international cap, but soon players like Paddy "Ginger" O'Rourke, Willie Peyton, Ronnie Whelan Sr. and Harry Boland became just as talked about on the terraces as St. Pat's went on to win the title again in 1955.

A Waterford side spurred on by the great Jimmy Gauld (who hit 30 goals that season) pushed a Saints' side managed by Alec Stevenson all season long, but the Dubliners held firm winning the league by three points with the loss of just three games. Dundalk came off particularly bad one mid-January game, losing 10-3. St. Patrick's had become so dominant that they won the first nine games of the following season. Having won the last four of 1954/55 it created a record sequence of 13 straight wins. Again, the League of Ireland Championship stayed in Inchicore after St. Pat's saw off the challenge of Shamrock Rovers. Once again the magnificent Gibbons hit 21 goals, topping the goal scoring charts for the third time that decade, one of only a handful of players to ever do so (though Evergreen's Donal Leahy managed the same that decade). Having been hammered 8-2 as a non-league side just eight years earlier by the Glenmalure club, it was a massive achievement to pip Rovers to not only win but retain their title in 1956.

The only problem Athletic had at this point was their nomadic existence. Despite paying rent to play at Richmond Park, the ground was deemed unsuitable for League of Ireland standards and the Saints had to spend time in Chapelizod, Dalymount and even Milltown during the fifties whilst looking for a plot of land to call their own.

The decade finished with the capture of their first FAI Cup in 1959. The campaign started with a 3-1 home win over Sligo before hammering four past non-league Chapelizod. A Pascal Curtin goal was good enough to see off Cork Hibernians in the semi-finals, and on April 19, 1959, St. Patrick's lined up against Waterford in the final. To add spice to the encounter the Blues were now managed by ex-Pat's boss Alec Stevenson, but were without their gifted young striker Alfie Hale, who had damaged his ligaments in a clash with Tommy Dunne in their league game against the Saints just two weeks previously. A crowd of 22,000 people saw one of the best cup finals of its era.

The Dubliners got off to the perfect start when Waterford's Jack Hunt sliced the ball into his own net in an attempt to clear a Johnny McGeehan shot, but within five minutes Waterford was level when Peter Fitzgerald drove an unstoppable shot past Dinny Lowry. A game already bubbling over with excitement exploded in the last eight minutes, when Dixie Hale set up Peter Fitzgerald to crack home his second of the game and the cup looked destined to cross the River Suir. St. Pat's equalised directly from the kick-off. Again, it would be Johnny McGeehan. Pascal Curtin won the ball in midfield and unleashed a shot which Vinny Dunphy in the Waterford goal could only parry and the in-coming McGeehan pounced to send the game to a replay.

Three days later at Dalymount, St. Pat's finally settled the tie. Despite the hassle of being a midweek game, 25,000 fans, a bigger crowd than the first game, turned up to see St. Patrick's take the lead after only two minutes through Johnny McGeehan yet again. The Saints backline was inspired that day, particular Johnny White who made one remarkable goal-line clearance, and Dougie Boucher who gave an outstanding performance belying his 19 years. In the second half Waterford won a penalty which Dixie Hale missed and to compound his misery Willie Peyton scored for the Saints sixty seconds later. Waterford did get one goal back but the day belonged to the club from Inchicore and their first ever FAI Cup.

It didn't take long to add their second. Having finally moved into Richmond Park on a permanent basis in 1960, the Saints won their second FAI Cup in 1961 with a 2-1 victory over Drumcondra to deny them a double. It was an impressive victory against a club that had five FAI Cups (not to mention the same amount of League of Ireland titles) by that point. The Saints also finished runner-up in the league that year.

St. Patrick's line up at Tolka Park for a League of Ireland Shield game, October 1965
(photo credit: Connolly Collection/Sportsfile)

The following season saw St. Patrick's compete in European competition for the first time. Trips to Spain, France, Portugal and Austria could have been on the cards, but the use for sunscreen or the inevitable Irish sunburn (red head and peeling skin for three months) went out the window when the lads drew the Fife-based Dunfermline Athletic. Excited to be playing in Europe, but less enthusiastic about the only country in the continent with worse weather than their own, St. Patrick's Athletic lost 4-1 in the first leg in Scotland and went down by another four on their first home tie in Europe on September 27, 1962 to end the odyssey rather abruptly, though that solitary goal scored by Paddy "Ginger" O'Rourke was Pat's first in Europe.

The rest of the sixties saw St. Pat's well off the pace. The only highlight of that period was in 1967 when Gerry Doyle's side put together their first decent FAI Cup run since winning it in '61, beating Cork Celtic, Limerick, and Drogheda (all 1-0) on the way to the 1967 FAI Cup final. Unfortunately, they were up against a Shamrock Rovers side hotter than a Playboy bunny on a stove. Liam Tuohy's side had won three-in-a-row with a squad that would go down as arguably the greatest in the club's history.

St. Patrick's scored through Noel Bates and Noel Dunne but still lost the game 3-2. However it proved good enough to clinch an Inter-Cities Fairs Cup place where this time the boys got to avoid clubs by the Outer Hebrides and drew French opposition in Bordeaux. Again, there was an exit at the first level and although they conceded six in France, they became one of the first League of Ireland clubs to score three away goals in that second leg tie, having lost 3-1 at home, with Eddie Ryan and a brace from Noel Campbell making sure their names were added to the club's history books. Having been the club's top goal scorer in 1969 and '70, Noel Campbell then became one of very few Irishmen to go abroad at the time when he signed for German side Fortuna Koln in 1971.

In 1974 a FAI Cup run was put together by Jack Burkett's side, defeating non-league TEK United, Cork Hibs and Drogheda along the way, but the Inchicore club lost to Patsy McGowan's Finn Harps in the final 3-1. Fellow Dubliners Shamrock Rovers also struggled for a time and Shelbourne had dipped off the radar. The rise of provincial clubs like Cork Hibernians, Waterford and Dundalk meant that Bohemians was the only club from the capital to win a League of Ireland title that decade. The Saints also had to be content with mid-table finishes, an FAI Cup semi-final in 1977 and Gordon Banks turning out for the club against Shamrock Rovers in the one game he played for Athletic.

The 1979/80 season marked a return to form though it proved a bittersweet year as the Saints made two domestic cup finals but lost out in both. It started with a trip to the League Cup final in November. Having done the hard work in winning away on penalties against Bohemians, then defeating Dundalk at Oriel Park, a 2-1 victory over Shamrock Rovers in the semi-final put the Saints into their first League Cup final under the new format (it had replaced the League of Ireland Shield). However Athlone Town were kingpins of the land at the time and, despite goals from Jackie Jameson and Noel Browning, St. Patrick's lost 4-2 in the final. Waterford then added salt to an already open wound that April in the FAI Cup when a solitary goal from Blues defender Brian Gardiner broke the hearts of Charlie Walker's men and left St. Patrick's with an unwanted record of defeat in both domestic cup finals.

"As hard as it was losing in both finals, I felt a great sense of achievement. I had brought a lot of players into the side who had been playing junior football the year before, people like Mick Wright and Derek Carthy. I'll always remember a save Peter Thomas made from one Jackie Jameson effort. The ball was floated in from the wing and Jackie caught it perfectly, I just couldn't believe Thomas saved it, I think that single-handedly won him the Man of the Match award."
– **Charlie Walker**

Around that time former Manchester United scout Billy Behan was responsible for finding a shy, awkward, Ealing-born centre-half by the name of Paul McGrath. Having begun with Pearse Rovers in Sallynoggin, the Dubliner was now playing his football at Dalkey United and Behan made Matt Busby aware of his talent, though it was suggested he gain some experience with a League of Ireland club first. St. Pat's chairman Paddy Becton asked manager Charlie Walker to have a gander and McGrath was promptly signed and given a weekly wage of £25.

"On Saturdays I watched a lot of local games and had heard about this guy out in Dalkey. I also knew the club's manager 'Digger' Dalton as well and told him I'd be down for a look. Immediately he stood out. It was a hot day and everybody seemed to be going through the motions but there was this guy with a big Afro in the middle of the park taking down balls, making tackles, chasing people, doing little things that no-one could put into you. You just knew he was special."
– **Charlie Walker**

Thirteen years later at Giants Stadium in New York the former St. Patrick's defender turned in possibly the finest display ever seen in an Irish shirt, to deny Italy but particularly an astonished Roberto Baggio in Ireland's 1-0 World Cup win over the Azzuri.

Having been in the doldrums for a few years, the golden era at Richmond Park arrived when Brian Kerr walked in the door from 35 miles up the road in December 1986. The Drimnagh native had been Mick Lawlor's assistant at Drogheda but was a lifelong Pat's fan. Things changed. In 1986/87, Kerr guided them to fifth place, their best position since 1969, and brought in players like Curtis Fleming, John McDonnell, Pat Fenlon, Damien Byrne and Mick Moody. A year later the Inchicore club put up an almighty scrap with Dundalk but lost the league championship by a single point. What made matters worse for the Saints was the fact that winning the title had been in their hands.

On the last day of the season Bohemians were top but had played all their games. The Saints had a better goal difference so a win against Dundalk would clinch the title. The problem was that Dundalk only needed a single point from the game to snatch the championship from under their noses. Pat Fenlon scored early for the Saints but it wouldn't be enough as Dessie Gorman's equalizer just before half-time sent a jam-packed Oriel Park wild as the 1-1 draw handed the Lilywhites the league championship. Bridesmaids again.

However the wedding day finally arrived in 1990. After losing to Hearts in the UEFA Cup, Kerr brought the Saints a long cherished League of Ireland championship, their first in 34 years, which was secured on April 16, 1990. St. Patrick's only lost three games all season to leave the previous year's champions Derry City in their wake. A penultimate day win against Drogheda with goals from Maurice O'Driscoll and John "Trapper" Treacy clinched the championship. Part of that success was down to players like Mark Ennis, whose 19 goals made him the first Pat's player to finish league's top marksman since Shay Gibbons in 1955/56, John McDonnell, Pat Fenlon and influential winger Paul Osam who drew comparisons with Paul McGrath and Curtis Fleming and was nicknamed "The Black Pearl Mark 3" – no pressure there then!

> *"The atmosphere around the club, from players, staff to supporters that year was special. Winning that championship meant so much to everyone. I was only a young lad so you don't really take it all in, that it bridged a gap of 34 years since the last league title. Working under Brian was great. He had so much knowledge."* – **Pat Fenlon**

That championship season saw the Saints playing their football in Harold's Cross while development work went on at Inchicore. Financial woes hit soon after, leaving several of Kerr's star players to seek employment elsewhere, but not before a first European Cup tie.

The Saints were drawn against Dynamo Bucharest, a club with a solid pedigree in Europe having reached the European Cup semi-finals in 1984 and had just lost to Anderlecht in the Cup Winners Cup semis four months before this tie. A tough task and so it proved as the Irishmen went down 4-0 on September 19 that year. The return home leg would however salvage some pride with a Pat Fenlon goal in a 1-1 draw.

With his star players leaving Kerr had to build from scratch again and by moulding the young talent at the club and introducing players like Eddie Gormley from Doncaster Rovers, former favourite John McDonnell from Shamrock Rovers along with Liam Buckley, the Saints returned to the top of the table and took their fifth League of Ireland championship in 1996 by pushing Bohemians into second by five points.

> *"When the club was in financial difficulty I decided to stay, as I was a young man still learning the game. I had offers from other clubs but Pat's had given me my opportunity, when assistant manager Billy Bagster had seen me playing at Mount Merrion and asked me along to pre-season training. I felt Brian (Kerr) brought a new level of professionalism and organisation to St. Pat's. His attention to detail, his knowledge of the opposition, and of his own players and their attributes."* – **Paul Osam, Extratime.ie interview 2010**

Shelbourne then denied St. Patrick's a historic first league and cup double by beating them in the 1996 FAI Cup final 2-1 after a replay. It should have been so different however. Shels goalkeeper Alan Gough had been sent off for a professional foul after just 18 minutes of the final, and with Shelbourne forced to use midfielder Brian Flood in goal, Dave Campbell finally scored with 15 minutes left and Athletic were cast-iron certs. Amazingly, not only could they not find another one past Flood, the Saints conceded a late equaliser to Shels and lost the subsequent replay!

Again the club went to Europe in the 1996/97 UEFA Cup, losing 4-3 to Slovan Bratislava in a highly entertaining first leg at Richmond Park, with goals from Glynn, O'Flaherty and McDonnell, before bowing out 1-0 in the second leg. Brian Kerr left in 1997 and the appointment of Pat Dolan then raised some eyebrows!

> *"I signed a three year contract at St. Pat's but within weeks of coming into St. Pat's as a player the club went into liquidation. Obviously it was in my own interest not to let them die and I took the Commercial Manager's job. At the time we didn't have a phone let alone a mobile! There was no club car so I got myself a bike! We got back to Richmond Park which in the context of Rovers losing Milltown meant everything to us. Shamrock Rovers may have had a bigger brand and Bohemians bigger crowds, but I felt we could compete and evolve. I didn't want us to be 'little old Pat's', I wanted the 20,000 seater and a fan base that supported the Supersaints exclusively. I wanted professionalism and ambition instead of the mediocrity of the League of Ireland."* – **Pat Dolan**

A charismatic man, never short of an opinion, Dolan was then taken from his marketing manager's job at the ground and put in charge of team affairs at the request of Chairman Tim O'Flaherty. New players like Colin Hawkins, Trevor Molloy and Trevor Wood signed on, and in his first season as manager Pat Dolan delivered the 1997/98 League of Ireland championship by a single point over Shelbourne on a dramatic last day. Their fellow Dubliners needed just a draw away at Dundalk, but slipped to a 2-1 defeat whilst goals from Colin Hawkins and Eddie Gormley clinched the title for Dolan's men in Buckley Park against Kilkenny City.

Europe beckoned again. Drawn against Glasgow Celtic in the Champions League the Saints travelled to Parkhead for the first leg in July 1998 and held a Celtic side managed by Jozef Venglos scoreless, before losing out 2-0 at home in Richmond Park. By now Dolan had moved into a new job as the club's Chief Executive, leaving Liam Buckley to deliver the League of Ireland title for the first time in consecutive seasons in 1998/99. This time no last day favours were needed as Buckley's men finished three points clear of Cork City. Trevor Molloy also notched 15 goals that season. It would be the Dubliner's only season in charge.

St. Patrick's Athletic – 1997/98 Premier Division Champions Back (L-R): *Ian Gilzean, Colin Hawkins, Paul Osam, Trevor Wood, Mick Moody, Leon Braithwaite.*
Front (L-R): *Willie Burke, Keith Doyle, Eddie Gormley, Trevor Molloy, Thomas Morgan (photo Credit: David Maher/Sportsfile)*

An astonishing collapse to Romanian side FC Zimbru Chisinau 5-0 in both legs of a Champions League qualifier in July 1999 left one of the worst aggregate defeats in the more recent history of League of Ireland clubs in Europe, and the writing was on the wall. Dolan ultimately popped back in the hot-seat and delivered the club's first League Cup with a 5-3 aggregate win over the students of UCD in 2001.

But the 2001/02 season would prove the most controversial one in the club's history – a proposed merger with First Division St. Francis that caused an uproar, strained relationships between Pat Dolan and Saints' supporters but, most damaging of all, a 15 point deduction for the alleged wrong registration of Charles Livingstone Mbabazi. At first the club had been deducted 9 points for fielding an illegible player in Paul Marney early in the season, but fought back from a minus goal difference then had the points re-instated on appeal. Closest rivals Shelbourne took severe exception to this and there was some banter in the air to say the least!

The upshot of it all was a farcical ending to the season. The investigation into Mbabazi's registration subsequently cost the St. Patrick's side, which had already wrapped up the title on points, with Shelbourne taking the title after the Saints' points deduction. However Dolan examined the situation within the league as a whole and found, to his amazement, that incorrect registration of players was prevalant throughout the league. Subsequently, St. Patrick's was belatedly issued with championship medals as well!

A turbulent year put behind them, Athletic lost the 2003 FAI Cup final to Longford, but clinched a second League Cup by beating the same team in the 2003 League Cup final with a goal from David Freeman. It proved to be the last trophy of the decade.

In 2006 the Saints reached the FAI Cup final only to lose to Derry in a seven goal thriller. Despite taking the lead three times through Dave Mulcahy, Trevor Molloy and Sean O'Connor, an unfortunate Stephen Brennan own goal in the first period of extra-time saw the Candystripes take the cup and leave St. Patrick's empty-handed for the fifth final in a row. It's now been 50 years since the famous old cup resided in Richmond Park.

Brian Kerr returned as Director of Football in 2007 but stayed for only a year. Despite leaving, Kerr's legacy at Richmond Park was already confirmed as the Drimnagh man went on to take the head coach job at the Faroe Islands. Assistant manager Billy Bagster has fond memories of him from his time at Inchicore.

"We were playing Wayside Celtic in the Leinster Cup – all-ticket affair of course! – and I was sitting on the bench. It suddenly occurred to me I'd let my cigarette down and was wondering where it was until I heard this roar from the other side of the bench and saw Brian Kerr hopping up. The cig had rolled down to wear he was sitting and burnt him. He turned to me and said, 'Jaysus, Billy, that's a new pair of Chino's ruined – they cost me £30'." – **Billy Bagster**

The prodigal son returns – Brian Kerr back at Richmond Park in 2008
(photo credit: David Maher/Sportsfile)

Odense accounted for the Supersaints in the UEFA Cup in 2007, and the club then finished runners-up to Drogheda and Bohs in successive years. John McDonnell's team beat Latvian side Olimps over both legs 3-0 in the 2008/09 UEFA Cup, then impressively saw off Swedish club Elfsborg. That victory was earned the hard way, drawing away from home and then pulling themselves back from the abyss having gone behind at Inchicore, before Jason Gavin and an injury time Mark Quigley goal put the Saints through 4-3 on aggregate. Alas, German giants Hertha Berlin stopped any progression in the next round.

Former Blackburn Rovers and Irish international Jeff Kenna was in charge 12 months later when again the club went on a run in Europe. They overcame Maltese opposition in Valetta (Declan O'Brien with the vital away leg winner) and then shocked Russian counterparts FC Krylia Sovetov. Declan O'Brien had given the Saints a one goal advantage in the first leg, but with 13 minutes left in Russia, the Irishmen had conceded three goals and were going out. Amazingly, an own goal and another O'Brien strike made the game finish 3-2, thus Pat's went through on away goals to become the first League of Ireland side to reach the play-off round of the Europa League. In a lovely gesture at the final whistle, three supporters from Dublin (apart from club officials), who attended the game, were paraded around the ground and given a standing ovation by the Russian people, despite the home crowd's disappointment.

A typical Irish evening! The Saints Grimsby-born striker Danny North gets a taste of our fabulous weather (photo credit: Ian Anderson)

They could have done with an easier draw than Steaua Bucharest in their attempt to reach the lucrative group stage, and it proved a step too far as the Romanians won 5-1 on aggregate.

Under current manager Pete Mahon, St. Patrick's reached the 2010 Setanta Cup final. The cross-border cup saw the Saints qualifying for the semi-finals in a group behind Linfield, then eased past Sligo Rovers in the semi-finals on a 6-2 aggregate score. However the final at Tallaght Stadium against Bohemians was decided by a 24th minute Anto Murphy goal and with it the cup went to Dalymount Park.

The Saints started their 60th unbroken year in League of Ireland football in 2011, still only one of two clubs (the other Bohemians) never to have fallen out of the top division in the land, and with a solid foundation built on sound business acumen and a loyal fan base, it's likely the team named after our most famed saint will be here for some time yet – even their ex-manager Charlie Walker is still going strong, teaching a whole new generation of kids how to play football at the ripe old age of 83.

> *"I was asked to teach the kids at DCU for one evening ten years ago. I'm still there! I train children aged between 6-11 three days a week and go to the gym in my spare time. It's better to wear out than rust out!"* – **Charlie Walker**

Ground Info

I often think some stadiums around the country could be missed among the terraced houses and greenery that surround them if it weren't for the floodlights, and Richmond Park is no different in that respect. Tucked away nice and snug off Emmet Road in Inchicore, St. Patrick's' ground is actually located on an area that was, prior to our independence, used as a recreational area for the British army who were stationed at the nearby Richmond Barracks, hence the name Richmond Park.

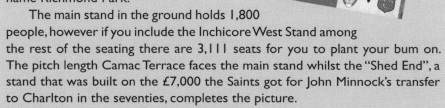

The main stand in the ground holds 1,800 people, however if you include the Inchicore West Stand among the rest of the seating there are 3,111 seats for you to plant your bum on. The pitch length Camac Terrace faces the main stand whilst the "Shed End", a stand that was built on the £7,000 the Saints got for John Minnock's transfer to Charlton in the seventies, completes the picture.

Record Attendance

5,250 v Waterford United (FAI Cup semi-final, April 13, 1986)

Cost

Adults: €15.00.
Concessions: €10.00
Children €5.00

Programme

€3.00 – The club has had to cut back on the programme this season which is a pity as St. Patrick's has always produced a high quality issue for every home game and were never short of contributors. However despite the reduced size, it's still worth buying when people like club historian Pat O'Callaghan have an input into it.

Rivals

Ground-sharing with a local rival will always annoy home supporters, which is probably why Shamrock Rovers topped my fans' survey, having spent time as tenants in Richmond Park at the start of the new millennium. Ironically, at one later point the club had thought of ground-sharing in Tallaght Stadium with Rovers, but plans were dropped after supporters made their feelings known!

Mascot

Paddy the Panther sounds harmless but if you're the club's office manager Gemma Fitzgerald then he's a man in a furry suit that strikes fear in the heart of the young lady. "He's forever popping his claw up at the little hatch in my office or sticking his head in when I least expect it. The man gives me nightmares!"

Food and Drink

Having arrived late (I had to cover the Bohemians v Galway game the same night) I didn't, for a change, sample the chipper inside the ground and instead settled for a lovely big mug of tea from three of the prettiest tea-ladies in the league in the hospitality room. Hilda Ogden they weren't.

In terms of drink, McDowell's pub has consistently popped up as a favourite among the hundreds of away fans all over Ireland that I interviewed for the book, and it is a cracking pre- or post-match pub, and extremely handy as it's just outside the ground on Emmet Road.

Club Shop

Located on Emmet Road, and opened in August 2010, the spacious new superstore is a credit to the forward thinking club and does brisk business considering there are over 60 different products with the St. Patrick's emblem on it, including St. Patrick's Athletic coasters! The club naturally has an online store as well.

Websites

www.stpatsfc.com – club website
www.saintsforum.net – fans' forum

Local Radio

WDAR (West Dublin Access Radio) 96 FM.

The Match – St. Patrick's Athletic v Dundalk (Premier Division, March 25, 2011)

I'm claiming an assist here folks. Having arrived late and done my rounds interviewing people, I finally sat down with the Saints 2-0 behind and more chance of a one-legged man winning an arse-kicking contest than Athletic pulling off a victory.

Inspired by my entry, the home side scored two goals in three minutes from Ewan and David McMillan midway through the second half, and completed an unlikely win for Pete Mahon's side with a last minute goal from Dave Mulcahy on his 100th appearance, sending the Lilywhites back to Oriel Park empty-handed.

UCD

Formed: **1895**
Ground: **UCD Bowl**
Capacity: **3,000**
Nickname: **The Students**

**"I went to go watch UCD playing in Belfield Park to cure my
fear of wide open spaces." – Dermot Morgan**

Some clubs wait a lifetime to play League of Ireland football, and to many outside Dublin UCD may have seemed like a fledgling club when they joined the top flight over 32 years ago, but the Students from Belfield are actually the fourth oldest club in Ireland with a proud history and tradition behind them. The club's origins go back over 116 years ago when in 1895 the Catholic University Medical Football Club entered a team in the Leinster Junior League. Their first game under that moniker was against a Bohemians B side, which they won 2-0. Thirteen years after their foundation, Catholic University merged with University College Dublin, changed its name to UCD, and have kept it that way for over a century now.

Although it would still be a full 71 years before the club took its place in the League of Ireland proper in 1979, UCD still had notable success in the

261

early years. The capture of the Collinwood Cup (the main football tournament for Irish universities) in its inaugural season of 1914, and the defeat of Portadown to win the IFA Intermediate Cup a year later, were notable. At the time, the IFA was the governing body in Ireland as we were under British rule, though a year later in 1916, Padraig, James, Michael, Eamon and a few lads tried to remedy the problem that Easter.

UCD also had the honour of playing in the inaugural Free State Cup in 1921, but lost 6-2 to a fellow non-league club called Shamrock Rovers, in the brilliantly named Windy Arbour. At the time, Dublin clubs made up almost all the teams in the Free State League (West Ham Belfast and Athlone Town were the only sides outside the capital in the cup) so even progressing in a cup competition with clubs like Bohemians, Shelbourne and double winners that season St. James' Gate was always going to be difficult. To rubberstamp the quality of teams from the capital, the very next season Shamrock Rovers gained entry to the Free State League and won it at their first attempt.

By this stage UCD had floated from ground to ground, playing their matches in Sandymount, Cowper Road, Croydon Park, Fairview and Terenure, but in 1935 the club ended their nomadic existence by moving into Belfield Park. The FAI Intermediate Cup was captured with a 4-2 win over Cobh Ramblers in 1945, and there was an FAI Cup first round defeat to Sligo Rovers in 1953. The Student's last appearance as a non-league side in that competition came on February 16, 1957 when Cork Athletic beat them in one of the Leesiders' very last games as a league club – they folded within three months of this match.

That was the last seen of UCD on a national scale for another 23 years as the team had to be content with football in the Leinster Senior League until 1970 when the club was elected to the League of Ireland B Division. It was around this time the influential Tony O'Neill joined the club.

A medical student graduate of UCD, O'Neill first got involved with UCD as club secretary but went on to make a huge impact within the club before his untimely passing in 1999. When most League of Ireland clubs in the seventies were making collections to fund trips to places like Kispest Honved and Ujpest Dozsa, little B Division UCD was flying all over the world playing matches in far-flung places like India, Hong Kong, Taiwan, Malaysia, Jordan, the Philippines and Australia!

Dr. O'Neill initiated the tours. Individual players were sponsored by local businesses and Tony produced a tour brochure for every country they played in, giving the companies' maximum exposure (and making sure Joe the Butcher could have his advert for streaky rashers seen in Hong Kong). Later he oversaw a new system where players could be offered a scholarship and sit for a degree whilst playing top flight football in Ireland. Keith Dignam became the very first player to avail of this new procedure when they entered the League of Ireland.

> *"I remember signing for UCD as a 17 year old. I was with Tony and my father in a bar and had several pints in me when he got me to put pen to paper – so essentially I was drunk when signing for the club! But Tony was a great mentor to me. He always evoked a lot a respect and though he wasn't necessarily a 'hand on the shoulder' manager I owe him my start in football. I ended up playing U-21 for my country and being nominated for FAI Player of the Year in amongst five professionals."* – **Tony McDonnell, who went on to make over 300 appearances with UCD**

Nine years after entering the League of Ireland B Division, UCD finally got their chance to sit at the top table. Attendances had fallen off the charts around the country and clubs were finding it hard to make ends meet. None more so than Cork Celtic, who had been fighting a losing battle financially for several years, and on the July 20, 1979 Celtic was expelled having failed to live up to certain conditions required at the League AGM. It allowed UCD the chance to make the step up from the B Division with Tony O'Neill as general manager and Theo Dunne as coach. UCD finally took its place in the League of Ireland playing its first game in the top flight on August 26, 1979 in the League Cup against Drogheda United. Tony Evans became the Students' first goal scorer at senior level in a 2-1 defeat that day.

The first season was a struggle. Five wins from thirty games saw the club finish second-last, with only Shelbourne padding their arses from the bottom position, and UCD's first four seasons were spent firmly in the bottom half of the table, having to apply for re-election twice in that time. Former Leeds United stalwart Peter Lorimer joined in 1983, but decided he didn't like the look of things and sodded back over to Elland Road a mere three games later.

UCD may have been the most intelligent side in Ireland, but it meant sod all in terms of points, so the club's student-only policy was abandoned and the door opened to anyone who wanted to play for the college. The change was dramatic. By introducing players like Alan O'Neill, Paddy Dunning, Robby Gaffney and Robbie Lawlor, UCD turned the corner which had been annoying them since entering the league. It was a clear road now.

Nine wins were collected in 1983/84 and a very healthy sixth place attained. Dermot Keely had started the ball rolling that season before leaving for Shamrock Rovers after just two months, but the good work was continued by Theo Dunne. Actually "good work" is probably an understatement. UCD conceded only 23 goals, finished with a plus goal difference and doubled their wins from the year before. Oh, and they won the FAI Cup for the first time in 89 years!

It started in the first week of February with a 3-3 draw against Sligo Rovers at the Showgrounds, and ended with the biggest moment in the club's domestic history with victory over Shamrock Rovers in the final. The replay against Sligo was a 5-0 rout, whilst Home Farm was the next victim in the quarter-finals. In the first week of April, Dunne's men travelled to Tolka Park in Dublin to play Waterford United (I remembered spending four hours on a bus with my Uncle Jess and his slab of cans thinking, who in the name of Christ decided to put the game on there?) and a solitary Joe Hanrahan goal which put UCD into the Blue Riband of Irish football on April 29, 1984.

Their opponents were a Shamrock Rovers side just crowned League of Ireland champions for the first time in 20 years and about to begin a period of total dominance under Jim McLaughlin. One of the culls from McLaughlin's sweeping changes at Rovers was Alan O'Neill. The goalkeeper had spent a decade at Glenmalure and was surprised to find himself surplus to requirements and, along with Robbie Gaffney, both ex-Milltown men, lined up against their former club that day.

A disappointing crowd of 6,500 watched the game finish scoreless at Dalymount Park, but a week later on May 4 at Tolka Park a goal from Joe Hanra-

UCD celebrates winning the 1984 FAI Cup (L-R): Aidan Reynolds, Martin Moran (almost completely hidden), Robbie Gaffney, Theo Dunne, Dr. Tony O'Neill, Brendan Murphy, John Cullen (photo credit: Philip Bourke/UCD FC)

han with a Ricky Villa moment (except Joe knew what he was doing, unlike Ricky and the Manchester City defence), and a winner from Ken O'Doherty captured the FAI Cup for the Students. It's a game Ken can vaguely recall!

> *"Oh lord, I remember it alright. I remember missing a penalty on the stroke of half-time! We were already 1-0 up from Joe's goal and my spot kick would have given us a two goal cushion bang on half-time. As if I wasn't under enough pressure, referee John Carpenter said, 'Ken, you better put it in first time as there's no time for the rebound!' I struck it well enough but Jody Byrne saved it. I laughed about it after and told him he just fell on the ball, but Jody reckons it's one of the best saves he ever made! Rovers levelled but luckily enough I ended up getting the winner. Mind you, when I rambled up for the corner Paddy Dunning shouted, 'Where in the name of Christ do you think you're going young lad? Come back!'"* – **Ken O'Doherty**

Reports of wild celebration were recorded that night, however Dublin bars overflowing with student grant cheques may be a bit wide of the mark!

> *"I remember getting annoyed with one journalist after the first game. He'd basically said we'd come to spoil and stifle the game. That we had no interest in actually playing. That was an insult to the players we had. The truth of the matter is we'd done our homework on Rovers and proved that in the replay."* – **Theo Dunne**

This placed the college team into Europe for the first time in their history and a plum tie against English counterparts Everton. Now if UCD had a crystal ball and peered into it to see exactly what Everton would do that season it's quite possible Joe Hanrahan and the boys would have locked themselves in their bedrooms, let alone the dressing room, and write the game off as a no-show as the Toffees would go on to win the Cup Winners Cup and take the English Division One title by a full 13 points. Only Manchester United and one Norman Whiteside stopped the Merseyside club winning a historic treble.

A side containing players like Trevor Steven, Neville Southall, Kevin Sheedy, Andy Gray (tut tut) Kevin Ratcliffe and managed by Howard Kendall (who later somehow thought he could do a job managing Ireland after ten years out of the game) came to Tolka Park and took away a 1-0 win courtesy of a Graeme Sharpe goal. Job done? Pat on back from Howard? It's understandable if the Toffees flew home with their minds on Southampton that weekend, whilst Andy Gray still dreamt of a satellite station with a computerised tactics

Paddy Dunning heading clear for UCD with Everton's Graeme Sharpe nearby during the Students Cup Winners Cup tie in September 1984 (photo credit: Ray McManus/Sportsfile)

board to annoy everyone with, along with the odd female presenter. If so, boy did they get a shock.

What the general football public would have expected to be a cosy tie with a gutful of goals at Goodison turned out anything but. Though under the cosh as expected for most of the game, UCD came within a couple of manky inches of dumping Everton out of the 1985 Cup Winners Cup. A side that went on to win their next two ties 4-0 and 5-0, and only concede two goals in the entire competition, had the width of a crossbar to thank at Goodison Park on October 2, 1984.

"Graeme Sharpe scored for Everton but we thought he may have been marginally offside as it was a part of our game we had worked so well on. I'd come close to equalising from a corner soon after then with five minutes left, Joe Hanrahan got hold of the ball on the left wing, cut inside and fired an effort that beat Neville Southall but hit the bar. They would go on to win the tournament - we'd come that close to knocking them out." – **Ken O'Doherty**

"I had made sure to pop across to Goodison Park to watch them before we visited. Tactically I always felt I was astute enough - and we needed to be against Everton. They were a magnificent side that season. Myself and Tony agreed fitness was most important so for the build-up to the game it was a professional set-up, training every single day. It was the one thing over ninety minutes we wouldn't be beaten on – I always thought we were fitter then Everton at Goodison." – **Theo Dunne**

Hanrahan signed for Manchester United on the back of the performances and UCD eventually finished fourth.

However there's always a kick in the nuts waiting around the corner for League of Ireland sides and UCD got it full force a year later. The club was forced to release the bulk of their semi-professional players, leading to the worst possible impact. A decimated side saw UCD relegated in April 1986 for the first time with a mere two wins from 22 games, amassing just eight points. It was uncharted water for the Students in a First Division which had just been operating for one year, and there was no "big fish in a little pond" scenario either as the club stuttered to a mid-table finish, a distant 14 points from champions Derry City.

Fed up with EMFA on a cold Tuesday night, and one man and his dog at Newcastlewest, the lads flew off to New Mexico where UCD won the World Collegiate Championships in 1987, and a year later inflicted a second round FAI Cup defeat to Shamrock Rovers, bringing to an end a sequence of 15 undefeated games for the then three-in-a-row champions in the competition. Ironically, that run had started after UCD in the 1984 final.

Before the end of the decade of shoulder-pads, make-up and highlights (and of course I'm taking about the men), UCD regained their Premier Division status under Theo Dunne as First Division runners-up to Drogheda United. A mere four goals separated the Students from third-place Bray Wanderers, due mainly to the fact Bray failed to win an outstanding last league game away to Monaghan, where United goalkeeper Damien McCorry had the game of his life in a 1-1 draw.

Alas, the high seas and choppy waters of the Premier Division had Theo and his charges feeling seasick on their return in 1989, and UCD was relegated after just one season, going down with Drogheda United – the club that had pipped them to the First Division title.

The club endured a few more seasons in the First Division, winning the most forgotten of domestic competitions – the First Division Shield. Although confined to lower league clubs and attracting an average of about 47 people per game, the First Division Shield had its place. It started Derry City on the road to silverware and was even won by little EMFA. UCD won it in 1991/92, beating Waterford over two legs 2-1 (the first of those games was the club's first game under floodlights), with Darren O'Brien scoring the all important goal to give UCD its first domestic silverware since the FAI Cup in 1984.

Having spent four fruitless seasons in the bottom tier, UCD finally produced a season worthy of plaudits to win the 1994/95 First Division Championship, again under Theo Dunne – their first league title in their centenary year on the back of 10 straight wins and 64 points. Mick O'Byrne set a then record goal-scoring tally of 14 goals and once again the rumour of student grant cheques being handed in over the pub counter surfaced. There was even a second victory in the First Division Shield against runners-up Drogheda United (though it remains to be seen whether more than the man and his dog turned up to watch it). Despite losing almost half their Premier Division

*Eamon McLoughlin just making sure Dundalk's Brian Byrne isn't going anywhere
(photo credit: Brendan Moran/Sportsfile)*

games the next season, UCD still finished a happy eleven points clear of relegated Drogheda as they reasserted themselves to life at the top table.

The 1995 season was also the club's centenary and they celebrated it in style by bringing over Liverpool for a game that was played in Lansdowne Road. It took a bit of lobbying from the good old IRFU to actually get the game on, but a crowd of 22,600 turned up to watch the match that finished 3-1.

By this point Jason Sherlock was a regular for UCD and for a brief time in the late nineties it was absolutely impossible to open a back page or sports supplement without seeing the Na Fianna man. Every Gaelic football side outside Dublin dreaded him, Liverpool courted him, and practically half of Ireland wanted to marry him. He scored over 30 goals for UCD, gained an under-21 cap and won a Leinster title with Dublin. Not bad for a guy who, if he'd dared to play soccer 70 years earlier, would have been shot by firing squad.

Still plodding along nicely in the Premier Divsion, a second trip to Europe arrived rather surprisingly in the 1999/2000 season. Under Martin Moran the Students made a late burst to pip both Shamrock Rovers and St. Patrick's Athletic to an Intertoto Cup place by a point. When I say a late burst I mean late. On the last day of the season the club needed an away win against Drogheda coupled with a St. Pat's defeat at Galway. The college boys hammered five past the Drogs, whilst Billy Clery's injury time winner at Terryland Park denied St. Pat's the point they needed and sent UCD into Europe.

It meant UCD taking on a Bulgarian side whose name sounded something like a wino ordering a kebab in a chip shop – Velbazhd Kyustendil. The Students did the country proud that August, twice coming from behind to draw 3-3 at Belfield with a brace from Robert McCauley and one from Ciaran Martyn, and defiantly held out for a scoreless draw in Bulgaria. However it meant they would go out on away goals.

The club went on to the League Cup final in January 2001 but lost out to St. Patrick's Athletic 5-3 over two legs. Ironically enough, it had been the first time the club had actually made it past the first round stage! Not only that, the Students didn't concede a single goal in the 360 minutes (four games before you start to calculate!) it took to get to the final. Paul Doolin would then become boss.

> *"I'll always be thankful to Martin Moran at UCD for giving me my first break into management. I'd been lucky enough to play football until I was 38 when Martin approached me to take a coaching role at the club which I was happy to oblige. The first thing I done was to get my badges as I firmly believed no matter how successful you've been as a coach or manager you needed your badges. Later on I was offered the manager's job which proved to be my first break."* – **Paul Doolin**

A nine-year top flight status was ended in November 2003. Despite a long, hard struggle all season (they took just five points from their opening dozen games), it seemed UCD would escape the drop with a last day 2-0 win against FAI Cup champions Longford Town. It should have been enough to survive, but second-bottom Derry, with one away win to their name all season, travelled to a well-placed Waterford United side and won 1-0 to relegate the Students.

Pete Mahon was left to pick up the pieces, which he promptly did, losing just two of 33 games and finishing runners-up to First Division champions Finn Harps. By now, men like Conor Kenna, Darren Quigley and Willie Doyle were some of the players uncovered by a now revalitised scholarship scheme. Doyle was top goal scorer that year with 15 goals. Their return to the top flight in 2005 saw Mahon's men finish a comfortable ninth and go on a League Cup run that resulted in the Students contesting their first domestic cup final since the 2000/01 season.

*Theo Dunne and Martin Moran share a laugh during the 1999/2000 season
(photo credit: David Maher/Sportsfile)*

A first round win away to Dublin City 3-1 was followed by a single Paul Whitmarsh goal to knock out Shamrock Rovers. Another one goal win was achieved in the last eight against Waterford United, with Tony McDonnell the man on target, but all the drama was seemingly saved for the semi-final. One goal down to Shelbourne with the 90 minutes up at Tolka Park, UCD seriously annoyed the home crowd with two goals in injury-time. If Brian Gannon's equaliser was painful, you can be sure the swift kick in the nuts that Rob Martin delivered a minute later was enough to floor Shelbourne and their fans for at least a few days.

On September 20, 2005 the League Cup final (the first live TV game to be screened from Belfield Park) saw UCD with home advantage over Derry City. Had it been any other club than Ulster's second city in the final, the result may have been a different outcome, but Derry City were (and still are) simply possessed when it comes to the League Cup. Eleven finals, nine wins and the only club to win four in a row, no team even comes near Derry in this competition. So despite a Conan Byrne goal, despite a crowd of almost 2,200 cramming into the ground, and despite the promise of a student grant hammering and another night on the lash with silverware to boot, UCD went down 2-1 to Stephen Kenny's Derry City.

Having spent over 70 years at Belfield Park the Students moved to their new home of the UCD Bowl in 2008. A redevelopment plan on the ground had started a year earlier, and by the time they moved in floodlighting, improved fencing and a 1,500-seater stand had been sorted. Not that the home advantage meant much as for the first season the last word you could associate with the Belfield Bowl was "fortress".

> *"Home advantage my arse! We only won two games in our first season at the Bowl. People said it would take time to get used to it, but our opponents seemed to be doing that in the first five minutes of each game!"* – **Declan Hughes, UCD historian and fan**

Ten home defeats played their part, and UCD was relegated long before the last day of the 2008 season, a massive eleven points from safety. It was a hugely disappointing start to life in their new home. The times they were a-changing. The collapse of the building industry, bank bail-outs and a leader announcing he'd get out of Dodge with them. However at the now seemingly cursed Belfield Bowl there was change too. For the 2009 season Pete Mahon was replaced by Martin Russell and the Students went on to win 23 of their 33 First Division games, and even had the luxury of celebrating a last day home defeat to Waterford United knowing the 2009 First Division title had effectively been sealed the week before with a 5-0 win away at Athlone Town. The one point that separated UCD and second place Shelbourne gave the club only their second league championship. Thankfully for the Students, there was

UCD 2011 Squad (photo credit: Ed Scannell)

consolidation on their return to the Premier Division with a comfortable seventh place finish in 2010.

From strange sounding monikers to a visionary doctor who wanted to bring the club forward, UCD remains one of the oldest and most respected clubs in the league, hoping that some day soon a chance will come again to collect silverware, grab headlines and cash in those cheques at the nearest watering hole on campus.

> *"Tony O Neill was quirky if nothing. I remember him once telling me about a guy he was going to sign who was a fantastic athlete, all-rounder, great swimmer, built like a tank and fantastic ball control. When the guy finally turned up he couldn't kick a f****** ball – but Tony was quirky like that – he saw things in people that others didn't! I can't really say his judgement was that wrong as he signed me."* – Tony McDonnell

> *"We really had some great times with UCD. Travelling the world with the team was fantastic and one of my most vivid memories was playing the Indonesian national football team in a stadium of around 85,000 people. We were touted as 'FC Dublin' but I'm sure many thought we were the Irish national side! We lost 2-1 but whilst we were playing we were constantly hissed and jeered at. We thought we'd never get out of the place alive, until we found out after the game that in Indonesia if a visiting team is playing well they get abused. If they are crap they clap them!"* – Ken O'Doherty

Did You Know?

UCD actually had four players that represented their countries in the World Cup playing for the Students at one point or another. Peter Lorimer played for Scotland in two World Cups. Dave Norman, who had been on loan from Vancouver Whitecaps, played in the 1986 World Cup. Kevin Moran, who played briefly for UCD, would of course represent the Republic in the 1990 World Cup and the fourth was, well, it's a bit of a cheat. It was Hugo McNeill, who scored 46 goals for the club in one season at university and did get capped in a World Cup all right – the 1987 Rugby World Cup, after his path took him down the road of the oval ball!

Ground Info

Mentioning the words "students" and "campus" among football fans doesn't conjure up images of a Premier Division football team with over a century of history and honours to their name, but nestled nicely in Dublin suburbia on the UCD campus lies UCD Bowl – home of UCD, a football club as welcoming as any in the League of Ireland despite the location.

The ground consists of one main 1,500-seated stand though it is only partially covered so if you're lucky enough to be seated smack bang in the middle when the proverbial cats and dogs pour down you'll be fine – otherwise it's umbrella city! There is standing room on the south terrace, though the grass bank on the opposite side to the stand is off-limits apart from the television gentry.

The Bowl was a concept thought up as far back as the late seventies by the late great Dr. Tony O'Neill, which finally came to fruition in 2008 when the club moved out of Belfield Park, which is also on the campus.

There is parking space at the ground (from the north and south entries) for roughly 200-250 cars.

Record Attendance

3,750 v Shamrock Rovers (at Belfield Park, December 1986) – UCD had 9,000 at their "home" game against Everton at Tolka Park in September 1985

Cost

Adults: €15.00
Students: €10.00
Concessions: €10.00
Children: €5.00

Programme

€3.00 – and stays away from 18 pages of "Pat the Butcher's half price sausage sale". There are some dedicated contributors, among whom is club historian Declan Hughes who is always on hand to give a few history lessons on each visiting team and their clashes with the Students down through the years. Retro pieces are a cornerstone of good programmes – thankfully, UCD realises this as well.

Rivals

Shamrock Rovers are the pick of the capital teams that tick all the boxes here. Logistically, when the Hoops played in Miltown the Students were the closest club with a lot of UCD's players crossing over to Glenmalure Park through the years, which probably didn't help relations!

Mascot

Collee is the faithful mascot of UCD. Mind you, he's still only a pup as it's his first year since the club introduced him in 2011.

Food and Drink

I've got to give credit to the cosy little tuck shop inside the ground as practically everything on sale was an uncomplicated €2.00. "Want a cheese and tomato sarny? That'll be €2.00." "Chicken or Veg soup my friend? €2.00 please!" They also had the cunning idea of selling those foreign pot noodles as well. Price? Should you really ask? There is also a burger van inside the ground.

The nearest pub to the ground (bar the student one on campus) is The Goat in Goatstown, which is a good sports pub and UCD supporters frequent it often.

Club Shop

Located just inside the main turnstiles.

Websites

www.ucdsoccer.com – club website
www.ucdsupporters.ie – fans' forum

Local Radio

Declan Hughes is the man on Dublin City FM 103. He hosts a one hour show on Mondays called "The Absolute Game", which covers a huge amount of League of Ireland stories and discussion.

The Match – UCD v Derry City (Premier Division, March 11, 2011)

Despite having over 25,000 students in the college UCD is starved of fans, though it's a situation the club has long since adapted to. Whether it's the fact most students travel home on weekend or support other sports or other teams in Dublin, UCD is reliant on a small number of hardcore fans.

Derry scored after eight minutes and finally finished the game off eighty minutes later having hit the post twice in-between. The half-time interval was one of the busiest I've ever seen on a football ground with a crossbar challenge going on in one half and an Under-7s match in the other, which produced one great moment when the goalkeeper saved a seven-on-one effort. Sign him up!

Waterford United

Formed:	**1930**
Ground:	**Regional Sports Centre**
Capacity:	**5,200**
Nickname:	**The Blues**

"When I first crossed the bridge into Waterford I saw a big parade along the Quay. Someone said to me, 'Johnny, this is because you signed for us!' I felt great. Little did I know it was the St. Patrick's Day parade."
– Johnny Matthews

There was a time in this land when thousands flocked to see a team in all blue every Sunday afternoon. A time when a team from the banks of the River Suir was the most dominate league team in the country. Football was their religion and Kilcohan Park the church in which they worshipped. It's been almost 40 years now since Waterford United won their last league title, but the memories evoked from a side of such skill in a time of uneven pitches and leather and lace footballs still resonate around the city by the Suir. Through changing times the club has survived and celebrated their 80th anniversary in 2010.

In 1930 Ireland was not a republic, Uruguay were champions of the world and women were denounced for not wearing stockings in public. The shame! Having played under the moniker of Waterford Celtic in the Munster Senior League in 1929 (they lost out to Cork Bohemians in the Free State Cup that year), Waterford FC gained entry to the league in 1930, dropped the "Celtic" tag and a committee was formed in order to bring in some overseas players to make sure the team could actually mix it at a competitive level with the likes of Shamrock Rovers, Shelbourne and St. James Gate. The task of managing Waterford FC in their inaugural season went to Jack Doran, a former Celtic international with the club's first League of Ireland fixture a ten goal thriller away to Dundalk (OK, they were beaten 7-3).

Though Waterford finished ninth, picking up just 19 points from 22 games, they went on to stun the league by winning the 1930/31 Free State Shield, humbling Bohemians in Dalymount Park 4-1 in front of almost 15,000 people. Back home in Waterford the score was flashed up on the screens of the local picture house when word got through, and there were scenes of bedlam when the team arrived back over the River Suir.

In 1932 the club was forced to resign from the league, largely due to the fact that the government imposed an "entertainment tax" on all Free State clubs which took a fifth off their gate receipts. Teams such as Cork Bohemians were one of the first to hit the wall with this tax and Waterford followed suit.

Waterford FC, 1937 – League of Ireland Shield and Free State Cup Champions

For a club with such a rich history it's still a source of bewilderment that in 80 years of competitive football the FAI Cup has only ever resided twice in the trophy cabinet of the Blues. The first of those triumphs came in 1937. Having earlier won the Free State Shield again that season, the cup campaign saw victories over Dundalk and Shamrock Rovers before a 4-1 semi-final win over surprise package non-league Longford Town put the Blues into the final.

On April 18, 1937, 24,000 turned up at Dalymount to see Waterford take on St. James Gate. The Blues selectors had dropped a bombshell before the game, dropping Johnny Walsh and replacing him with defender Eugene Noonan in attack (the modern day equivalent of dropping Robbie Keane and replacing him with Paul McShane) – but it turned out to be a masterstroke as Noonan scored and along with Timmy O'Keeffe's goal Waterford saw off the challenge of St. James' Gate 2-1. Tom Arrigan collected the cup, the players earned a £5.00 win bonus and even the Lord Mayor of Dublin, Alfie Byrne, was at Knightsbridge Station to wave goodbye to the Waterford supporters after their day in the capital. Oh, for the days of genuine sportsmanship! Darker days were to follow.

In 1941, despite the club getting to the Free State Cup final, losing to Cork United 3-2, the club had to resign from the league after an amazing internal bust-up between players and management. Having finished joint top with Cork United on 30 points, a play-off game was needed to decide the league championship. Seven of the Blues players then demanded a "defeat" bonus, only to be rebuffed by the club's directors who made it known exactly what they thought of the that demand and Waterford FC was thrown into turmoil.

Ultimately, it meant the Blues failing to fulfil the fixture and Cork United was handed the 1941 League of Ireland title by default. Waterford was fined, but the seeds had been sown and the knock-on effect proved disastrous for the Blues. As Cork lifted their first championship title, Waterford was forced to resign from the league. There was a four year exile before re-joining the league, and in 1955 Waterford finished second to St. Patrick's Athletic in the Championship, with Jimmy Gauld notching 30 goals that season – a club record that still stands over 55 years later.

There was a League of Ireland Shield success in 1958, a competition Waterford has won five times, but there's also been many "close but no cigar" moments in the Suirside club's history, and one of the biggest came a year later in the 1959 FAI Cup final. Having worked their way to the final via Transport, Dundalk and a single Tommy Coady goal against Limerick in the semi-finals, Alex Stevenson's Waterford side contested their first FAI Cup final in 18 years against St. Patrick's Athletic on April 19, 1959.

The final will always be remembered for the story of two brothers who suffered agony of two kinds, both equally painful. A couple of weeks prior to the final, Waterford played St. Patrick's Athletic in a dress rehearsal for the cup final, and a young Alfie Hale, already a youth international at the time and the Blues top goal scorer, was stretchered off after a clash with Pat's skipper Tommy Dunne. Hale spent six months in plaster with torn knee ligaments and missed the cup final. Alfie watched on with 22,000 others in Dalymount as the teams played out a pulsating 2-2 draw with Peter Fitzgerald notching Waterford's two goals. However the replay proved harder on Alfie's brother Dixie, who after spearheading the Blues to within eight minutes of victory in the first game, missed a crucial penalty in the replay as Waterford went down 2-1.

> *"In fairness to Tommy there was nothing malicious in the challenge. I was young and a bit naive as had I have been older I would have pulled out of it. It was hard watching it from the stand, even more so when Dixie missed the penalty in the replay, as I regularly took our spots kicks. When it came to the penalty Con Martin didn't want to take it, Peter Fitzgerald and Dixie had a chat and of course my brother stepped up to take it. Even to this day he's still reminded of that miss!"* – **Alfie Hale**

The sixties saw the emergence of Waterford as a true power of the national game. Not only did the Suirsiders win honours, they dismantled everything in front of them with a style of football that won admirers the country over. A sea of Blue travelled the length of the land supporting Waterford and it took the return of a prodigal son to ignite this revolution. The great Paddy Coad started it all off in 1965/66, and by the end of the 1972/73 season Waterford had won an astonishing six league titles in eight years.

After the Blues had re-gained their league status in 1945, only Cork United, Cork Athletic, Dundalk and Limerick had taken the title outside Dublin clubs in the next 20 seasons. Coupled with the fact the FAI Cup had resided in either St. Pat's, Shelbourne or the marauding Shamrock Rovers' trophy cabinet from the late '50s, the capital's monopoly on the major trophies in Irish football was getting all too depressingly familiar.

Coad had been instrumental in a superb Shamrock Rovers side that had won all around them in the 1950s. Between 1952 and 1959, "Coad Colts" went on to win the league three times, the FAI Cup twice, a brace of Top Four Cups and four League of Ireland Shields, just for good measure, in a glorious era for the club from Glenmalure Park. It is still arguably the greatest side to have been spawned by the Ringsend club.

Paddy joined Waterford in 1962, and along the way brought in players like Jimmy McGeough from Derry City, Johnny Matthews from Coventry and Mick Lynch, adding them to a side consisting of the likes of Tommy Taylor, Shamie Coad, John O'Neill, Vinny Maguire, and Al and Shamie Casey. There were also players like Noel Griffin, Paul Morrissey, and Peter Fitzgerald, a veteran of the 1959 Cup final.

Strangely enough, Waterford was firmly beaten 4-0 by Bohemians at their former home, Kilcohan Park, on the opening day of the 1965/66 season, but a string of results from December onwards, including a record-breaking 12 straight wins, climaxed in a memorable day at Lourdes Stadium that April where a travelling Blue and White army watched Waterford beat Drogheda with two goals from Mick Lynch and a Shamie Casey penalty to clinch their first League of Ireland championship.

> *"I don't think anybody thought we'd win the league at the start of the season, but we had made some good signings who fitted in straight away and began to put a run together. The game at Lourdes Stadium was special. Every car, van or bus from Waterford seemed to follow us up to that match! It was such a good team, one of which was Noel Griffin who I felt never really got the recognition he deserved. After all, this was a guy who marked George Best at Lansdowne and kept him quiet!"* – **Shamie Coad**

That league title success meant a first trip to Europe for the Blues. Waterford drew East German opposition in Vorwaerts, a side that had lost on their last visit to Ireland, just twelve months previously against league champions Drumcondra. However the Germans weren't going to make the same mistake twice (the five hour training session they had under the lights at Dalymount the night before was indication of that), and Waterford was overrun the next day, losing 6-1 with Mick Lynch becoming the Blues first European goal-scorer. The second leg saw Waterford ship another six and they were more than happy to get back to domestic matters on their return home.

> *"Playing German side Vorwaerts was a real eye-opener. Everything was fine on the West side until we crossed into East Germany. Our coach was stopped and police had mirrors looking under it which was a real shock to us. The place was desolate and bombed out. We were put up by Vorwearts in a local barracks and they treated us very well. I felt so sorry for the people there. Football was their only escape from what was around them."* – **Vinny Maguire**

The greatest league side of the sixties – Waterford FC pictured here in 1967.
Back (L-R): *Mick Lynch, Jackie Morley, Peter Bryant, Peter Thomas,*
Paul Morrissey, Seamie Coad, Terry Stafford. Front (L-R): *Alfie Hale,*
Johnny Matthews, Vinny Maguire, Jimmy McGeough, Al Casey, John O'Neill
(photo courtesy of Trueblues.zoomshare.com)

Although they relinquished the title a year later, Waterford, now managed by Vinny Maguire, won the League of Ireland championship again in 1967/68, finishing four points clear of Dundalk, the side that had taken their title a year earlier. On the last day of the season St. Patrick's Athletic formed a guard of honour for Maguire's men at a packed Kilcohan Park, where goals from O'Neill, Morrissey, Coad, Lynch and two from Johnny Matthews gave Waterford a 6-1 win and the league title.

There could have been a first double only Waterford's great nemesis intervened. For every hero there's a villain. Batman had the joker. Superman had Lex Luthor. For God, see the Devil. And a certain club from Glenmalure Park had always been Waterford's. Shamrock Rovers beat the Blues convincingly in the 1968 FAI Cup final 3-0, one of the many great run-ins between the clubs, to ruin the dream of that double with goals from Mick Lawlor and a brace from Mick Leech.

> *"My worst memory with the club was the '68 final. Rovers had such a good side. I'll always remember my tussles with Frank O'Neill. He was Rovers outside right in those days and an Irish international. If you let him turn with the ball at all he'd kill you. We had quite a few tussles though I was one player he found hard to get the better off. But they were just too good for us that day."* – **Paul Morrissey**

The astonishing goal rate of O'Neill, Hale and Matthews was the springboard for some astonishing success on the domestic front. In the 1968/69 season alone they hit an astounding 76 goals between them. What the Blues were doing in the league, Rovers were replicating in the cup. By the end of the sixties, Waterford had three league titles, whilst Rovers bagged six FAI Cups. But the summer of '68 also saw Waterford land a plum tie against then European Champions Manchester United in the European Cup.

The game immediately caught the attention of the public. With an unprecedented demand for tickets (some changing hands for £10.00, which was real money back then), and with the Best-inspired victory at Wembley against Benfica still fresh in the memory, over 50,000 packed into Lansdowne Road only to see Denis Law having the bare-faced cheek to ruin the fairytale ending with a hat-trick, though Waterford did score through Johnny Matthews and Al Casey missed a good chance late on in the 3-1 defeat. The return leg at Old Trafford was one-way traffic in a 7-1 hammering, though Al Casey made his own little piece of history by scoring the Blues' first away goal in Europe.

"Our away leg of the 1968 European Cup tie against Manchester United will always be special for me. With Vinny Maguire out injured, I captained the side that night. Walking out alongside Bobby Charlton at Old Trafford against a team defending their European trophy will always be a special memory." – **Alfie Hale**

It would be unfair not to mention the role of Frank Davis in this glorious era with the Blues, as the former Waterford Chairman is regarded as the man responsible for making the club the major force they were in the sixties. Frank famously took heed of a warning in 1965 from then League of Ireland Chairman Sam Prole, who was also Chairman of Drumcondra – reigning champions at the time – for Waterford to "get their house in order, or else". The transformation in the team was astonishing and the success rate unprecedented. It was Davis who paid the princely sum of £3,000 to bring Jimmy McGeough to Waterford, and sorted Johnny Matthews' move from Coventry.

Having retained the title again in 1968/69, seeing off Shamrock Rovers by five points, yet another trip on the continent beckoned, this time against Turkish club Galatasaray. Despite being late September, the heat in the Ali Sami Yen Stadium was stifling in what was already a difficult tie. Peter Thomas picked the ball out of his net twice that afternoon in a 2-0 defeat. Phil Buck and Jackie Morley did notch for the Blues in the return leg (also played at Lansdowne Road), however Galatasaray scored one more, won 3-2 and went through 5-2 on aggregate.

Get in there my son! Johnny Matthews hammers one past Sligo
(photo courtesy of Johnny Matthews)

Under player-manager Alfie Hale, Waterford took a third successive League of Ireland title in 1970. Their arch-nemesis from Glenmalure Park again pushed them hard, but one defeat in four months resulted in the title being clinched on the penultimate weekend of the season when goals from Casey, O'Neill and two from Matthews gave Waterford a 4-2 away win against a Finn Harps' side that had been unbeaten at home to that point.

The club then pulled off a major coup by signing Manchester United full-back Shay Brennan, a man who'd played his first game for United just two weeks after the Munich '58 crash. Hale then decided to revert back to playing duties, leaving Brennan to lead Waterford into a European Cup tussle that autumn with north of the border Glentoran. The usual bragging rights, pride and political divide were churned out by the press, but a well-drilled Waterford side recovered well from going behind and won 3-1 at the Oval. A solitary Al Casey goal in the second leg wrapped up proceedings and put Brennan's men into a second round tie with Glasgow Celtic.

Just three years previously, the "Lisbon Lions" had tamed Inter Milan to win the 1967 European Cup final, and just four months before the Waterford tie had agonizingly been beaten in extra-time of the 1970 European Cup final by Feyenoord. The side boasted players like Billy McNeill, Jimmy Johnstone, Lou Macari and Bobby Murdoch. And orchestrating this Scottish symphony – the great Jock Stein.

Lansdowne again was the venue for what proved a mammoth task. Celtic had got to this round with an absolute annihilation of KPV Kokkola from Finland 14-0, and on October 21 they weren't in the mood for letting up. The Blues endured a harrowing ninety minutes, losing 7-0. Two weeks later Brennan's men travelled to Parkhead. Famously that day, a local newspaper declared in bold print, "Come See the Slaughter of the Leprechauns!" to the Scottish public. The Blues took to the field and John O'Neill scored after 17 minutes and Johnny Matthews added another on the half hour and at half-time the score read Celtic 0, Part-time Leprechauns 2. Jock Stein read the riot act at half-time and Celtic went on to win 3-2 and deny Waterford a famous victory. Although one man thought it was a great result. Johnny Barnes, Waterford's trainer, came out late for the second half and missed Celtic's first goal just seconds after the re-start. At the end of the game Johnny was hopping around with delight at what he thought was a 2-2 draw!

Brennan's transition to player-manager had been seamless and despite losing the title to Cork Hibs' in 1971 they regained it a year later with the most dramatic ninety minutes of any game the club has played in their 80-odd year history. It came on the last day of the 1971/72 season in a match neither Waterford nor Cork Hibernians fans will ever need to be reminded of.

Waterford was two points clear at the top, needing only a point to secure the title. Hibernians needed to win to force a play-off. To add spice to the game, it was a forerunner for the FAI Cup final, which both sides would contest as well. The Hibernians side boasted names like Tony Marsden, John Herrick, and a certain Miah Dennehy. Add the likes of Lawson, Sheehan, Wiggington and manager Dave Bacuzzi into the mix and it was easy to see why this Cork side were the league champions at the time.

A crowd of 25,000 streamed into Flower Lodge to watch this clash. Even before a ball had been kicked in anger, Cork manager Bacuzzi brought his team on a lap of honour in an act of naughty gamesmanship aimed to overawe the Waterford side. It certainly worked . . . for a while. Hibs took the lead through Lawson and Wiggington and were up 2-0 after 32 minutes. To make matters worse for Waterford, Paul Morrissey had gone off injured and with Vinny Maguire already on as a substitute for Jimmy McGeough, and only one substitute allowed at the time, Waterford had to play the entire second half with ten men and already 2-0 down. If you're a Blues fan, read on. If you support Cork Hibs, it might be wise to stop now.

In the proverbial "game of two halves", Brennan's men came storming back out after the break, scoring first through Carl Humphries and then levelling with just four minutes to go from a Johnny Matthews penalty after John Herrick handled Jackie Morley's shot.

"The penalty obviously sticks out in my memory. I always remember Joe O'Grady, the Hibernians goalkeeper, coming up to me and saying, 'You've got no chance of scoring past me you little Englishman', to which I replied, 'Get back on goal you big thick Irishman, I'm putting it to the bottom right hand corner!' Later in the dressing room whilst I was in the bath, Joe came in and pushed my head under the water and said, 'Jesus, I didn't believe you would!'" – **Johnny Matthews**

Astonishingly, in the 90th minute Alfie Hale headed home John O'Neill's free-kick to give Waterford a 3-2 win, leaving Hibernians bewildered and substantially increasing the takings of every pub between Flower Lodge and Redmond Bridge in Waterford that evening. Cork and the magnificent Miah Dennehy gained their revenge in the FAI Cup final, however, with the Corkman becoming the first player to score a hat-trick in a final.

A disappointing exit in Europe to Cypriot side Omonia Nicosia followed before a sixth League of Ireland title in eight years. That came in 1973 when Waterford saw off a highly determined Finn Harps challenge, led by manager Patsy McGowan, by a single point on the last day of the season. Again there was defeat at the first hurdle in Europe, going out to Hungarian outfit Ujpest Dozsa, and a lean period followed with dwindling attendances, poor results and managerial merry-go-rounds only interrupted by a 1974 League Cup final win over Finn Harps.

By the time Tommy Jackson took over in 1978 the club had been drifting around mid-table, but the former Nottingham Forest man breathed new life into the Blues and they contested the 1979 FAI Cup final, going down 2-0 to an impervious Dundalk. It meant dusting down passports that had six years of dust on them and a trip into Europe, where they performed admirably against IFK Gotenburg, losing out 2-1 despite a Tony Keane goal holding the Swedes to a 1-1 draw in the home leg.

A year later, on April 20, 1980, Suirside's finest went one better and bridged a 43-year gap to win only their second FAI Cup in their history. Having beaten Thurles Town, Athlone Town, and seeing off Eoin Hand's Limerick in a cracking 3-2 semi-final replay at Milltown with goals from Syd Wallace, Tony Dunphy and Paul Kirk, Waterford reached its second FAI Cup final in a row.

That Sunday afternoon Brian Gardiner, a 21-year-old Preston-born defender, put a 22nd minute header past Jim Grace in St. Patrick's Athletics' goal to give Tommy Jackson's men the cup, with goalkeeper Peter Thomas, the last remaining link to the great Blues side of the sixties, producing a "Man of the Match" performance.

*"I was immensely proud to captain Waterford in 1980. I remember
the tension in the town in the lead-up to the game. The fact that it
had been so long since the cup had been over the River Suir, so it was
great to get that monkey off our back. I felt confident we'd win – we
had such a strong side. I had captained Limerick in '71 when we won
the cup so to do it twice in one decade is an achievement I'll always
treasure." – Al Finucance*

1980 FAI Cup Winners Back (L-R): *Larry Murray, Mark Meagan, Al Finucane,
Ger O' Mahoney, Mick Madigan, Tony Dunphy, Brian Gardiner.* Front (L-R): *Eamon
Coady, Syd Wallace, Vinny McCarthy, Peter Thomas, Tommy Jackson, Paul Kirk.*
(photo credit: Waterford News & Star)

The 1980/81 Cup Winners Cup paired Waterford against Hibernians of
Malta and, despite losing the first leg 1-0, the Suirsiders hammered four without replay in the return leg to advance. Exciting stuff, which is more than can
be said for the destination of their next opponents. Dynamo Tbilisi in Russia
(or Georgia, if you want to be geographically correct) was about as appetizing
as a week old taco-chip with a rusty fork stuck in the middle. It also presented
a financial burden as Chairman Joe Delaney estimated it would cost £20,000
to send the club to Russia. The first leg had a bumper 3,000 crowd at Kilcohan,
and unfortunately a goal by Russian international Slengelia, before the Iron
Curtain mob finished the job off 4-0 at home.

There was a change of name to Waterford United in 1982 and a League
Cup final victory over Finn Harps in 1985. The Blues had worked their way to
the final having come out of a group containing Limerick, Cork and Athlone,
then dispatched Shamrock Rovers in the semi-finals, all with just the loss of

one goal. On a windswept March afternoon goals from Pat Morley and Mick Bennett sealed the cup at Kilcohan Park against a Harps side who had initially taken the lead through Ian Arkwright.

By this stage former Blues great Alfie Hale was back in charge and the club also contested the 1986 FAI Cup final as well. Unfortunately, they came up against an all-conquering Shamrock Rovers side destroying everything in its path who won through goals from Kevin Brady and Noel Synott, with a bullet of a header any striker would have been proud of – unfortunately, Noel was a Waterford defender.

It produced, however, an 11th and so far last visit into Europe that autumn. A Bordeaux side with the likes of Bernard Lacombe, Jean Tigana and Patrick Battison came away with a 2-1 victory in front of 7,000 in Kilcohan, before the French aristocrats finished off the tie 4-0 at home two weeks later.

Waterford lost their Premier Division status for the first time in 1988/89 but regained it a year later through another ex-player, Johnny Matthews. The nineties proved a real rollercoaster.

Despite Matthews bringing them up after one season in the First Division, the club went straight back down, then up, then down, as United changed divisions almost every single year. One common theme with the club was the revolving door that was installed in each manager's office. Former players Shamie Coad and Michael Bennett also managed, along with former Leeds defender Brendan Ormsby. Incredibly, between 1985 and 2011 United has gone through no less than 17 managers, with Stephen Henderson the latest casualty this June – though he did last a massive four seasons!

Silverware was denied three times in the early nineties as the Blues made a habit of losing in the First Division Shield. The Students of UCD foiled them in the 1991/92 final, whilst Sligo Rovers and Bray Wanderers inflicted the same dose in 1994 and '96. A cup run a year later under Tommy Lynch saw United defeat Monaghan, Shamrock Rovers and Drogheda United on the way to an FAI Cup semi-final defeat on April 4, 1997 to Shelbourne, where a record 8,200 crammed into the RSC to watch the Dubliners win 2-1. Dundalk also defeated Lynch's side in the promotion/relegation play-offs that season, but 12 months later a 1-0 away win to Athlone Town on the penultimate day of the 1997/98 season gave Waterford the First Division championship and promotion back to the Premier Division after an absence of five years.

One of the more painful relegations occurred in 1999/2000, when United lost its Premier Division status to near rivals Kilkenny City in the promotion/relegation play-off that season. The fact a host of ex-Blues players played for "the Cats" made it harder to swallow.

John Power (left) and manager Tommy Lynch celebrate winning the
1997/98 First Division championship (photo credit: Gerry Carroll photography)

In 2003 a third First Division championship was landed by manager Paul Power with Celtic striker Daryl Murphy scoring the winner in the penultimate game away to Dundalk to clinch the title, before another former player Alan Reynolds carried on the good work by securing a fifth place finish in the Premier Division and getting Waterford to their first FAI Cup final in 24 years. That 2004 final is one that still rankles with the Blues faithful. One goal up, four minutes to go, Europe on the horizon. And then? Do I really have to explain this again (as every Longford fan reading this book smiles and nods their heads in unison)? With four minutes left and leading through a Willie Bruton goal United conceded two goals in two minutes (one ironically scored by Waterford native Alan Kirby) to snatch defeat from the jaws of victory.

In 2005 the club looked doomed to relegation as new manager Brendan Rea struggled to keep United in the Premier Division, but the recruitment of Pat Dolan helped steer the club out of choppy waters.

> *"Brendan was a great man doing a difficult job and just needed a*
> *little help. As a player he was an absolute lionheart for the club and*
> *we struck up a good relationship straight away. I'll always remember*
> *the 2-2 draw with Cork in the league that season. We were trying to*
> *avoid relegation, Cork were going for the league title - great crowd,*
> *great passion, a fantastic Munster derby. We had an unbelievable*
> *run and a lot of that was down to Brendan."* – **Pat Dolan**

There should have been relegation in 2006, losing out in a relegation/promotion play-off to Dundalk, only for Shelbourne to offer a reprieve by not securing a Premier Division licence to give Gareth Cronin's men another shot in the big time. Unfortunately, Finn Harps weren't as nice in 2007 beating Waterford 6-3 over two legs in yet another promotion/relegation play-off to send United down.

Out of nowhere a run to the 2009 EA Sports Cup final developed to bring Waterford United into their first League Cup final since 1985 in the same year they lost out in the semi-finals of the FAI Cup. Now managed by Stephen Henderson, the Blues had one of their most successful domestic cup campaigns in years, beating FC Carlow, Shamrock Rovers and UCD on the way to an September 26 showdown with Bohemians in the League Cup final. Despite the home advantage and a large crowd, the damage was done early with two Killian Brennan goals and another from ex-United striker Neale Fenn to rub salt into an already gaping wound, though United did grab a consolation through Kenny Browne.

The FAI Cup saw Henderson's men take out non-leaguers Carrigaline and Crumlin United before taming Premier Division side St. Patrick's Athletic in Richmond Park on the way to a semi-final that saw them lose to a Matthew Blinkhorn goal for Sligo Rovers.

Things were looking up and Henderson's side put together six straight wins at the start of the 2010 season as the club looked primed for promotion. But form dipped and the club was forced into a play-off game against their bogey side Monaghan United. The Northerners hadn't lost to Waterford in a dozen games and that didn't change at the RSC that October when Monaghan came away with a 3-1 win.

Henderson left in June this year (ironically, after another defeat to Monaghan) as the Blues look again destined for another year in the First Division. Sometimes trouble rains on those who are already wet, but despite those who hark back to a bygone day of league titles, cup success and nights in Europe, the club still endures, still operates and still hopes for a new set of heroes to inspire a new generation. And nothing happens unless we first dream.

> *"Waterford and Shamrock Rovers games evoked such great memories throughout the years. I remember the 6-5 game in March of '59 where the Blues had come back from 4-1 down to win 6-5. It was a game straight out of schoolboy fiction. At one point Denny Fitzgerald turned around to Con Martin and said, 'Con - what's the score now?' To which Martin replied, 'I don't have a clue just keep on playing!'"*
> – the late Leo Dunne, one of Waterford's and Ireland's finest sportswriters

Ground Info

If you're worried about grounds hidden in residential areas and sneaky little turnstiles you miss and end up miles away from your destination, then you'll be relieved to hear you simply can't fail to spot the RSC.

The Regional Sports Centre is a modern facility located about a mile from the city centre, just opposite the Ring Road roundabout. It's been home to the Blues since 1993 when United moved from the memories of Kilcohan Park to this current location, though both grounds are similar in that a track separates the supporters from the pitch. In Kilcohan, it was a greyhound track; here it's the two-legged variety.

The main stand which houses 1,300 people was opened in 1996, whilst the Tramore End Stand was added in May 2008 to bring the seated capacity to 3,100. Parking is not a problem with ample room inside the ground on the Ring Road side.

Record Attendance

8,200 v Shelbourne (FAI Cup, April 4, 1997)

Cost

Adults: €10.00
OAPs/Students/Concessions: €6.00
Children (U-16): €3.00

Programme

€3.00 – The match programme has steadily improved over the years to the extent the opening day programme had seven solid, well researched stories from past and present. Shane Murphy's weekly column is worth a mention for the time and research it takes dealing with Waterford games from the past.

Rivals

Cork clubs have always been high on the rivalry agenda. Be it Cork United in the '40s, Cork Hibernians in the '70s or Cork City in the '90s to the present day, any clash with the Leesiders is always anticipated. However, if there was any one club to top that look 90 miles up the road to a team now residing in Tallaght, as Shamrock Rovers for many have been the Blues' biggest rivals throughout the years.

Mascot

Just recently BTID – the unofficial club website – ran a poll to have a new mascot elected with "Bilberry the Goat" coming out tops. Hopes are high his horns might be on show next season.

Food and Drink

Hot food is available from the tram-shaped chipper inside the main gate, whilst there is also a shop under the main stand. An upstairs bar is available also in the same stand, though it is limited to season ticket holders and their guests.

Club Shop

Located on the right-hand side off the main entrance. Gets a little crowded at half-time and swinging a cat in there is not recommended, but it's always doing business so the lads there don't mind! The club also has an online shop whilst the BTID website also sells supporters' merchandise.

Websites

www.waterford-united.ie – club website
www.btid.net – fans' forum

Local Radio

WLR FM 97.5.

The Match – Waterford United v Athlone Town (First Division, March 4, 2011)

First game of the season – new signings, young opponents in Athlone Town and renewed hope of a long-waited promotion. That'll be a scoreless draw then!

From about twenty minutes in it looked as if the game was only going one way. Despite looking like there was nobody at the game almost 800 had turned up in the biting cold. Below me in the stand a father cuddled his son and told him of glory days gone by in Kilcohan as the youngster was clearly attending his first Waterford game. Whether it was his last remains to be seen.

Wexford Youths

Formed:	2007
Ground:	Ferrycarrig Park
Capacity:	2,200
Nickname:	The Youths

"It takes balls to choose pink as your team colours. It takes even bigger ones to get eleven guys to run out on the field wearing them!"
– Dan O'Leary, Wexford Youths Supporter

Every accomplishment starts with the decision to try. For a handful of years players in the youngest club in the league have been crossing the white line with an owner that's testament to the philosophy, "Life is short. Work hard. Play Hard" emblazoned on their chests.

That's something that Wexford Youths' owner Mick Wallace knows all about. The property developer from the local village of Wellingtonbridge is no fly-by-night character or sugar daddy who wanted to buy himself a little plaything with eleven men running around for his amusement, as the Independent TD for Wexford has long been the face of Wexford football. A charismatic, likeable individual who graduated from UCD with a degree in English, History and Philosophy, and built up a successful construction business – if ever the headline "Local boy comes good" could be identified with one person, Wallace fits that profile perfectly.

Mick's links to Wexford soccer are deep-routed. For the best part of two decades he's been coaching the county's U-16 and U-18 sides, presiding over the most successful period in their history and guiding the Wexford Youth League to four U-18 FAI inter-league titles. Another huge achievement was masterminding a Wexford Youths side that won the 2008 FAI Youth Cup, hammering Dundalk 4-0 with current Youths striker Danny Furlong scoring all four goals in the final. In all, the club's underage sides have reached four finals in seven years.

The league's youngest club (mere pups at four years of age) was founded in 2006. Wallace himself funded the construction of Ferrycarrig Park, a state-of-the-art complex comprising of clubhouse, training pitches, Astroturf and a floodlight pitch at a cost of €6 million.

Despite being a predominantly GAA-based town, Wexford still had a thriving soccer community in Junior League terms. Whether they expected to eventually have a League of Ireland club may have been the dream, but reality intruded for many years. Then a chance presented itself unexpectedly with the demise of Dublin City in 2006. The Dubliners had formed out of the ashes of Home Farm Everton and achieved success under owner Ronan Seery, who had pumped a large chunk of his own money into the club winning the 2003 First Division title under manager John Gill and finishing runners-up two years later but fell, like many, into financial difficulty. The Vikings' resignation from the league midway through the 2006 season opened the door for a number of clubs, and Wexford Youths was one of them.

The FAI then took over the running of the Eircom League and immediately stated that all existing clubs had to apply for entry to the league under the new licensing laws brought in by UEFA. It meant every club's infrastructure being looked at and houses needing to be put in order. All were – except one.

Limerick FC was denied a licence and the franchise went out to tender. They came back in the shape of Limerick 37, but it still left one place up for grabs that Dublin City had vacated, and Wexford would grab it like a fly to a cow pat.

"By the time 2007 came about the complex had been built a few years and we knew we had the infrastructure to compete at that level. To be honest, when I started the senior team it was more to promote the under-age rather than vice versa. That said, it was still a huge opportunity for us to have a League of Ireland side. People may have doubted if we had the players but the way I looked at it at the time

was we were the best in Ireland U–18, so why couldn't we be at least decent at U–21, 22 or 23?" – **Mick Wallace**

On entering the league, Wallace called on former St. Patrick's and Cork City manager Pat Dolan to help out (Dolan became head coach) and stuck with a policy of recruiting only Wexford-based amateur players from the local league. Some may have said it was suicidal, but you look up the phrase "stick to your guns" in the dictionary and you'll likely see a picture of Mick Wallace smiling back at you . . . and probably in pink.

> *"I understood completely that if we were going to stay amateur whilst other clubs were professional that we'd lose our best players, and in some cases that's how it turned out, but that's the nature of things. The same as a young player would leave a Wexford Junior League side and come here, to one of our players leaving for money to go somewhere else, and if an English club then came in for him he would move again, so in that respect I accepted it. Our plan was always to stay amateur."* – **Mick Wallace**

A local derby with Waterford United (photo credit: Sean Dempsey)

On February 6, 2007 Wexford Youths were granted a League of Ireland licence, just weeks before the start of the 2007 season – a truly rapid rise to top flight football. Wallace was under no illusions about their inaugural season in the league. With a side made up of local Junior League players with an average age of 20, the Youths weren't expecting to move any mountains for a couple of seasons, but it was important to get acquainted with the league even if it meant a rough ride most weekends.

Despite that, the club's first League of Ireland game didn't end in defeat. An away trip to Monaghan United on March 9 ended in a 2-2 draw. Conor Sinnott had the honour of being the first player to score a League of Ireland goal for the club, while Tom Elmes had his Buzz Aldrin moment scoring the second.

> *"To be honest, getting the draw was the most important thing as we were 2-0 down against Monaghan in that game. Obviously it's a historic goal but it wasn't something I thought about at the time as only weeks earlier we'd been told we were entering the League of Ireland so for a while it was all helter-skelter at the club." –* Conor Sinnott

A week later Ferrycarrig Park hosted their first game at senior level as over 2,100 fans showed up to see a Tom Elmes' goal give Wexford Youths a 1-0 win over Cobh Ramblers to send everyone home happy.

> *"We had a storm the night before the game and all the temporary security fencing around the ground had blown down so Mick was on the phone to me at 8.30 that morning and through hail, rain and showers myself, Mick and one or two others had to try and erect the fencing before the crowd arrived which we just about did in time for kick off!" –* Simon Aust, Event Controller

Four points won. Two games in. Still undefeated. Piece of cake this League of Ireland lark!

There were local derbies with Kilkenny City and a higher profile one in the shape of Premier Division Waterford United when the sides clashed in Wexford Youths' first League Cup game. That clash happened on April 2, 2007 at Waterford's Regional Sports Centre, and although United won comfortably 3-0 the clubs would get better acquainted over the next few seasons!

Everything was a brave new world and wide-eyed adventure for Wallace's youngsters that season. A first game, first win, first goal scorer and soon the inevitable first FAI Cup match at this level. That took place against another newly formed club – Limerick 37. The meeting of both new boys had ended in a draw when they met in the league in April, and the cup game followed suit when they clashed in Ferrycarrig Park that June. A Joey Wadding cross was turned into his own net by Limerick's Nigel Keady before the visitors equalised through Ross Cosgrave. Limerick won the replay before going out to Longford in the quarter-finals.

The Warriors (as they are also called) defied the doubters and notched seven wins that season, collected 31 points and avoided finishing bottom – that misfortune going to near neighbours Kilkenny. That first season in the big time finished with a 3-1 away win at former Premier Division champions Shelbourne, a fixture no doubt Mick Wallace had given considerable dream-time to when Shels were winning league championships and competing in the Champions League a few years earlier.

The 2008 season began the way Wexford would have wanted – a local derby at home. Despite still being in their infancy the Youths built up a bona-fide rivalry over the next few seasons with their neighbours Waterford United. The Blues lay 30 miles to the south, with a league history that marked them as a "big fish in a small pond scenario" to some. With Cork City playing Premier Division football, and the demise of Kilkenny City the same season, both clubs had to settle on trying to outdo each other over the next eight months. Close to 2,000 supporters turned up for that league opener on March 7, only to see the Warriors lose 2-1 against United after Paul Murphy had scored on his Youths' debut.

Again the league was hard work for the Youths, but there was a marked improvement. Ten wins and 11 points on the happy side of relegation meant the club that had, in an act of sheer bravery on the part of Mr. Wallace, adopted pink shirts as their kit, were safe for another season.

In researching this book I went to my local bookie and asked him what price Wexford Youths were to win the 2008 EA Sports League Cup. He replied with, "Get out of my shop you gambling degenerate", but after I explained I'm not so demented that I'd try to place money on a competition played two years' previously, he found out that at the beginning of the competition Wexford Youths were 125/1 to take home the trophy.

Had anyone faith in the Youths that season? Did any of the Ferrycarrig faithful have a sneaky each-way bet? Did the players think they could appear in a League Cup final on national television in pink shirts? If the answer was yes to all three then you had a nice little nest-egg that year as the Warriors ripped up, poured petrol on and set fire to any form book by becoming the first side outside the Premier Division since Limerick FC in 2002 to reach the final of the League Cup.

It all started with an extra-time win against Premier Division strugglers Cobh Ramblers in the last week of March 2008. After a second round victory against the Kerry League (with a brace from Conor Sinnott), the obstacles were beginning to clear and a magnificent away win at UCD with goals from John Flynn-O'Connor and Sinnott, yet again, saw the Youths into a semi-final meeting with another Premier club – Cork City.

If winning away at UCD had raised an eyebrow or two, the semi-final triumph at Turner's Cross produced a collective sit-up-and-take-notice from the rest of the league. Despite being 6/1 underdogs (yes, my bookie checked that as well) Wallace's men produced yet another shock by beating the Corkonians in their backyard courtesy of a Paul Murphy goal on 24 minutes.

A fairytale in the making, 3,000 supporters converged on Ferrycarrig Park on Saturday September 27, 2008 to see could Wexford Youths add just one more Premier Division scalp to their collection when the Warriors faced off against Derry City in the EA Sports Cup final. It wasn't to be.

Despite having the other 24 counties in this country rooting for them, the Youths were brushed aside as Stephen Kenny's men took no prisoners, scoring five in the first half hour and killing any chance of a revival. Danny Furlong had given the Youths brief hope at 2-1, but a Sammy Morrow hat-trick for the visitors inflicted terminal damage and made sure Derry collected their fourth League Cup in a row. In the FAI Cup, St. Patrick's accounted for Wallace's men after a third round win against non-league Killester.

> *"Derry were a great side but we froze on the night as well. We had so much youth and I suppose inexperience in the side and the best part of 3,000 supporters looking on that it got to us. The damage was done very early and we had no way back."* – Conor **Sinnott**

> *"Beating Cork in the semi-final at Turner's Cross was one of the greatest nights we've had as a club, but the final was also a very proud moment for me despite the defeat. Only three players out of our fourteen that night were over twenty-one."* – Mick **Wallace**

Again in 2009 considerable progress was made. Winning 15 of their 33 games, Wexford finished a comfortable sixth, amassing 50 points and gaining a first win over local rivals Waterford United – doing it in style with a 2-1 away win at the RSC.

The League Cup heroics of 12 months' previous couldn't be repeated in 2009 and Premier Division Bohemians shaded an entertaining quarter-final in Ferrycarrig Park that May on the way to winning the trophy, however Wallace managed to bring through nine U-18s into the senior squad – something almost unheard of in League of Ireland terms.

Mick stepped down in 2010 and left team affairs to Limerick native Noel O'Connor and another season of mid-table safety followed. Any cup progress was halted by Shamrock Rovers in the FAI Cup and Cork City in the League Cup. The 2011 season has been a struggle on and off the field for Wallace's warriors. The building boom going bust has obviously had a knock-on effect at Wexford Youths, particularly when the club had finally got planning permis-

Wexford Youths owner Mick Wallace with current manager Noel O'Connor
(photo credit: Sean Dempsey)

sion for a state-of-the-art, 2,500 all-seated stadium after years of red tape, and construction on a new gym has stopped.

But the club still have people of purpose to fall back on. Everyone who works for the club does it voluntarily – from all the match day crew to the people who serve in the bar.

On the field a battle for survival ensued, however they've had bright spots – the hammering of Derry City in this year's FAI Cup being one and Mick remains defiant and typically philosophical about his club. One look at the heading in his programme notes explains that. "The world belongs to the optimist."

> *"Mick has been a great, great friend and a big influence on me. When he asked me to help start a League of Ireland side in Wexford it was a delight to return one favour after him doing me so many and I said I'd give him two years. The facilities he built with his own money with no support was incredible. I'd make him Sports Minister tomorrow if it was down to me." – Pat Dolan*

Ground Info

Ferrycarrig Park is located in Newcastle, Crossabeg less than three miles from Wexford Town. Although you can see the ground from the main road don't be deceived (like me) that you can gain entry from there. Take the first left past the Ferrycarrig Hotel and then the next right and you won't go wrong.

Record Attendance

3,100 v Wolves (Friendly, November 2, 2009)

Cost

Adults: €10.00
Students/OAPs: €5.00
U-16s: €5.00
U-10s: Free

Programme

€3.00 – Short yet sweet with some interesting articles. Brian De Salvo pens a good column as does media officer Peter Crimmings, whilst Mick adds a philosophical edge to his notes: "We don't expect our players to play like Barcelona each night, just a consistent honest approach."

Rivals

To my surprise it wasn't Waterford United, rather a team almost three hours away in a different province! Limerick FC has been the focus of the supporters' ire for a while, so little did I know I had stumbled across a grudge match.

Mascot

The Pink Panther strolled around the ground on previous visits but hasn't been around the vicinity for a while now.

Food and Drink

The Wexford Youth clubhouse is an absolute credit to the club. Finished in 2003, the downstairs houses changing rooms whilst the bar upstairs has ample space and is extremely cosy (especially on a cold night). Quite probably the best place to watch a game of League of Ireland football and have a glass of wine.

The shop on the far side of the ground will do you coffee, choc's and the hottest hot dogs in Ireland (I didn't need gloves after wrapping my hands around them – not bad either!).

Club Shop

Located just inside the turnstiles with witty banter and chat from the lads inside there as well. So much so I even thought about purchasing something pink from inside!

Website

www.wexfordyouthsfc.ie

Local Radio

South East Radio 95.6 FM.

The Match – Wexford Youths v Limerick FC (First Division, June 24, 2011)

By far the worst weather I've experienced but also one of the best games. You could have given me 500/1 on the Youths winning this game after the first 45 minutes and I wouldn't have taken you up on it in a lifetime, however Noel O'Connor's men battled their way back from 2-0 down with two goals from Ben Ryan (the first direct from a corner) only to lose to an unfortunate Craig Wall goal less than a minute after levelling the game. Best moment of the match? The kids sitting in front of me who were convinced the Youths had added a bit of continental flair with a new goalkeeper called "Taykurtime", only to find out it was Noel O'Connor shouting "take your time" every time the ball came to goalkeeper Packie Holden.

Gone But Not Forgotten

A look back at clubs that once graced the League of Ireland.
Some are defunct, some are still fighting fit. All have brought
wonderful memories to many.

---

*"It was an amazing experience which included a mix of emotions.
Fantastic highs and hurtful lows, but still a wonderful journey. I'd like
to think that somewhere down the line someone might relight the fuse."*
– Jim Rhatigan, Kilkenny City FC

Bray Unknowns (1924–1943)

When Bray Wanderers were playing as a local Sunday League side in the late
1920s, Bray Unknowns were already proudly representing County Wicklow in
the Free State League. Entering the league in 1924 as a replacement for Midland Athletic, Unknowns struggled to make any impact on the competition,
finishing top half of the table just once in their first decade, but managed to
reach two consecutive Free State Cup semi-finals in 1925 (losing to Shamrock
Rovers) and in 1926 where Fordsons of Cork beat them 4-1.

The club tied with both Waterford and Dundalk on 24 points behind
eventual champions Sligo in the 1936/37 season, but three consecutive bottom
placed finishes between 1940-43, where the club won just four games, eventually saw the demise of the team as a League of Ireland club. They continued as
a Leinster Senior League club and eventually merged with Bray Wanderers in
the mid-seventies.

Brideville (1925–1945)

Hailing from the Liberties area of Dublin, Brideville entered the Free State
League in the 1925/26 season as a direct replacement for Brooklyn. The club
became the first winners of the Free State Junior Cup in 1925 and twice came
close to winning the Blue Riband itself. In 1927, despite finishing bottom of
the league with just two wins all season, Brideville reached the Free State Cup
final only to be denied by then non-league Drumcondra. Three years later a last

minute goal by David Byrne of Shamrock Rovers foiled Brideville again in the final. The club temporarily said goodbye to the Free State League at the end of the 1931/32 season, re-emerged in 1935, but checked out permanently in 1945.

Brooklyn FC (1923–1925)

Elected to the Free State League for the 1923/24 season, Brooklyn lasted just two seasons. Though they finished third bottom those years, their 6-2 away win against Jacobs in the 1924/25 Free State Cup was the biggest away victory in the cup to that point. They also produced Joe Kendrick, who represented the Irish Free State League when they played at the 1924 Olympics.

Cobh Ramblers (1985-2008)

The best known of Ireland's third tier sides, with a rich history in the League of Ireland, Cobh may be in the shadow of their near rivals Cork City but "the Rams" have also tasted success, played in the top tier and ironically lasted longer than any of one of Cork's eleven incarnations.

The club dates back 89 years and were kicking a ball about the same year as the first full season of the Free State League, however their first impact on national level came in the 1976 League Cup topping a group of Waterford, Cork Celtic and Kilkenny, before losing to Shamrock Rovers 3-0 in the semi-finals.

In 1983, whilst a Munster Senior League side, they reached the last four of the FAI Cup beating Dundalk and Finn Harps en route to a semi-final defeat against Sligo Rovers which went to four games, equalling the longest cup tie in League of Ireland history, Rovers eventually winning 3-2 at the Showgrounds after 1-1, 2-2 and 0-0 draws.

In 1985 the club made its debut in the League of Ireland playing their first match against Cork City in a League Cup game on September 8, 1985 and won promotion from the First Division under Liam McMahon in 1988. Their stay in the top flight was brief, finishing second bottom with 21 points, however St. Coleman's Park saw promotion once again in the 1992/93 season, just seeing off Monaghan United to clinch a First Division runners-up spot behind champions Galway United.

Though they survived their first season back in the top flight via a promotion/relegation play-off against Finn Harps, the Rams were relegated in 1995. In 1999 a First Division play-off spot was earned, but also a 7-0 hammering from surprise relegation candidates Bohemians.

Under Stephen Henderson, 2007 proved the most successful league campaign in Cobh Ramblers' history. A season which had started unimpressively with a 2-0 home defeat to Limerick soon gained momentum, and on November 10, 2007 a goal from Kevin Murray against Athlone Town was enough to clinch Cobh Ramblers the First Division championship in a season where they kept 22 clean sheets.

Unfortunately, the club couldn't hold on to their Premier Division status for more than a year, and worse was to follow when Ramblers failed to obtain a League of Ireland License in 2009. In 2010, now as an A Championship side, the club reached the First Division promotion/relegation play-off decider against Salthill Devon but lost 3-1 over two legs.

Cork Clubs – See Cork City FC chapter.

Dolphin FC (1930-1937)

A very successful side for the short period of time they played League of Ireland, Dolphin Football Club won the League Championship once in the mid-thirties as well as playing bridesmaids in the Free State Cup on two occasions. The Dublin outfit entered the Free State League in 1930 when the championship had been extended to twelve clubs – finishing fifth in their first season. In 1932 they surprised St. James Gate, Cork and Shelbourne on the way to the Free State Cup final before losing 1-0 to Shamrock Rovers on April 17. Twelve months later the club again reached the final. Again it was against Rovers, only the margin of defeat was three goals this time. The club's luck changed and soon after Dolphin cliched the 1934/35 league title, seeing off St. James Gate by a point, in a year they also won the first Dublin City Cup. A treble was denied in the League of Ireland Shield – yet again by Shamrock Rovers. The club was denied a successful title defence only by Bohemians before resigning from the league in 1937.

Drumcondra (1928-1972)

The first non-league winners of the FAI Cup, the first Irish team to win a tie in Europe, and a club that's boasted a huge array of talent and honours throughout the years. Formed in 1924, "Drums" first entered the league in the 1928/29 season, however it was their success in the Free State Cup two seasons previously that brought them to national attention. Drums beat Jacobs then Bohemians on the way to winning the Blue Riband with a Johnny Murray goal in a replay over Brideville on April 9, 1927, in a year where they also won the Intermediate Cup.

They finished fourth on their League of Ireland debut and caused a real upset by winning the 1943 FAI Cup by beating an all-conquering Cork United side who had won three League of Ireland titles in a row as well as coming into the final for a third year running with goals from Dick McGrane and Tommy McNamara. Three years later the club won their third FAI Cup, defeating Shamrock Rovers 2-1 in the final in a year the club also clinched the League of Ireland Shield (which they won another three times.) A first League of Ireland championship was finally clinched in the 1947/48 season, seeing off Dundalk by a point with players like former Irish internationals Kevin Clarke, John "Kit" Lawlor and Benny Henderson. The 18 points gained from the 14 games played that season remains the lowest points tally ever to win a league title. Not that it bothered the Drums – they successfully defended the title a year later. The FAI Cup was won twice more in the fifties.

Another League of Ireland title was clinched in 1958 with a side including former Irish international Alan Kelly Sr. and the club played Athletico Madrid in the European Cup as a reward – their first trip into Europe. Another title was clinched in 1961, pipping St. Patrick's Athletic, then Drums became the first League of Ireland club to claim an aggregate win in Europe by beating 1909 Odense in the 1962/63 Inter-Cities Fairs Cup.

The club's home ground of Tolka Park was packed during this golden era. Sam Prole was Chairman of the club and the League of Ireland when Drums won their final league title in 1965. In 1972, Drums merged with Home Farm as Home Farm–Drumcondra, but the famous club title vanished off the name in 1973 (Home Farm continued to play at Tolka). The club still survives now as a Lenister Senior League side.

Dublin City (1999-2006)

Formed in 1999, the Vikings achieved promotion to the Premier Division twice and won a First Division championship, but all too soon became a statistic among the growing trend of League of Ireland clubs that fell into financial difficulty in the twenty-first century which eventually consigned them to the annals of League of Ireland history.

Home Farm Fingal CEO Ronan Seery renamed the club as Dublin City and under John Gill the club surprised everyone to win the 2003 First Division championship, losing just four of the 33 games. Life in the choppy waters of the Premier Division however proved anything but plain sailing. Six wins and Gill's resignation proved a season to forget. City regrouped and bounced back at the first attempt.

Roddy Collins, who had taken over from the departed Gill, made a well publicised move three weeks before the end of the 2004 season to manage Premier Division Shamrock Rovers. City finished runners-up to Sligo Rovers in the First Division, but claimed the scalp of the Hoops in their promotion/relegation play-off, sending Rovers down for the first time in their history. However poor attendances and the fact the club had no permanent home ground, playing in places like Dalymount Park and Morton Stadium, eventually took its toll and on July 19, 2006, 17 games into the season, the club resigned from the Eircom League citing financial difficulties.

Dublin United (1921-1923)

Played in the first season of the Free State league, finishing seventh with their games played at Angelsea Road. The following season was their last in the league. Became the first team to score eight goals in the Free State Cup with a hammering of fellow league side Frankfort 8-1 on January 14, 1922.

Frankfort FC (1921/22)

Formed in 1908, the Dubliners played in the first Free State League season – 1921/22 – finishing sixth of eight teams. They were not re-elected for the following season, however Frankfort FC still exists as a junior club and celebrated their 100 anniversary in 2008. Former Irish international Tom Davis started his career with the club before enjoying success at Tranmere Rovers.

Home Farm (1972-1999)

Founded in 1928 as a merger between two street football teams from the Drumcondra and Whitehall districts of Northside Dublin, Home Farm is a name synonymous with decades of young, precocious talent. Winners of the FAI Intermediate Cup on three occasions (1963, '67 and '68), as well as the Leinster Senior Cup (1964), the club has produced some of the finest players in Ireland through their youth set-up. People like ex-Manchester United legend Johnny Carey, and fellow Red Devil Liam Whelan who lost his life on a snow-ridden tarmac in Munich 1958, plus Irish internationals like Paddy Mulligan, Ray Treacy, Ronnie Whelan, Kenny Cunningham, Richard Dunne, and Darren O'Dea, whilst Liam Brady and Johnny Giles were also on Home Farm's books before crossing the pond to Arsenal and Leeds respectively.

Whilst the Leinster Senior Cup defeat of Dundalk on St. Stephen's Day 1964 shocked many, the club's finest achievement was capturing the FAI Cup in 1975, thus becoming the first amateur club since Bohemians in 1935 to collect the Blue Riband. Under manager Dave Bacuzzi, and with players like Dermot Keely, Martin Murray and Noel King in their side, Home Farm worked their way past Dundalk, Cork Celtic and St. Patrick's en route to meeting Shelbourne in the final. Despite being overwhelming underdogs, a goal from Frank Devlin after just seven minutes was enough to win the cup which loyal club servant Jack Dempsey lifted above his head on April 27. The club went on to represent Ireland in the 1975/76 Cup Winners Cup against Lens, drawing 1-1 at home but shipping six goals without reply in France. By that stage the club had already been a League of Ireland club having merged with Drumcondra as Home Farm Drumcondra in 1972, then reverting to

Home Farm a year later. Despite the cup success the club's league form was consistently poor, finishing just once inside the top nine before relegation to the First Division in 1987.

The club signed a sponsorship deal with Merseyside giants Everton in 1995 which allowed the Liverpudlians first choice on the best of the club's players, eventually resulting in Richard Dunne moving from Whitehall to Goodison Park. At this point the club changed its name again to Home Farm Everton. Promotion was achieved for the first time in almost a decade by beating Athlone Town in the 1995/96 promotion/relegation play-off, and under Dermot Keely the club won its first silverware in 23 years by winning the First Division Shield beating Cobh Ramblers 5-3 over two legs in 1998.

The deal with Everton ended soon after and with Ronan Seery, son of Home Farm co-founder Don Seery, taking over the club there was a split. Home Farm FC would play in the Leinster Senior League (as they still do today) whilst the League of Ireland licence was kept under the heading of Home Farm Fingal (later renamed Dublin City).

Jacobs (1921-1932)

One of the original eight of the Free State League in its inaugural 1921/22 season, Jacobs played their football at the Strand, and chalked up over a decade in the league reaching two Free State Cup semi-finals in 1923 and '26 before bowing out in 1932. They consistently qualified for the FAI Cup as a non-league side in the 1950s and '60s.

Kildare County (2002-2009)

When St. Francis withdrew from the league in 2001, Newbridge Town FC was approached to fill the gap the Saints had left in the First Division, however to reach a broader fan base it was decided to enter a team with Kildare in their name – hence the birth of Kildare County.

The Thoroughbreds played their first game on August 24, 2002, losing to Limerick FC in a First Division clash. Playing their games at Station Road with Dermot Keely as manager County finished fifth just two points off a play-off place. The club kept up its solid start to life in the First Division – again finishing fifth and two points off a play-off spot in 2003 (the interim year) whilst a fourth place placing in 2004 with 62 points under Eric Hannigan proved the highlight of the club's tenure in the league.

Former Bray striker John Ryan took charge for the next four seasons, however the Thoroughbreds horsed around in the bottom half of the table, though the club's U-21 side did reach the final of the Enda McGill Cup in 2006 – losing out to Cork City. In 2008 Tony Cousins replaced the departing Ryan, but the club finished bottom and then lost out to A Championship side Mervue United in the promotion/relegation play-off match. It should have meant demotion, however Kildare County was granted a First Division licence after Cobh Ramblers failed to meet the necessary criteria.

It only proved a short respite. With ongoing financial difficulties, despite some high profile friendlies against Dundee United and Sunderland, the club's board and management team resigned before their final game of the 2009 season against Shelbourne, though a fantastic effort by the players and fans ensured the game went ahead, even if it meant a 5-1 defeat. The club then disbanded, unable to fulfil their promotion/relegation play-off with A Championship side Salthill Devon, meaning the Galwegians received a walkover and took Kildare's place in the First Division for 2010.

Kilkenny City (1985-2008)

Not many clubs have been formulated by a bunch of Leaving Cert students with a free class in a Christian brother's school, but Kilkenny City can claim this original beginning. Founded in 1966 originally as EMFA (the EM for Emmett Place and the FA for Fatima Place, where co-founder Jim Rhatigan grew up), the club played locally until they gained entry into the inaugural First Division in 1985. Stationed at Buckley Park, a ground they bought for £16,000, EMFA played their first league game at home to Derry City on October 20, 1985 with Jim Rhatigan in charge. Jim Leahy had the honour of scoring the club's first league goal in that 1-1 draw against the Candystripes. That first season proved a harsh introduction to League of Ireland football. One win in 18 games meant "the Black Cats" finished bottom on eight points, however just a season later the club picked up its first piece of top flight silverware. By beating Finn Harps 4-2 under manager Joe McGrath, City had surprised many to take the 1986/87 First Division League of Ireland Shield.

The club changed its name to Kilkenny City in 1989 and two years later beat UCD, non-league Port Laoise and Ashtown Villa on the way to a semi-final showdown with Premier Division Shamrock Rovers in the FAI Cup. A record 6,500 turned up at Buckley Park to see the dream die courtesy of a Derek Swan goal. City continued to struggle in the league; their 94/95 campaign produced just two draws and 25 defeats – the worst season of any club in the history of the league but amazingly within two years the club gained promotion as First Division champions under Alfie Hale, winning the title by a massive 11 points from Drogheda United – still the biggest winning margin for any champion of the First Division.

The Premier proved choppy waters for the good ship Kilkenny and the Black Cats were relegated after just one season, however they regained Premier Division status again in 2000 under Paul Power with a promotion/relegation play-off victory against near neighbours Waterford United. Only one victory was harnessed on that return to the Premier Division and Kilkenny was relegated again in 2000/01 after just one season. Pat Scully then cut his managerial teeth at Buckley Park before Shamrock Rovers came calling in 2005. The club finished bottom the next two seasons, and a 3-1 defeat at home to Finn Harps on November 10, 2007 proved to be the club's last league game. Kilkenny City resigned from the league in January 2008, their place being filled by Sporting Fingal.

Midland Athletic (1922-1924)

Lasted just two seasons in the top flight, playing their games at the Thatch. Finished ninth in their first season, but 16 defeats from 18 games in 1923/24 put paid to the club and they would not be re-elected.

Newcastlewest FC (1985-90)

Limerick side Newcastlewest played in the inaugural First Division championship of 1985, finishing eighth in a season that former Cork Hibernians great Miah Dennehy turned out for them. Indeed, the Munstermen also had former Irish international Al Finucane and Des Kennedy finish their career with the club, whilst also being managed by former Waterford winger and seven time league winner Johnny Matthews. The club's highest position came about in 1988/89 when 27 points were taken from 27 games, however their last season saw them just avoid the First Division wooden spoon on goal difference from Monaghan. Left the league in 1990 but went back to being a successive junior league club in the Limerick Desmond League.

Olympia (1921-1923)

Played in the inaugural Free State League, finishing fourth and losing out to Shamrock Rovers in the first Free State Cup. A year later only Rathmines finished below them in a poor season and the club would not be re-elected.

Pioneers (1922-1925)

Joined the Free State League in 1922/23 and lasted four seasons, the last two of which they spent propping up the table. Went down 6-2 to non-league Lindon in the Free State Cup in January 1926 – the first time a non-league side scored six goals against league opposition in Free State Cup history.

Rathmines (1922/23)

Resigned from the league after one season, where they lost 19 of 22 games and gave the first walkover in FAI Cup history when they failed to fulfil their fixture with non-league Fordsons of Cork on January 13, 1923.

Reds United (1935/36)

When Shelbourne had a high profile disagreement with the FAI during the 1933/34 season it lead to their resignation from the league in a move that shocked League of Ireland football. Reds United took their place for a solitary season. Their 1935/36 campaign saw the club finish fourth, whilst Dundalk accounted for the club in the Free State Cup. They then resigned so Shelbourne could rejoin the league for the 1936/37 season.

Shelbourne United (1922-1924)

Not to be confused with a certain team from Tolka, United played their games at Anglesea Road on entry to the league in 1922. A moderately successful first season saw them finish fourth but lose to non-league Alton United of Belfast in the cup. The following year the club finished sixth playing their games at Glenmalure Park before withdrawing from the league.

Sporting Fingal (2008-2011)

The most recent high profile casualty. The idea of Fingal County Council, who wanted to establish football in the area, Sporting were supposed to compete in the A Championship, however the demise of Kilkenny City created a window of opportunity which the club took playing their first game in top flight Irish football in the First Division against Longford on March 8, 2008, losing 5-1. Despite this the club finished fourth on 62 points, and with an increased budget for 2009 Fingal produced a fairytale season of First Division promotion an FAI Cup triumphs.

The league campaign had seen Fingal finish third behind Shelbourne and champions UCD but achieve promotion via the promotion/relegation play-off over two legs against Bray Wanderers, whilst the FAI Cup would take on Roy of the Rovers proportions, beating Blarney United, Athlone Town, Shamrock Rovers and Bray Wanderers on the way to a showdown on November 22, 2009 against Sligo Rovers. The scriptwriters may have packed up and gone home by the 85th minute with Rovers leading 1-0, but a Colm James equalizer and a dramatic injury-time winner from Gary O'Neill clinched the Blue Riband for Fingal.

That victory brought the fledging club into Europe where they performed admirably against Portuguese side Maritimo in the Europa League, going out 6-4 over two legs. Despite the success the club soon ran into financial difficulty, players' contracts were cancelled and on February 10, 2011 Sporting Fingal withdrew their application for a League of Ireland licence bringing and all too abrupt end to the club.

St. Francis (1996-2001)

Founded in 1958 and hailing from the Liberties in Dublin, St. Francis had a brief flirtation with the league for five seasons before reverting back to Leinster League status. The club had been successful at Junior League level, winning the FAI Junior Cup in 1969, progressing through Intermediate level on to Leinster Senior League status, winning it in 1989.

An FAI Cup odyssey that began on the March 11, 1990 with a 1-0 win away to Kilkenny City ended in front of 33,000 people at Lansdowne Road with defeat at the final hurdle to Bray Wanderers in the FAI Cup that May. Along the way Pete Mahon's men also accounted for Cobh Ramblers, Newcastlewest and Bohemians, before a John Ryan hat-trick for the Seagulls killed the dream.

In 1996 the club replaced St. James Gate in the League of Ireland First Division, playing their first league match on October 11, 1996 against Waterford United – losing 4-0. They won seven of their 28 games to finish ninth, but never finished outside the bottom three during their five-year tenure. Current St. Patrick's Athletic manager Pete Mahon ended a 26-year association with the club in 1998, 16 of them as manager. A highly publicised proposed merger with St. Patrick's Athletic was expected to breathe new life into the club after they'd finished bottom with just three wins from 36 games at the end of the 2000/2001 season, however the plan outraged St. Pat's fans. Talks soon broke down, the merger never materialised, and St. Francis exited the league despite having been re-elected to play in the 2001/02 season. In 2003 they re-joined the Leinster Senior League.

St. James Gate (1921-1944, 1990-1996)

Winners of the inaugural Irish Free State League and the first champions of the FAI Cup. Established in 1902, the club won that first title in 1922 with players like Charlie Dowdall and Bob Carter in a side that beat Bohemians by two points. The double was completed with a victory over a non-league Shamrock Rovers courtesy of a Jack Kelly goal in front of 10,000 spectators at Dalymount. The club spent the rest of the decade in mid-table obscurity before winning the League of Ireland Shield in the 1935/36 season.

Having lost Free State Cup finals to Cork (1934) and Waterford (1937) St. James clinched their second Blue Riband with a 2-1 defeat of Dundalk in the 1938 final, whilst a 6-0 hammering of Cork City gave the club the Dublin City Cup a year later. Another title arrived in the 1939/40 season with Irish international Paddy Bradshaw hitting 29 goals, topping the goal scoring charts for the second season in a row. In fact, between 1932-40 St. James players accounted for top goal scorers in six of those eight seasons: George Ebbs in

1932/33, Alf Rigby in 1933/34 and 1934/35, Willie Byrne in 1937/38 and Paddy Bradshaw in both 1938/39 and 1939/40.

However in the 1943/44 season, the club finished bottom and were not re-elected. They spent another 46 years outside the league until re-entry as a First Division side in 1990, finishing fifth in that first season. The club spent five further years as a mid-table First Division side before resigning in 1996, though they still exist as a Leinster Senior League club playing their games at the Iveagh Grounds and will celebrate their 110th anniversary in 2012.

Thurles Town (1977-82)

Elected to the league in 1977 along with Galway Rovers, Thurles Town managed to sustain League of Ireland football for five seasons until departing from the top flight in 1982. The Tipperary outfit had gained entry to a League of Ireland that had expanded for the first time to 16 teams. It wasn't a pleasant first season: one solitary win from thirty games meant the Munstermen finished bottom. A tenth place finish in 1979/80 was as good as it got in the league whilst the cups offered little solace – in their five seasons in top flight football, Town never once won an FAI Cup tie but did reach the semi-final of the League Cup in 1980 before going down to Galway Rovers. Two poor seasons of finishing bottom followed and the club checked out of the league in 1982 though they still continue as a successful side locally in Tipperary.

Transport (1948-1962)

Enjoyed 14 unbroken years of service as a League of Ireland club, winning the prestigious Blue Riband in 1950, the club had been elected to the league in 1948, finishing a healthy fifth in their maiden year. Twelve months later the club beat Waterford, Bohemians and Sligo Rovers on the way to a meeting with Cork Athletic in the FAI Cup final. The first game at Dalymount Park ended 2-2, with goals from Barney Lester and Jimmy Duggan, as did the second three days later (Bobby Smith and Jim Loughran scoring) before Transport finally sealed their first and only FAI Cup with goals from Jimmy Duggan and a brace from Lester in a 3-1 victory on May 5, 1950. Transport also won the Leinster Senior Cup in 1951/52, beating Shelbourne 3-0, but spent most of their league existence in the bottom half of the table. A fifth place finish in '56/57 was as good as it got before failing to get re-elected after the 1961/62 season.

YMCA FC (1921/22)

Formed as early as 1893, the club featured in the inaugural 1921/22 Free State League season, failing to win a game, collecting just three points from their 14 games and losing out to non-league Athlone Town in the Free State Cup.